Only One Child

BRIAN BOHUN BARLOW

Brian Bohun Barlow

Sheila Barlow O'Brien

Malcolm Bohun Barlow

SWB
Just Write Books

Published by

𝒥𝒲ℬ

Just Write Books

47 Main Street #3, Topsham, Maine 04086
207-729-3600 • www.jstwrite.com

Library of Congress Catalog Card No. 2006931833

Barlow, Brian Bohun
Only One Child/Brian Bohun Barlow
p. 204
1. History–United States–General.
2. Biography & Autobiography–General.
1. Title.

ISBN-13: 978-0-9777614-9-4
ISBN-10: 0-9777614-9-5

Printed in the United States of America

Dedication

To my Father, Horace Victor Barlow, and to
my Mother, Violet Layman Jamieson,
who unknowingingly made a fateful decision
when they sent their four youngest children
to safety in America.

The author's thanks go:
To my wife, Posey, who never wavered in her support
for the writing of this book.
To my friend, Pam Lunday,
of Santa Fe, New Mexico,
who pleaded so eloquently
that I write this book.

To Margaret M. Betts
without her this book could not
have come together in one piece—from
typing the manuscript, hunting through
photos, patiently reworking paragraph
after paragraph—she is a part of this
book and our family.

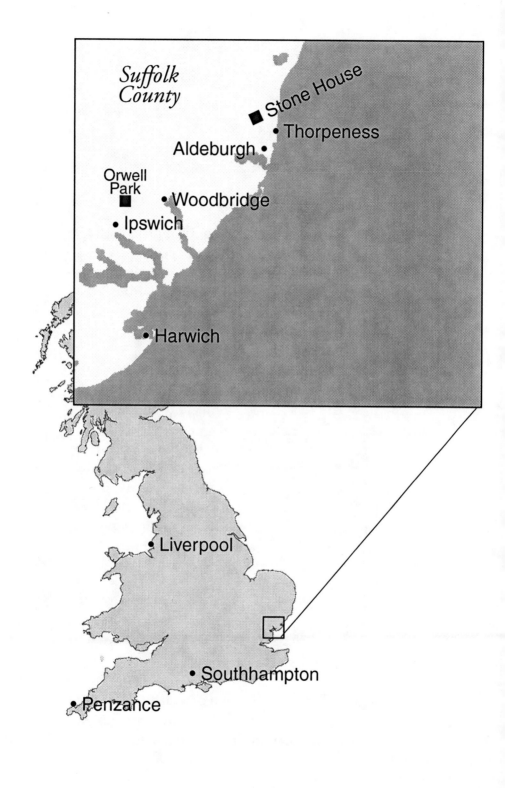

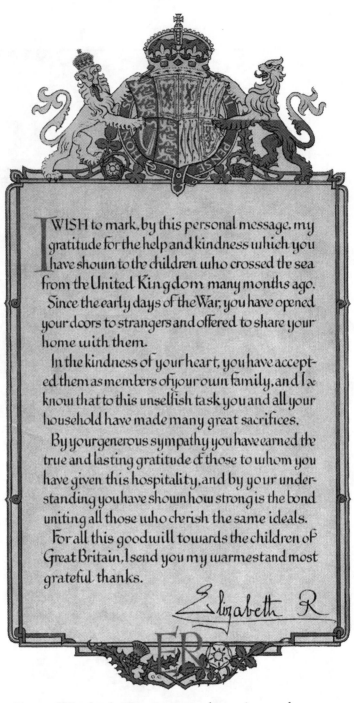

I WISH to mark, by this personal message, my gratitude for the help and kindness which you have shown to the children who crossed the sea from the United Kingdom many months ago.

Since the early days of the War, you have opened your doors to strangers and offered to share your home with them.

In the kindness of your heart, you have accepted them as members of your own family, and I æ know that to this unselfish task you and all your household have made many great sacrifices.

By your generous sympathy you have earned the true and lasting gratitude of those to whom you have given this hospitality, and by your understanding you have shown how strong is the bond uniting all those who cherish the same ideals.

For all this goodwill towards the children of Great Britain, I send you my warmest and most grateful thanks.

Elizabeth R

Queen Elizabeth II sent a proclamation to honor Aunt Peg, as well as other families who hosted evacuee children in the United States.

CHAPTER ONE

Before drifting off to sleep that August evening in 1940, I reflected on the day just past. My school had played its last tennis match of the season that afternoon. It had been a warm and sunny day. The grass tennis courts were in front of the main school building, and the crowd of spectators was large. I thought our team looked very smart in their immaculate whites and navy blazers with yellow piping. By the end of the afternoon, the match was tied. The outcome of my sets would determine which school won. After hard-fought sets, my opponent went down to defeat. Both masters and boys rushed up to congratulate me on my victory. It had been a very satisfactory day.

My English public school, Orwell Park School, was in the process of settling into new quarters on an estate in Devonshire. The entire school had recently been evacuated from Ipswich, Suffolk, north of London, because England was once again at war with Germany. In April 1940, a German bomb had killed the first English civilian. Because the most direct air route between Germany and London was over Suffolk, it was thought that Devonshire would offer the school a safer haven from German bombs.

That evening, the sunset had been an unusual blood color,

The author's father, Horace Victor Barlow.

Violet Layman Barlow, before the war.

Derrick and the author's parents in front of "Overdeben," their home in Woodbridge, 1941.

and it took more time than usual for the dormitory of unruly twelve-year-old boys to settle for the night. Our normal bed-time behavior included pillow fights, and insults bantered back and forth amidst cries of "shut up" from boys anxious to get some sleep. We quieted down only after threats from a harassed master that he would send culprits to the headmaster for a caning.

I had been asleep for some time, when a hand on my shoulder shook me vigorously. Half asleep, my first reaction was to wonder how my latest misdeed had been discovered so quickly. A couple of times in the past, a shake in the middle of the night had meant a visit to the headmaster's study with its unpleasant consequences. It was a relief to hear the master say, "Barlow, your father wants you on the morning train to London. You are going to Canada." After his departure, whispered inquiries came from the darkness. The other boys were suitably impressed by my forthcoming adventure.

Before falling back to sleep, I thought over this summons from my father in the middle of the night. It must mean that my whole family was going to Canada. Most likely, it had something to do with an engineering project my father was involved in. In any case, I assumed the move would involve not only my father and mother, but also five children—my older brother, Derrick, myself and my twin sister Sue, my younger sister Sheila, and my younger brother Malcolm. As for Canada, about all I knew was that it was a country across the Atlantic Ocean and still part of the British Empire.

It did not occur to me that the summons from my father had something to do with Hitler's plan to invade England in 1940. Like any schoolboy, from time to time my attention was caught by outside events. The German attack on Poland in September 1939 had, I knew, caused England to declare war on

Germany. I knew that British efforts to help Norway had failed, and that consequently both Norway and Denmark had been occupied by German troops. I had followed with keen interest Hitler's "blitzkrieg" against the Low Countries and France. I shared in the feeling of relief when the British Army was rescued at Dunkirk on June 22, 1940. With other schoolboys, I listened in hushed silence to Churchill's broadcast that "what General Weygand called the Battle of France is over. I expect that the Battle of Britain is about to begin … Let us therefore brace ourselves to our duties, and so bear ourselves that, if the British Empire and its Commonwealth last for a thousand years, men will say, 'This was their finest hour.'" I realized that England now stood alone against Hitler, but I had no real understanding of how perilous was England's position.

The next morning I was on the earliest train to London. Traveling alone did not bother me, because I had been going away to boarding school since the age of seven. In those days, public schoolboys traveled like royalty. We carried only pocket money on our persons. The school made all the arrangements for us to travel first class and then billed our parents. Any taxi fares were paid on arrival.

That particular morning the train compartment was full, and in the customary manner we sat facing the other passengers with our knees almost touching. After polite "Good mornings" made the round, silence reigned. It was not considered well-bred for a traveler to inflict his opinions or personal affairs on strangers. Passengers spent their travel time hidden behind newspapers or books, or looking out the train window. I was bursting to tell someone I was off to Canada, so I can well recall the oppressiveness of the silence on that train ride to London. What tales we passengers might have told each other if we had been with Chaucer on a pilgrimage to Canterbury that day!

CHAPTER TWO

*T*he train arrived at last at the cavernous London Station, blackened by soot from years of coal-fired trains. I had never seen such a huge railway station before. My amazement grew at the sight of dozens of giant locomotives, half-obscured by hissing steam, lined up on parallel tracks. The station bustled with hurrying passengers and the shouts of porters.

Trains had fascinated me since the age of five when I was given my grandfather's Victorian train set as a Christmas present. The set consisted of exact replicas of several famous British trains, and there was enough track to cover the floor of a good-sized room in the thatched cottage we used as a playhouse. I remember the trains had to be wound up with a large key. One morning the playhouse burned to the ground, and the train set was destroyed. My parents were too relieved by the fact that none of their five children were inside the playhouse when it burned to pay much attention to my tears at the loss of my favorite toy.

It was all I could do to tear myself away from the trains and London Station. I took a taxi to the house my parents had rented on Davies Street, across from the world famous Claridge's Hotel.

6   On the way to Davies Street, I looked out the taxi window with interest at the city of my birth. A 1928 photograph in a family album shows my mother holding me and my newborn twin sister, Susan, in front of a London hospital. Mother looks a bit uneasy, but there is the reassuring figure of a nurse in a starched uniform in the background. (The only other time I recalled having been in London was to attend a pantomime one Christmas at the invitation of Sir Malcolm Campbell, the racing car driver, who had set a world's speed record with his Bluebird car. He and my father had been friends for many years, and my younger brother had been named Malcolm after him.)

Now on my second sojourn to London, the city basked in sunlight and its streets were full of shoppers. Hitler had invaded Denmark and Norway in April, but in August the war still seemed far away to London citizens. However, there were signs that London had prepared itself for German air raids. Out the taxi window I could see sandbagged store fronts with their plate glass windows criss-crossed with tape. Next to colorful flower beds in the parks were anti-aircraft gun emplacements. Air raid shelter signs were everywhere. I saw my first barrage balloon—a blimp—floating like a large sausage in the bright blue sky, and moored to its truck by long wire cables. In his book *The People's War,* Angus Calder writes, "The barrage balloons were wound up and down and controlled by crews from R.A.F Balloon Command, operating on sites in parks and open spaces. It was harder work than it looked, but later achieved its modest purpose in discouraging dive bombing and low-level attacks. In the first months of war, however, the blimps inspired an irrational sense of immunity among civilians. This was encouraged by an early propaganda film, *The Lion Has Wings,* which depicted a mass raid by Luftwaffe bombers turning back in fear and confusion at the sign of Britain's terrifying balloon barrage." [1]

Upon my arrival at the Davies Street house, I was greeted enthusiastically by Malcolm, Susan and Sheila. I don't remember my older brother Derrick being there that day. Although I don't recall it, I would have gotten a firm handshake from my father and a kiss from my mother. I quickly learned that the whole family was not going to Canada—only we four youngest. Derrick would not be going because the British government would not let persons over the age of 16 leave the country. At 17 they would be called up for military service. The news came as a bit of a shock to me. In the excitement of the moment I did not realize its importance.

The decision by my parents to send their four younger children to safety in Canada was made at the urging of an American friend of my father, Caldwell Johnston, who had worked in the American Consulate in London. He had just been posted to Montreal, Canada, and he offered to have two of us children live with him, and the other two would live with a friend of his on the same street in Montreal. Consul Johnston would obtain American visas for the four of us. Hitler's planned invasion of Britain seemed imminent, and the British government was urging parents to send young children to safety overseas. My parents must have been greatly relieved to know exactly where the four of us would end up in Canada. In many cases the parents were sending their children to Canada, the United States, Australia, New Zealand, and the Union of South Africa without knowing who would give them refuge.

CHAPTER THREE

$\mathcal{T}$he outbreak of World War II in September 1939 marked the beginning of my family's moving into one rented house after another. The move to London in 1940 had not been the first of such moves, nor would it be the last. By late 1942 my parents would have moved seven times.

The rented house I had grown up in, the one I remember best, and where my parents had lived for 17 years, was called Stone House. It was located in Aldringham, Suffolk County, north of London, near the seaside village of Thorpeness. Stone House was an L-shaped manor house that looked hundreds of years old with its ivy-covered stone walls. (Later in life, I was surprised to read in a sales brochure that the house had been built shortly after World War I.) Like other country houses of that period, the servants' wing was as large as the main part of the house.

While I lived at Stone House, the staff was in a constant state of turnover. Normally there were five maids to run the house and a nurse to care for the children. The servants disliked Stone House's rural location and with only one afternoon off each week, they stayed for such a short time that they made little impression on me as a child. I had no favorites among the servants. Perhaps the English system—unlike the American—discouraged close bonds among family members and staff. I remember reading that Churchill adored his nanny all his life, but I don't remember reading that he felt the same way about other members of his family's staff.

My father was at heart a country squire, and he loved Stone House, which met all the needs of a country squire. He even looked the part—as he was stout and round of face, with a florid complexion—looking in appearance remarkably like the traditional figure of "John Bull." I remember him inspecting the grounds at Stone House in well-worn tweed plus-fours, a tie, a tweed cap, and sturdy walking shoes. Despite his weight, he moved lightly on his feet. He gave the impression of solid respectability. He liked people, and was much more open and friendly, and showed less English "reserve," than many from his rural background. He had been born in and grew up in the village of Woodbridge, Suffolk.

Sadly, like Churchill, he suffered from bouts of depression, followed by periods of ebullient spirits. I remember one strange incident, which took place at Stone House, when I was quite a young child. One day, Father announced to Mother that he was dying. He said he was coughing up blood. Mother's reaction was to tell him it was all nonsense, and she refused to curtail her daily golfing. With that, Father hired a trained nurse and retired to bed. Over the next few days, Mother continued to show no concern over his condition. Mother was habitually afraid of illness and never could deal with it directly. Whenever we children were sick, we were sent to an infirmary, to be cared for by nurses. Father soon got bored in bed, dismissed the nurse, and went back to his engineering projects.

Father loved Stone House for its attached shooting woods.

Each spring the woods were a mass of yellow daffodils, because gardeners had been planting old bulbs there for many years. Father was a crack shot, and always kept a superbly-trained black Labrador as a gun dog. As a young boy, I used to beat for him, along with the gardener and other local men called in by the day. I never saw him miss a pheasant in flight, nor did his gun dog ever fail to retrieve a downed bird. I can still recall my surprise at finding the pheasant's body warm to the touch as I stuffed it into the leather game bag. Father's most famous gun dog was Mike. When Mike died he was buried in the garden at Stone House. He was replaced with a young black Labrador named "Slick." Slick had to be given away when the outbreak of war forced my parents out of Stone House on twenty-four hours' notice. The smell of a spent cartridge still reminds me of the gun room at Stone House with its odors of gun oils, rubber boots and oil skin mackintoshes.

The four brick kennels with wire runs at Stone House had great appeal for Father, although his gun dog always lived in the house as a family pet. Father once came home with a dun-colored greyhound, which he was sure would make his fortune at the dog racing tracks. The greyhound would curl up its lips and expose all its teeth whenever I came near him. Father said it was the greyhound's way of being friendly, but I was never quite convinced. Also, I didn't like the fact that the greyhound looked half-starved with all his ribs showing. Evidently the greyhound proved to be a disappointment, and one day he was no longer in the kennel.

As an engineer, Father was intrigued that Stone House had its own electric plant in a building off the greenhouses, which were located to the left of the entrance courtyard. I remember the huge glass tanks filled with a green-colored acid, although we were forbidden to play there. In a 1942 letter, my father observed that "country mansions, like our Stone House, are things of the past, because it is no longer possible to get domestic staff or gardeners and chauffeurs to run electric light plants and pump water with engines."

The only change Father made at Stone House was to build an elaborate, tiled goldfish pond on the lawn in front of the dining room windows. The goldfish ended up the size of trout, so well did they flourish in the pond. We children were surprised that as the goldfish grew, they lost their golden color becoming a translucent white with gray and black markings.

Mother was equally fond of Stone House. "Golf was at one time the chief interest in her life," according to a 1944 letter from Aunt Cecile, my father's sister. Mother was delighted at being able to enter on to one of the holes of the Thorpeness Golf Club through a garden gate. I understand the Thorpeness Golf Club is still full of silver trophies won by my mother. Since the championship Aldeburgh course was only three miles away from Stone House, Mother often played there, too. My interest in playing golf as a young boy stemmed from watching my mother play, and playing with her old clubs.

The grounds were in a sad state of repair at Stone House when my parents first rented the place. With Mother's flair for gardening in the English "natural" style, she soon had colorful flowerbeds highlighting the extensive green lawns surrounding the house. The most noticeable feature of the grounds was a magnificent oak tree, one of the oldest and largest in Suffolk, if not in all of England. Its huge outspread limbs had to be supported with guy wires and wooden props. Behind the oak tree was a wide belt of woodlands, chiefly pine and fir, which protected the house and gardens from the prevailing winds. Each spring, the woods were a mass of yellow daffodils and delicate yellow primroses.

On the front side of the house were kitchen and fruit gardens, which were partly enclosed by brick walls. I remember the taste of sun-ripened purple figs, which had been espaliered against the walls. The fruit trees grew in wire cages to keep the birds from eating the ripened fruit. More tropical fruits grew in heated greenhouses. The gardener was always having to chase us out of the greenhouse where bunches of green and plum-colored grapes hung within our reach. Other greenhouses held orange and lemon trees in large wooden tubs. From this Garden of Eden, Mother was able to bottle all sorts of fruits—raspberries, black currants, red cherries and green gooseberries. Her marmalade, with its tangy bits of peel, could not be equaled.

Father was very proud of what Mother had been able to do to beautify the grounds at Stone House. But Father was even more proud of the air of glamour Mother added to his country establishment. Mother was tall and striking-looking with her silver hair, marvelous English coloring, and unusual violet-blue eyes. (Elizabeth Taylor, as a young girl, was the only other person I've seen to have the same colored eyes.) When in the country, she always wore beautifully-tailored tweed suits, often in a heather-like lavender color. With these, she wore pearls, or her favorite brooch, a sapphire and diamond wing-shaped pin. I noticed at a young age that when Mother entered a room, all eyes turned in her direction, and the men in the room would find some excuse to talk to her. At times I think Father was jealous when other men paid too much attention to her. Mother never sought such attention, and her "independent" means allowed her to ignore my father's remonstrances whenever she chose to do so.

When we first moved to Stone House, there were four children in the family. At 16, my brother, Derrick, was the oldest; then came my twin sister Susan and me, and finally my younger sister Sheila. My youngest brother Malcolm, was born at Stone House in 1935, when I was seven. Most of the time, Derrick was away at boarding school and, being older, lived his own life when home. The four youngest spent a good part of each day in the so-called nursery, where three of us were looked after by a governess, and Malcolm was looked after by a nanny. The nursery was a large sunny room with a bay window—and was located above one of the formal drawing rooms—which had French doors opening on to the lawn. To one side of the French doors was a cast iron boot scraper with sharp arrow points at each end. While still an infant, Malcolm fell out of the bay window, and narrowly missed being impaled on the boot scraper. The incident made the local newspaper with a photograph of the bay window and arrows marking his descent. His nanny was discharged on the spot, and a new nurse took her place.

My two sisters had very different personalities. Sue, my twin sister, had inherited Father's artistic abilities. Like him, she loved old things. She spent many happy hours dressing dolls and decorating the dollhouse. In a 1943 letter to "My Darling Daughter Sue," Father praised her for a painting she had sent him. "Your painting is very good. Your ideas of proportion are excellent. The angles of the shed are perfect; your shadow background very good. Only fault—little too heavy in the background. Your Mum is having it put in a proper picture frame." In the same letter he described an old fire screen he purchased at auction. "I bought a very old fire screen with heavy plate glass. I knew by the design of the fire screen frame

BABY FELL FROM
WINDOW, LAUGHED

Malcolm Barlow.

BABY Barlow, nineteen - month - old toddler, crawled to the window of his nursery at Stine House, near Thorpeness, Suffolk, reached up 3ft. 6in., opened the window, dived out 12ft. to the hard gravel below, and sat up chuckling !

His only injury was a slight scratch on his forehead.

"It was a miracle," Mr. Bill Barlow, the father, told the *Daily Mirror*. "Two doctors have been to see him, and they say there is not a thing wrong with him.

Photograph of Stone House from a brochure offering the property for sale after the war.

The Meare at Thorpeness.

16 (wood) it was very old, about 200 years. I removed the glass with screwdriver in the Auction Room and as I anticipated found a highly colored floral picture worked in silk and wood—a wonderful work of art. It must have taken several years to work. The stitches are so fine as to require a magnifying glass to see them. It cost me twenty-four shillings. I had it put in an old antique picture frame, and today it hangs in your Mother's bedroom—a really beautiful floral picture with every color under the sun."

Sheila, my youngest sister, had a very different personality and talents. She never showed much interest in dolls, much preferring to share my train set and other boys' toys. She had inherited Mother's athletic ability, and was good at all sports. She was always winning athletic prizes at her day school.

Malcolm was a miniature version of Father. He had his sturdy build, and his ability to make friends from all walks of life. On Saturday mornings, Father would take me and Malcolm to the Lunatic Arm's Inn in Aldeburgh-on-Sea for a glass of beer. We would listen with rapt attention to Father and the pub owner discussing the local news. In a 1942 letter to Malcolm, Father wrote, "Will you, please, write your friend who kept the pub at Aldeburgh, where Daddy took you every Saturday for a glass of beer. Be sure to mention his wife, who gave you cakes. They still keep your special mug in memory of you, Malcolm. Can you remember the fishermen played shove half-penny for pints of beer?"

Sheila and I were enough alike in personality and interests that we usually teamed up together—often against Sue. Malcolm, being younger, was often left out of our games. Derrick was enough older that he wasn't interested in playing with us. While at Stone House, Sue, Sheila, and I roamed freely about the grounds, making up games which often failed to amuse the gardener. One day he found me daring Sheila to jump off the roof of a high shed into a pile of straw. She jumped before he could stop her, and fortunately wasn't hurt. Unlike Sue, who could always think of a hundred reasons not to take one of my dares, Sheila could never think of a single reason not to do so.

Our other favorite place to play was in the seaside village of Thorpeness, only one and a half miles away, so we could walk or ride our bicycles there. The big attraction for us was The Meare, a man-made lake dotted with islands with names like Crusoe's Island, Peter Pan Property, and The Happy Isles. Rowing boats, punts and sailboats could be rented by the hour or by the season. These could be used to follow a numbered trail by water to such attractions as a Pirate's Fort, or the House of the Seven Dwarfs. The water was quite shallow, so parents could let their children play there without supervision.

Once a year a regatta was held on The Meare and all the boats would be decorated with flags and streamers. The three of us would take part in all sorts of races. Sheila was always one of the big winners. The most elegant boat in the regatta was a miniature yacht that belonged to two boys we used to play with. It made the rental sailboats look like very ugly ducklings.

Our unfettered play came to an end when I was seven years of age. I was sent off to boarding school at Aldeburgh. About this time the reign of governesses also came to an end, and Sue and Sheila were enrolled in a day school. Malcolm was still under the care of a nurse. From then on, I was only at Stone House during school vacations.

When home from school my favorite pastime was to play golf on the courses near Stone House. Mother always played with men's clubs, so I used her old clubs to learn the sport. Slick, Father's young gun dog, used to come along. Somehow he had learned to retrieve lost golf balls from the rough. As the rough at the Thorpeness Golf Club consisted of wiry heather—kept short in those days—there was no lack of lost balls for him to retrieve. Slick was always pleased that so many of my golf balls ended up in the rough.

In reflecting back on our childhood years at Stone House, I realize now how formal our relationship was with our parents. English parents expect children to adjust to their schedule, not the other way around as in the U.S. My parents did not expect to take their children with them when they visited friends or went on vacations. We were often left under the care of servants, although occasionally Father would ask his unmarried sister, Aunt Cecile, to look after us whenever she was free to do so. I remember being taken by the nurse or governess to see my parents before bedtime as a young child. They would be seated at the dining room table, before dinner. Father would ask us questions about what we did that day; Mother usually remained silent. Any misbehavior would call for immediate banishment back to the nursery. The end result was that we were invariably polite to our parents, and did not question their right to order our lives. Even so, Stone House continued to evoke happy memories for the four youngest of the Barlow family, even after our departure.

Aunt Eileen Powers, sister of the author's mother.

The author's maternal grandfather, Frederick Layman, dirctor of the Morny Perfume Company.

The author's paternal grandfather, Alec Charles Bunn.

Violet Barlow Jamieson after WWII.

CHAPTER FOUR

$\mathcal{T}$he culmination of "The Gathering Storm," as Churchill phrased it, occurred in September 1939 when, on September 1, the Germans invaded Poland. On September 3, Neville Chamberlain, the British Prime Minister, announced in weary tones that England was once again at war with Germany. Twenty minutes after this announcement, air-raid sirens sounded in London. It turned out to be a false alarm.

The most dramatic sign for my family that war had come to England was the sudden arrival in the summer of 1940 of a small group of school-aged children in ragged clothes. They had been evacuated from the East End of London by the British government. I don't recall how many children turned up on our doorstep, but I think the group included both boys and girls ranging in age from six to ten or twelve. I do remember clearly that we had great difficulty understanding their Cockney accents. I also remember being impressed by their impressive vocabulary of swear words. Father took all the children to the garage to give them a good scrub in a galvanized tub, normally used for washing the dog. The children were infested with lice, and my parents were afraid to let them in the house without a bath first.

Children who were evacuated from London went

through an upsetting experience. One evacuee, who was seven at the time, wrote after the war, "I know that we rehearsed the evacuation every morning for a week. Each morning my sister and I would leave home with our packed sandwiches and clothes. We would say good-bye to our parents. Our labels were pinned on and I felt sick. We were not told the date of the real departure in case the Germans bombed the train. That seems hard to believe now, but at that time people seemed to find spies under their beds every night. So we had to leave home without knowing if we would return that day or not. We went through this awful ritual of good-bye every morning for a week. Every morning I felt sick and kissed my parents and felt I was leaving my name and identity with them."

The children's arrival at Stone House was in fulfillment of a British government pre-war plan to evacuate some two million children from the cities to safer areas in the event of war. A census of accommodations in every country house throughout England had been made in advance. Our vacant maids' rooms had evidently made us eligible to receive evacuees on a quasi-voluntary basis.

The government's evacuation scheme received a mixed reception from some of the owners of country houses, who suspected that the voluntary acceptance of children would be made mandatory in time. The *New York Times* reported that many owners were in agreement with Viscount Hailsham, who "served notice that he will take no children until the government can satisfy him regarding a whole series of legalistic questions, including who will pay him for the damage they do." The same article reported that "an organization calling itself The United Ratepayers Advisory Association contends that protests have been made against billeting in 150 districts. Its slogan is 'Think of the Danger—Dirt, Disease, Theft, Vandalism, Immorality and Strife.'"[1]

To offset such criticism, the government persuaded the aged Duke of Connaught, great uncle to the King, to announce he would permit 200 Cockney children to find refuge in his country home in the event of war, without seeking any compensation from the British government. (The children would not be admitted to the Duke's house itself, however, but placed in servants' cottages instead.)

Common sense eventually prevailed, and it was reported by the government that "1,100,000 Britons offered billet aid before half the census had been completed." As far as I know, my parents were in this group.

How our particular group of evacuee children was chosen to fill our vacant rooms is not known to me. In *The People's War*, Angus Calder writes, "Methods of billeting varied greatly. In the well-organized city of Cambridge, volunteers were waiting on the station platforms as each train came in to take the evacuees to 'dispersal centres' organized in different wards, and efforts were made to keep school parties together. In many areas, however, local householders had assembled to pick their evacuees when the trains or buses arrived, and scenes reminiscent of a cross between an early Roman slave market and Selfridge's bargain basement ensued. Potato farmers selected husky lads; girls of ten or twelve who could lend a hand in the house were naturally much in demand; nicely dressed children were whisked away by local bigwigs. Those who got 'second pick' were often resentful, and there was likely to be a residue of unwholesome looking waifs whom nobody wanted, but whom somebody would have to take when the billeting officer began to mutter about compulsory powers. The alternative was usually a more or less haphazard distribution of children by the billeting officer and his helpers."[2]

Our children were obviously not the prize pick.

However, my parents greeted them warmly and seemed unfazed by their ragged appearance and foul language. Mother attempted to feed them a healthy diet of fruit and vegetables from our gardens, but the children refused to eat it. The only food they liked was bread and drippings (white lard). Their reaction was more common than not. *Mass Observation*, a British government publication, reported that, "One boy, 13, refused to eat cereal and milk, saying 'I want some bloody beer and some chips.'"[3]

I never got to know our evacuee children, because about a week after they arrived I returned to boarding school in Ipswich. Soon I learned that our children had gone back to London. Mother summed up her experience with the evacuee children when she said, "We tried to do everything for them, but having come from the East End of London, they simply hated the country." Little did I suspect that before 1940 was over, we four youngest would ourselves become evacuees, seeking a safe refuge from Hitler's bombs.

Another sign for us that our lives were changing was the British Army's abrupt commandeering of Stone House for quarters for military personnel. As a result, my family had to move, this time into a small rented cottage known as The Sundial, located in the nearby seaside town of Aldeburgh (now famous for its Benjamin Britten music festival). The Sundial had been the infirmary for my boarding school when it had been located in Aldeburgh. To return to The Sundial to live, where once I had spent time recovering from various illnesses while a student, was a curious experience for me. Where there had been rows of white iron bedsteads, presided over by a matron in starched cap and cuffs, now stood some of Mother's furniture. Having to leave Stone House was quite a blow for my family, but The Sundial's location right on the beach helped soften the blow somewhat.

A final sign for me that my life was changing was coming into personal contact with the machinery of war. My only vacation at The Sundial was spent walking along the beach looking for amber. On one of these early-morning hunting expeditions, I saw my first mines. They were close enough to the beach for me to see clearly their covering of spikes. I watched fascinated as the waves would push two mines toward each other, and then pull them apart just as they were about to strike each other. I finally lost interest when I realized the mines would not hit each other. When I got home, I told Father about the mines and he immediately called the authorities, so the mines could be disposed of. He explained to me that if the two mines had collided, the explosion would have blown me to smithereens, along with some of Aldeburgh's seaside cottages.

On that same vacation, I went to the beach one afternoon and came across a startling sight. The stone beach was covered with thick black oil and the bodies of what seemed to be hundreds of naked babies. Upon closer inspection, the naked babies turned out to be celluloid dolls that had drifted ashore from a cargo ship sunk by a German torpedo or mine during the Battle of the Atlantic. By the end of 1939, 79 Allied ships of 262,700 tons had been lost to mines; some 114 ships had been torpedoed by German U-boats.

Soon summer was over and it was time to turn our attention to school again. At the beginning of the summer Mother would put away the clothing that I had worn at Orwell Park School. When it was time to return to school mother would check the previous year's clothing. She would replace lost buttons and darns socks. She would knit a new sweater; if I needed one. If I had outgrown any of the items she would order more from stores near the school. When we went to the store the clothes were neatly folded and the clerk added them to my footlocker in the trunk of the car. The next stop was to buy shoes. I enjoyed this because I could slip my feet into the x-ray machine, common in those days, and see my bones in their ghostly outlines. Then Mother and I would stop for lunch at a fancy restaurant. At age 12, I was always hungry but my favorite part of the meal was dessert. My favorite dessert was chocolate eclairs which in those days were filled with real cream. After lunch we would see a movie together—often about pirates or a film featuring Charlie Chaplin.

As my anxiety mounted, we could delay no longer. It was time to go to Orwell Park. Upon arrival at the school Mother would park the car and take me to meet the Headmaster and his assistant. She would depart for home. In the meantime a staff member had removed my footlocker and placed it in my dorm. Joining the other boys I would stand outside the entrance hall to watch parents drop off their boys. Cars driven by uniformed chauffeurs earned the most respect. That fact that I had

The author's father, Horace Victor Barlow.

The student body at Orwell Park School in front of the ha-ha wall in 1939. Brian, 11 years old, is inside the circle.

The cricket team at Orwell Park School, 1939. Brian (front center).

Orwell Park School, reconstructed by Horace Victor Barlow,

Hembury Fort House, Devonshire, 1940. Orwell Park School relocated here from Suffolk to escape the bombing. The author attended the summer term here.

arrived in a Rolls Royce with Mother at the wheel put me in the same category as the boys who were driven by chauffeurs.

I was seven when I first went away to school. The pleasant ritual of Mother taking me, and our having a day out, just the two of us, had been well established by the time I was twelve.

Once back at Orwell Park School in Ipswich, I found school routines had changed for the better as far as twelve-year-old schoolboys were concerned. Classes were often interrupted to hear radio broadcasts of the latest war news, or to practice air raid drills. The deep cellars under the school buildings now used as air raid shelters opened up new possibilities for exploration. I remember being fitted with a gas mask and a tin helmet. Even today, I can recall the rubbery smell of the gas mask, and the claustrophobic feeling it engendered in its wearer. The gas mask, in its cardboard box with a string shoulder strap and the tin helmet, had to be taken to all our classes. The dormitory windows had to be carefully blacked out each night, and I remember cutting out a circular piece of cardboard for my flashlight. Pinpricks in the cardboard of my flashlight were the only source of light allowed. The most exciting change of all was the drilling we did with wooden rifles under the masters, who were shortly to leave for military service. As time went on, our masters began to pay less and less attention to classroom work, and suddenly to our delight, we found ourselves with more freedom than we had ever known in the past.

I had always felt at home at Orwell Park School in Ipswich because Father was a frequent visitor to the school. When he drove through the marvelous iron gates at the front entrance in his Rolls Royce, I would be called to the headmaster's study for a visit with him no matter the hour. Throughout my time at Orwell Park, Father worked on various engineering projects for the school. He considered the conversion of the largest private house in England into a preparatory boarding school his most outstanding engineering feat. From 1936 to 1939 my father worked on the reconstruction of the buildings, together with the help of two hundred skilled craftsmen. In a 1942 letter to me, Father wrote, "Yes, my Son, your Father is very proud of his achievement and engineering skill he displayed at Orwell Park. The name of BARLOW will live for the next 50 years—the man who had the courage to buy the largest building in Great Britain—all its contents, pictures, and furniture (the majority of the library books were sold to America, I understand, for nearly £100,000), when all the leading architects and engineers had pronounced it obsolete, impossible to reconstruct or modernize, not being a commercial proposition. Your Father proved that they were all wrong."

Orwell Park had been built in 1862 by Colonel Tomlinson, who, according to Father, had made a profit of £2,000,000 by cornering the silver market and compelling the government to mint more silver coins. With the money he made, he bought 22,000 acres of the best land in Suffolk, reaching from Ipswich to Felixstowe and then to Woodbridge. The estate was laid out for sport shooting—pheasants, partridges, wild duck and hares. Col. Tomlinson then built Orwell Park at a cost of £980,000. The interior under cover totaled approximately one million square feet.

Father told me that all the kings and queens of Europe had stayed at Orwell Park, including the late German Empress and Crown Prince, King Edward VII, his son George V, and all the royal family who came for the shooting. He

30   told me, "Until your Dad bought it and sold it to Orwell Park School, no Commoner had ever put a foot inside the mansion, not even our County families. It was reserved for Royalty." In its heyday as an estate, Orwell Park had required a staff of 280 men and women to keep the place running, according to Father.

As a student at Orwell Park School, I delighted in exploring the enormous range of buildings, as well as the deer park on the other side of the ha-ha wall and ditch. One of my favorite buildings was the Observatory, which was 97 feet high and had a revolving copper dome. It contained the second largest telescope in England. Father told me that in the old days the estate retained a private astronomer. I used to sit in the seat at the base of the telescope and pretend to be surveying the stars. Another favorite building was the Clock Tower, which was 77 feet high and contained a four-face clock from Germany. Between three and four o'clock in the afternoon, it played Old English folk tunes and songs for one hour. These tunes could be heard for over a mile on a quiet day. In the deer park my classmates and I built elaborate brush forts with intricate escape tunnels. Mock battles were fought long and hard, with horse chestnuts the preferred weapon.

CHAPTER FIVE

*D*espite its fashionable location, the Davies Street
house seemed very small and dark to me that August of 1940.
The only sunlit room in the house was the kitchen with a
glass skylight. After my sudden removal from school and arrival in London, life now centered on obtaining American
visas for the four of us with the help of Father's friend, Caldwell
Johnston, in the American Consular Department.

The procedure for obtaining American visas for children
to be sent overseas was at first a cause for great confusion.
With a German invasion expected any day, there were many
complaints about the slow processing of papers by the American Embassy in London. The American ambassador, Joseph
Kennedy (father of the future U.S. president, John Kennedy),
found it necessary to issue a public statement that the U.S.
was not to blame for the small number of British children
sent to the U.S. He blamed the delay on the British government. The end result was that procedures were speeded up
by the issuance of "new" instructions. These required that an
Application for Visa Examination be filled out and mailed
immediately to the American Embassy in London.

On the appointment day designated by the American
Embassy, English parents were to bring with them valid British

passports for each child, two birth certificates for each child, and five photographs, 2 ½" square, of each child. Also to be brought was a cable from the American friend or relative guaranteeing support of the child or children while in the U.S., and a cable from their banker stating that in the bank's opinion the sponsor was financially able to comply with the terms of his or her undertaking. In addition, the English parents were required to pay a visa fee of $10, and they had to sign a consent form in triplicate if the applicant children were proceeding to the U.S. unaccompanied by father and mother. Finally, the instructions required that every applicant for an immigration visa, even an infant in arms, must appear in person on the appointment date for Visa Examination. Because my father's American friend, Caldwell Johnston, would be taking the four of us under his personal care, we could meet these regulations. However, many other refugee children, especially those Jewish children who were fleeing from Hitler, had no hope of meeting these requirements. Eventually, groups aiding refugee children were allowed to guarantee financial support, and the children were allowed to come on visitor visas, rather than immigration visas, which had quota restrictions.

While Father struggled to complete the necessary paperwork, Mother was busy outfitting the four of us for our stay in Montreal, Canada. Consul Johnston had already taken up his post there. I remember that whenever we went to the cinema, Mother would knit one of us a sweater. She would knit away in the darkened cinema, and by the end of the film the sweater would be finished. On one of our shopping expeditions to Selfridge's department store, Malcolm, my five-year-old brother, bought himself a small white horse to take with him to Canada. Unfortunately, in the flurry of our departure, he forgot to take it with him. Mother would later write on October 31, "Give Malcolm a big kiss for me and tell him I am very sorry he left behind his little horse that we bought in Selfridge's. Perhaps I shall be able to slip it into a Christmas parcel."

There was no bombing going on when I first reached London, so the four of us were able to explore without supervision that part of London near the Davies Street house. We often walked to Hyde Park to feed the pigeons with breadcrumbs from the brown paper bags we had brought with us. We listened to the passionate speeches of the soapbox orators at Hyde Park Corner. We discovered a Trans-Lux cinema nearby, which showed news, travelogues and short comics in one-hour segments. Malcolm had his own way of dealing with the scary parts of films, which Mother recalled in a 1941 letter. "Do you remember when we saw *Pinocchio* in London, Malcolm would get under the seat during bits he did not like?"

Two adventures while we were in London come to mind. Sheila returned home one day with the news she had seen a "real" black person. This news startled us as much as Robinson Crusoe had been startled by the discovery of the black "Friday." Nothing would do but for the rest of us to go and see this "real" black person for ourselves. We all trooped to the hotel where Sheila had discovered him. He was the doorman for the hotel, and he dressed in a long coat with much gold braid. He must have been surprised to find himself being stared at so intently by the four of us. We decided that his skin was really black, and not put on with burnt cork. He was the first non-white person we had ever seen—a bit surprising when one realizes how many non-whites made up the British Empire and Commonwealth during our childhood years.

On another day, Sheila and I went to look at the display windows of Selfridge's, which were still well-stocked at that time. Just as we were walking by, a body came hurtling down from the sky and hit the pavement with a thud right in front of us. A crowd gathered so quickly that we didn't even get the chance to look at the body before being pushed back to the fringes of the crowd. That evening in the newspaper was a small paragraph saying the man had committed suicide by jumping off the roof of the store.

The four of us were completely unaware of the controversy surrounding the sending of British children to safety overseas for the duration of the war. The controversy started over the fact that the first English children to reach Canada (on July 3, 1940) were three hundred children from aristocratic homes. The *New York Times* reported that among the passengers was Lady May Cambridge, daughter of Princess Alice and the Governor General of Canada, who arrived with her three children. The passenger list also included five-year-old George St. Lawrence Ponsonby, son of the Earl of Bessborough; eleven-year-old Earl of March, son and heir of the Duke of Richmond; Gordon, a son of Viscount Rothermere and the young Lord Edward Cavendish. The *New York Times* article said that "their youthful names covered a large section of the entries in *Burke's Peerage*, but they came in baby frocks or short pants, hugging toys or sitting in perambulators, with nurses and governesses in attendance."[1] There was much criticism from the British press to the effect that only the wealthy could afford to send their children to safety and only the wealthy could afford to book passage for their children on the "fast" ships, which didn't require Naval escort, and therefore were less likely to be sunk by German submarines.

An overseas evacuation scheme was hastily proposed in Parliament, and approved. Its goal was to evacuate 30,000 children overseas by the end of August 1940—seventy-five percent of whom were to be from working-class parents. Although one-half of these children were eventually to be placed in U.S. homes, all would go to Canada first, because U.S. law prohibited the entry of children whose passage had been paid by the British government, rather than by the parents. By July 4, 1940, the British government had received 211,000 applications for billets overseas for children of school age, and had then to announce that no further requests could be entertained.

With the British government's overseas evacuation plan finally in place, a new difficulty arose. It was discovered that there were not enough British ships available for the transport of children. Towards the end of July, the British government was forced to announce a "temporary" suspension of the shipment of British children overseas. The "temporary" suspension triggered a remark in Parliament by Prime Minister Churchill that the exodus of children to the Dominions and U.S. was "most undesirable." He did not think the military situation required such a course.

Private groups in the U.S. then pressured Congress to allow U.S. ships to be used for the evacuation of English children. Despite the refusal of Hitler's government to guarantee the safety of U.S. ships used solely to evacuate English children, the U.S. Congress approved a bill allowing the entry of U.S. ships into war zones for the purpose of bringing out stranded children. The British government's overseas evacuation scheme was reinstated, only to be closed down for good on October 3, 1940 after *City of Benares* was sunk by a German torpedo in the Atlantic on September 17; and 85 children were lost. In *America, Lost and Found*, Anthony Bailey, an English child sent to America, records that "the total figures for children evacuated overseas were 2,664 by the (British) government, and around 13,600 privately—including the 838 children sent by the U.S. Committee."[2]

Two of our friends missed out on being evacuated overseas. In a 1941 letter Mother wrote, "Roy is now working in The Works and Peter has won a scholarship to the High School. They had their names down to go to their uncle in Canada, but were not so lucky as you to get there before the scheme was closed down."

At the same time as my parents were working on arrangements to send us to Canada, the *New York Times* reported on July 21, 1940 that the general attitude in England about sending children to safety abroad was that it wasn't "cricket" to send anybody out of England. The article said that "people are beginning to talk about other people who have sent their children away—signs already can be seen of trouble between evacuated and non-evacuated children." An example given was the Eton boy who wrote his mother that his best friend had gone to the United States. "I hope his ship sinks," the boy said.

Father and Mother never raised the issue with us. I suspect "public opinion" would not have changed their minds about sending us overseas, as they were not in the habit of paying attention to what other people thought.

My own feelings about being sent to Canada were ambivalent. On first hearing of the scheme, I was excited by the chance for new adventures. However, after finding out that my whole family would not be going overseas, my enthusiasm cooled. As the time drew near for departure, my feelings were not too different from those of the eleven-year-old son of a Labour Member of Parliament, who wrote his parents a letter which was published in the *London Times*. He wrote, "I am writing to beg you not to let me go to Canada. First, because I do not want to leave England in time of war. Second, because I should be very homesick. Third, because it would be kinder to let me be killed with you if such a thing happened (which is quite unlikely) than to be left to drift in a strange world and finish my happy childhood in the contrary fashion. Fourth, I would not see you for an indefinite time, perhaps never again. Letters would simply redouble my homesickness. These are my reasons, and I hope you will take them into consideration. I cannot do anything myself, but I implore you to be reasonable. I am not asking to live in London, I am merely asking not to leave the country. PS: I would rather be bombed to fragments than to leave England." Churchill wrote a congratulatory letter to the boy.

In our own case, the choice was never offered.

CHAPTER SIX

$\mathcal{I}$n July 1940 France surrendered to the Germans. Fortunately for Britain, in the so-called "Miracle of Dunkirk", in the last days of May, some 225,000 of its fighting men had been successfully evacuated from France prior to the French surrender to the advancing German army. As the fighting in France wore on, Churchill rallied the English on June 4 with the most famous of his great wartime speeches: "We shall fight on the beaches—We shall never surrender." On June 17, shortly before the final collapse of France, Churchill told the English people that the Battle of France was over and the Battle of Britain was about to begin. One month away from my twelfth birthday, I was stirred by Churchill's call: "Let us so bear ourselves that if the British Empire and Commonwealth last for a thousand years, men will say, 'This was their finest hour.'"

The English people rallied behind Churchill. They had nothing but scorn for Goering's threat, made on July 17, the day I turned twelve—"If Churchill does not prefer to free England of his presence, then the same inexorable fate will overtake England that struck down and destroyed France."

"The weather in the early summer of 1940 was glorious.

Day after day was warm, dry and sunny; in June the temperature reached ninety degrees," writes Angus Calder in *The People's War*. However, our peaceful days and nights at the Davies Street house in London came to an abrupt end on August 15, 1940.

According to Calder, "For the first and only time, all three German air fleets in the west, including Luftflotte 5 operating from Norway, were committed in simultaneous daylight attacks. The Luftwaffe flew nearly eighteen hundred sorties; more than it would ever be able to mount again.

"It [August 15] was a fine, warm day. The bombers of Luftflotte 5, attacking the north of England without cover from Me 109s, were ignominiously routed and forced out of the battle; not a single British fighter was lost in repelling them. The R.A.F., by the end of the day, was ready to claim the destruction of no less than one hundred and eighty-two German aircraft, and had in fact brought down seventy-five, for the loss of thirty-four of its own fighters. Though the Germans claimed over a hundred scalps, they were bewildered by the ubiquitousness of Fighter Command, still assisted by virtually complete radar coverage. They managed, however, to do a good deal of damage, notably at Croydon airport. The houses and factories around the airfield also suffered, and this was the first time that Greater London had been seriously bombed. About two hundred houses were affected by bombs or blast; sixty-two people were killed, and three times that number were made homeless. It was a small taste of what was to follow.

"Next day, the southern suburbs of London suffered again; but so did the Luftwaffe. On August 18th, a cloudy Sunday, another huge attack was combated successfully. Several days of relative calm followed, when the weather was

40   unsuitable for massed German assaults. On the 20th, Churchill sang the valour of Fighter Command in the House of Commons. 'Never in the field of human conflict,' he said, 'was so much owed by so many to so few.'[1]

"Everyone agrees that there was a Battle of Britain in 1940—the first battle fought over British soil since Culloden; and most concur with the American authority who describes it as 'the pivotal event of the war ...' The British official ac-

Brian in front of 39 Davies Street, London. This was the family home in September 1940 from which the Barlow children departed as evacuees.

count places the opening of the battle on July 10, but even this delimitation is somewhat arbitrary. The first phase involved attacks by the Luftwaffe on convoys passing through the Straits of Dover and was, from their point of view, unprofitable. The Luftwaffe lost twice as many aircraft of all types as the R.A.F. lost fighters, and not much merchant shipping was sunk ...

"Meanwhile, Hitler continued to hope that Britain would surrender without an invasion, encouraged by the fact that the Churchill government still kept open unofficial chan-

Brian in front of the Italian Embassy, London, on a return trip after the war. The Barlow family sought shelter from the Blitz in this building.

nels whereby peace might be negotiated. Dithering, he gave the R.A.F. and the ground defences of Britain a precious month of grace. On July 16th, he issued his direction for the invasion. But on the 19th, addressing his Reichstag, he called for peace ... 'A great Empire will be destroyed,' he warned, 'an Empire which it was never my intention to destroy or even to harm ... I consider myself in a position to make this appeal since I am not the vanquished begging favours, but the victor speaking in the name of reason.' Within an hour, to the amazement and disappointment of the Germans, the BBC on its own initiative had broadcast a blunt rejection of this offer, confirmed by Ambassador Halifax on the 22nd.

"On the night of August 1st, German bombers scattered green and yellow leaflets over Hampshire and Somerset entitled 'The Last Appeal to Reason,' and giving the text of Hitler's speech. These were gleefully collected and were auctioned successfully for the Red Cross. On the next day, Goering ordered the Luftwaffe to destroy the R.A.F. If Britain was to be invaded, it was essential that Fighter Command should be knocked out of the air. August 13th was set as Adlertag—Eagle Day—when the hitherto invincible German air force would commence its destruction."[2]

It was probably the final phase of the Battle of Britain that reinforced our parents' decision to send us to safety in Canada. This phase was an attempt by the Luftwaffe to crack civilian morale by indiscriminate bombing of civilian centers. According to Calder, this phase began when "certain German pilots lost their way on the night of August 24th ... Directed to attack aircraft factories and an oil refinery in the home counties, they bombed the central London area by mistake, contravening Hitler's direct and emphatic orders to his pilots. Considerable fires were started in the City; the

East End suburbs had their first scattering of bombs since 1918. Churchill ordered a reprisal. Next night, eighty R.A.F. planes were sent to bomb Berlin. Again, there was a mistake; those who reached the German capital damaged 'civilian' as well as 'legitimate' military targets. There were further raids on Berlin, night by night, and ineffectual though they were, the first civilians were killed there on August 28th …

"On September 24th, Hitler made a surprise appearance at a rally of women nurses and social workers in Berlin. He promised invasion. 'In England they're filled with curiosity and keep asking, 'Why doesn't he come?' Be calm. Be calm. He's coming! He's coming! Then he brought the women to their feet with hysterical applause as he swore, 'When the British Air Force drops two or three or four thousand kilograms of bombs, then we will in one night drop 150, 230, 300, or 400 thousand kilograms. When they declare that they will increase their attacks on our cities, then we will raze their cities to the ground. We will stop the handiwork of these night air pirates, so help us God!'"[3]

The four of us experienced in all their horror Hitler's reprisal raids on London. Once the German nightly air raids began, which I remember as starting at 6 PM and ending at 6 AM, my family was faced with finding shelter from the bombs. We were spared spending nights in a public shelter when my four-year-old brother Malcolm announced one evening to Father that Joe said we could use his shelter. I remember Father saying to Malcolm that he didn't know anyone named Joe in a tone which suggested he was unlikely ever to know a person named Joe. It turned out that Malcolm had met Joe on a street near our Davies Street house and struck up a friendship with him. Malcolm was in the habit of talking to anyone he met, unlike the rest of us who had

had a longer period of training in class distinctions. We had been carefully taught that friends should be made from one's own background on the theory that you would have something in common.

Joe turned out to be a big, friendly British man with a jolly wife named Mabel. He had been made caretaker of the Italian Embassy in London when the Italian diplomats were recalled at the start of the war. Before the war began, the Italians had constructed a bomb-proof, gas-proof shelter in the basement of the embassy. The shelter was furnished like an apartment. It was large enough to hold beds for all of us as well as over-stuffed chairs and tables. In a 1942 letter, Father described the shelter as the "best and safest underground shelter in London, fitted with anti-gas devices and an air conditioning plant. The [censored] [Italians] knew what was coming."

Each night during the London Blitz, as sirens wailed to announce the arrival of German bombers, we would hurry through the pitch-black streets to join Joe and Mabel in their shelter. The "we" did not at first include Father, who told Mother he had no intention of allowing Hitler to drive him from his own bed each night. He changed his mind when one night an incendiary bomb dropped through the glass skylight in the kitchen, hit the wooden kitchen table, and bounced onto the floor, only to fizzle out without starting a fire. That night Father arrived at the shelter out of breath after a dash through the streets now lit by burning buildings. From then on, Father was more reluctant to stay in his own bed during German air raids.

At first the four of us were frightened by the noise of bombs exploding around us, and by the terrific noise of the big Naval guns in Hyde Park, quite close to the shelter. In time we became accustomed to the noise, and spending nights in the shelter became extremely monotonous. After the rush to the shelter, we were all too keyed up to sleep. Cups of tea or chocolate would help pass the time for a while, especially for the adults. At first, Mother kept us occupied with coloring books or reading to us. Finally, in desperation, she hit on the idea of having us hook rugs. Our response was enthusiastic, and even my older brother Derrick, then a college student, hooked with the rest of us through the long nights. In a 1940 letter, Mother wrote, "The blue rug Derrick started to make when he was in the air raid shelter in London is getting on fine; he has nearly finished it." Mother started on a tapestry, but did not finish it before she left London. It was concentration on such mundane tasks that made it possible for people to withstand the nightly bombing.

From time to time during the night, Joe, who was an air raid warden, would appear in the shelter and give a report on what was going on outside. His reports made us feel as if we, too, were involved in the fight against Hitler. When we emerged from the shelter shortly after 6 AM each morning, it was with a sense of accomplishment. Like other Londoners, we were pleased to be able to thumb our nose at fat Reich Marshal Goering and his vaunted Luftwaffe. Walking back to our house in the early morning hours, we would quite often see shattered glass in the streets and the smoke from burning buildings off in the distance. Relatively little damage was done in the part of London where we lived, as the German pilots concentrated on the dock area.

This all changed after our departure for Canada. In November 1940, Father wrote, "Since you left Grovesnor Square, London, the Germans have played havoc all around Davies Street. The big block of flats over the Motor Showroom and above the shelter you sometimes used during the morning raids received a direct hit with a big bomb, and nothing is left of it. Berkeley Square—every window was blown out. The American Embassy had a delayed bomb, but it was removed before it exploded … You all know what bombs are and you can picture the noise and wuff wuff of the bombs." A December 1940 letter from Mother told us, "Several of those blocks of flats on the right hand of the Square where we used to shelter are just heaps of bricks now … It seems funny when you think how often we used to pass them on our way to the park."

Two incidents from the London Blitz are still vivid in my mind. The first happened during an afternoon raid, when on the way to the nearby public shelter, we witnessed a "dog fight" just above the rooftops. The duel was between a German bomber and a British Spitfire. It must have been a Junker 88 bomber, because it had a plexiglass bubble under the fuselage. We could clearly see the German machine gunner inside the bubble. Smoke was pouring out of the tail of the bomber, and the Spitfire was swooping in for the kill. We watched, fascinated, as the German gunner in the bubble fired frantically at the rapidly approaching Spitfire. Suddenly the German gunner slumped over his weapon, and a burst of red blood ran down the side of the bubble. The German bomber careened out of sight.

It must have been this incident which Father reminded us of in a 1942 letter. "Surely," he wrote, "you must remember the Battle of Britain, when 1,000 German planes came over at 5 PM, teatime. When I arrived by taxi from Mrs. A's, Chelsea, I found you all with Mother in 3 King's Yard (Mews) cheering and clapping your hands as you saw German planes shot down over the River Thames. The sky was a brilliant light blue without any clouds. The German planes looked like big silver dragon flies in formation and in squadrons of 60 planes."

The second incident, also still so fresh in my memory, was when we witnessed the burning of a large part of the dock area in London. As we were hurrying to the Italian Embassy shelter after dark, the sky above London was so lit up by raging fires that you could read the small print of a newspaper with ease. It was as if the blackout had been ended by turning on every street lamp and house light in the city.

"No one escaped the noises of the Blitz," writes Angus Calder in *The People's War*. "First there was the alert, a wail rising and falling for two minutes, 'warbling' as the official handbook somewhat inexactly put it. There was not one siren but a series, as the note was taken up borough after borough. Then there was the heavy, uneven throb of the bombers. 'Where are you? Where are you?' Graham Greene imagined them saying. Then there were many noises. The howling of dogs; the sound of a high explosive bomb falling, like a tearing sheet; the clatter of little incendiaries on roofs and pavements; the dull thud of walls collapsing; the burglar alarms which destruction had set ringing; the crackle of flames, a relishing, licking noise; and the bells of the fire engines. Each individual anti-aircraft gun, to the increasingly sensitive ears of Londoners, had its own voice. One set near John Strachey's warden's post in Chelsea was called 'the tennis racket' because it made a staccato, and yet plangent wang, wang, wang, wang. The shells shrieked and the splinters pattered on the pavements. A bomb falling half a mile away gave you ten seconds' warning by its swish and rush through the air, but the one 'with your number on it', the one which killed you or buried you alive, was heard only when it was almost upon you, because the sound waves caught up with themselves."[4] Malcolm, five years old, probably summed it up best when he told Father, "Hitler is a nasty, noisy old man."

Thanks to the kindness of Joe and Mabel, my family was spared the ordeal of spending our nights in the Tube stations under London. Calder describes them: "The public and communal shelters rapidly developed individual characters. There were quiet, genteel ones; noisy ones, where people brought beer in after the pubs closed; shelters on main roads which served drunks and casual passers-by; shelters favoured by taxi drivers or prostitutes. Specialized shelters developed where people had to work late or be on call all night; hospitals turned their underground vaults into nurses' sleeping quarters and casualty wards."[5]

"Some seventy-nine Tube stations in Greater London became de facto shelters, and at a peak near the end of September, 177,000 people were sleeping in the Underground system."[6]

Conditions in the public shelters were often appalling, but they did improve with time. As Calder stated: "For the first time in many hundreds of years, *Mass Observation* pointed out, 'civilized families conducted the whole of their leisure and domestic lives in full view of each other ... Most of these people were not merely sheltering in the Tubes; they were living there.' Queues began to form outside the stations as early as six in the morning. Children or servicemen on leave would be sent to establish priority for their families. 'The constant worry,' wrote Bernard Kops, 'was whether we would find a space for that night. We lived only for four o'clock when they let us down.' Spivs joined in, to reserve places on the platform for which they would charge half a

crown or more when the raid 'hotted up.' Rain, wind, and
even daylight did not shift the queues. Two white lines had
been painted on the platforms. Until seven-thirty in the
evening, shelterers must keep within the one drawn eight
feet from the edge, leaving the rest for passengers. From eight
until ten thirty, they might encroach as far as the second line
four feet from the edge. Then the Tubes stopped running;
the light was dimmed; the current was cut off in the rail.
People would sling hammocks over the rails, and would walk
a little way down the dark tunnel to relieve themselves. In
the early days, the platforms were packed tight, and people
slept on the escalators or even on the banisters between them.
The snoring rose and fell like a loud wind."[7]

War is a terrible curse to mankind, but it does stimulate
exciting changes. No sooner had the bombing started than
the social strictures I had grown up under began to fall away.
My parents raised no objections when I began to follow
Malcolm's example and talk to people I met in public air
raid shelters during the day, or at the cinema or on street
corners. Calder notes, "War had already weakened the famous English reserve; the blitz swept it away. The shift of
values which Priestly had exhorted was implicit in shared disaster and danger. A grocer excavating the ruins of his store,
handing tins of soup and milk to those who wanted them,
and saying quite solemnly, 'Put it on the account;' a pub sell-
ing drinks out of hours to the local raid victims; a manager
staying on late at the factory so as to give a lift in his car to
weary workmen—such things were unknown before September 1940. Neighbors forgot their censorious rivalries and
joined together in impromptu parties to fight fires, to repair
each other's houses, to look after children, to cook meals.
Life, briefly, seemed more important than money. Edward

R. Murrow observed that no one talked about the cash value of the damage, even when their own homes and offices had gone … 'It's much more important that the bomb missed you; that there's still plenty of food to eat—and there is.'"[8]

Father and Mother became real friends with Joe and Mabel, and they continued to visit each other after my parents left London for Woodbridge, Suffolk. This new sense of social harmony was extolled by the King in his 1940 Christmas message, when England stood alone against Hitler. The King told the English people, "Out of this suffering there is growing a harmony which we must carry forward into the days to come when we have endured to the end, and victory is ours. Then, when Christmas days are happy again and good will has come back to the world, we must hold fast to the spirit which binds us all together now. We shall need this spirit in each of our own lives as men and women, and shall need it even more among the nations of the world."

The London Blitz continued for many months after the four of us left England for Canada. Not until May 10, 1941, did what Calder termed "the last and worst night of the London Blitz" take place. "Fires raged over an unprecedented area, from Hammersmith in the west, and nearly as far as Romford in the east. A British record was set with 1,436 people killed in a single raid; 1,792 Londoners were seriously injured. Westminster Abbey, the Law Courts, the War Office, the Mint, and the Tower were hit. A quarter of a million books were burnt in the British Museum. There were altogether two thousand, two hundred fires, including a huge conflagration at the Elephant and Castle. Next morning a drifting cloud of brown smoke blotted out the sun. Charred paper danced in the woods thirty miles from the City. Churchill wept over the ruins of the House of Commons."[9]

The Battle of Britain came to a halt when, in June 1941, Hitler gave up on his campaign to bomb England into submission, and German air strength was transferred to do battle on the Russian front.

After our departure from London on September 16, 1940, my parents gave up the Davies Street house. They had rented it for the sole purpose of being London-based in order to secure passage overseas for us. They immediately returned to Woodbridge, where Father had been born; and where his sister, my Aunt Cecile, still lived in my grandparents' cottage. They rented a fair-sized house, called "Overdeben." From one of Father's letters I learned that the house was not far from the site where the Anglo-Saxon ship-burial at Sutton Hoo had been uncovered in 1939. It was considered the most remarkable archaeological find in England's history. In *The Treasure of Sutton Hoo*, Bernice Grohskopf writes, "For the first time scholars would be able to examine the actual regalia of a king who reigned in England during the Anglo-Saxon period. The abundance of gold, garnet, and silver revealed for the first time the level of wealth and the scale of life of an East Anglian king in the 7th century, and in all probability the treasure represents only a portion of the royal treasury."[10]

CHAPTER SEVEN

*A*bout the same time my parents moved into the Davies Street house in London, an American couple (unknown to my parents) was deciding to respond to an appeal, issued by the United States Committee for the Care of European Children, "to enable a child (or children), seeking to be safe from the dangers of war, to secure asylum and refuge in the U.S." On July 27, 1940, Mr. Henry Gibson Brock signed an affidavit agreeing to support for an indefinite period five evacuee children. The honorary chairman of this committee was Eleanor Roosevelt, the wife of the President.

Mr. and Mrs. Brock, who had no children of their own, planned to house the children at Muncy Farms, Pennsylvania, the property that had belonged to the Brock Family since 1806. Although their permanent residence was in Philadelphia, the Brocks moved to Muncy Farms in 1926, the year of their marriage, after restoring the 1769 mansion house on the property to its former elegance.

In addition to signing the support affidavit for evacuated children, Mr. and Mrs. Brock filled out a two-page registration form. The form included a section headed, "If the children are unknown to you, please fill out the following: boy or girl, how many, age range, religious affiliation, nationality, and backgrounds." The file copy does not indicate how the Brocks filled out the form. A deposit of $138.00 per child requested was to be sent with the registration form and affidavit to the U.S. Committee. On July 29, 1940, Mr. Brock received a Confirmation of Sponsor's Deposit in the amount of $690.00. Of that amount, $375 was to be used for "reception, care, and transportation," $250 went into a trust fund, and $65 was to be used for "tax, visa, and investigation."

The children Mr. and Mrs. Brock planned to take in would be looked after by Mrs. Josephine Gorham, widow of a former farm manager. She had remained a close friend of the Brocks after her husband's death, and she agreed to return to the farm to provide a homelike atmosphere for the evacuee children.

Mr. Brock had been born into a distinguished Philadelphia family, the only son of Col. Robert Coleman Hall Brock and Alice Gibson Brock. He was a direct descendant of Robert Coleman of Cornwall, the great iron king of the American Revolutionary War. Upon the marriage of Coleman's daughter and Charles Hall, Robert Coleman gave his daughter and her new husband "the great stone house and four thousand acres which formerly belonged to Samuel Wallis". (In the 1940s it was discovered that Samuel Wallis had been a British spy during the American Revolution.) The property became known as Muncy Farms. By the time Mr. Brock inherited it, the land holdings had been reduced to eight hundred acres.

Mr. Brock was a graduate of the University of Pennsylvania, which was founded by Benjamin Franklin. During World War I Mr. Brock paid his own way to France and volunteered to drive an ambulance. After America's entry into the conflict, he transferred to the U.S. Army and acted as liaison officer to the French. After the war ended, Mr. Brock worked in his family's private bank in Philadelphia until his retirement in 1926, when he and Mrs. Brock took up residence at Muncy Farms.

Mrs. Brock's family was also socially prominent. She was one of seven children born to Mr. and Mrs. George Collinson Burgwin of Pittsburgh. Her father was a distinguished lawyer. Mrs. Brock graduated from Dobbs Ferry School and, after her debut in Pittsburgh, spent her time on behalf of many charitable organizations in Pittsburgh. She was particularly fond of the Federation of Girls' School Societies, which supported the Harmerville Home for Convalescents. After her marriage to Henry Brock in 1926, she continued to serve on many charitable boards, all of which benefited from her outstanding ability to raise funds. The Brocks made frequent trips to Europe, and when World War II broke out, they were eager to give whatever support they could to beleaguered France and England.

Despite their wealth and social position, the Brocks had known tragedy. Just as they were about to announce their engagement in 1923, Mr. Brock was involved in a car accident in which three persons were killed. He had been returning from a party in the early morning hours when his powerful motorcar struck and killed three people alighting at a bus stop, and then "sped madly away," according to a newspaper account. At the time, it was rumored that he was not the actual driver of the car. That person was said to have been a well-known society woman, who fled before the police arrived at the scene. Mr. Brock, as a gentleman, refused to divulge her name, and always claimed the accident was his fault. He was charged with operating a vehicle under the influence of alcohol and indicted for murder. Despite a financial settlement reached with the families involved, Mr. Brock was deaf to all pleas by his family and lawyer to plead extenuating circumstances. He was found guilty of second-degree murder and sentenced to six to 10 years in prison. "At the time he was the first driver in the U.S. to be convicted of murder after a fatal crash," according to the *Boston Herald*. He served three years and two months in prison before being pardoned by the governor of Pennsylvania. More than 1,000 signatures were on the petition for his release, including those of relatives of the persons killed by his car. Upon his pardon, the soon-to-be Mrs. Brock met him on the steps of the prison, and one week later, on June 30, 1926, they were married in Pittsburgh. The Brocks moved immediately to Muncy Farms.

There is little doubt that this tragedy gave a new direction to Mr. Brock's life. He never drank or drove a car again in the U.S. He devoted his time and his own money to helping ex-prisoners. He was the first ex-prisoner to serve as a Prison Inspector in Pennsylvania, and to serve as a board member of the Eastern State Penitentiary, where he had served his prison sentence. He used his own money to set up workshops at that penitentiary and to open stores in Philadelphia that sold prisoner-made articles. Mrs. Brock helped design and find attractive items for the prisoners to make and sell. The money earned by the prisoners helped to support their families during their incarceration.

On September 21, 1940—not quite two months after Mr. Brock had signed the affidavit to support five evacuated children (and just six days after we four Barlow children set sail from Liverpool) tragedy struck the Brocks again. While on a visit to the University of Pennsylvania, Mr. Brock was stricken ill with appendicitis. He was rushed to the Presbyterian Hospital for emergency surgery. Complications developed and he died October 9, at the age of 54.

By October 9, the four of us were living at the Gould Foundation in New York City, anxiously waiting to see which American family would take us in, wondering if we four would be able to stay together, and learning to adjust to American ways.

There were many newspaper accounts of Mr. Brock's death, and many tributes. The warden of the Eastern State Penitentiary wrote, "There was a man who did more for penology than anyone I can recall. He was an ideal prisoner—in fact, one of the finest men I have ever met. When he left, we felt we had lost one of our closest friends, and it was with gratitude that we learned that he had decided to devote most of his remaining years to the rehabilitation of the unfortunate. Guards as well as prisoners are in mourning today."

A close friend wrote to Mrs. Brock on November 6, "I can't tell you how grateful we are that you have put our wreath on Henry's grave (at Muncy Farms). Mother writes about the iron fence and just how everything looks. Although Henry is cracking jokes somewhere else, I don't feel as if Heaven was ever really *fun* until he got there. Still, the human heart clings to the details of earth, too, and it seems a link with you and him ... Wasn't it wonderful the way Henry would be silent for ages and then come out with some one phrase that was so direct and humorous and made an absolute picture of the other person. He had more charm than any man that I ever saw, and it all came up bubbling warm from such kindness and generosity ... It must be so terrible for you to be without Henry, and you've been so ill and must still be so weak, and yet because you have lived so great a life, have had such richness and beauty and pain in it, it simply seems an enviable life. The people we are sorry for are the people who have missed life … It was so enchanting to see you together, such gaiety, and charm and fun and dearness, as well as all the hard work you were both doing for the world."

Mrs. Brock would speak of her husband in adoring terms until the end of her life, more than twenty years later.

CHAPTER EIGHT

*T*he four of us left London, bound for Liverpool, to board a ship headed for Canada on September 16, 1940, along with 112 other evacuee children. Our group included the future journalist and author, Anthony Bailey, who would later tell about the trip in his book, *America Lost and Found.* Some of the details about the voyage to Canada given in his book are the same ones I mentioned in a letter to my former headmaster at Orwell Park School, written at the request of my father.

"I'll start from the very beginning, when we left London. We all spent the last night in Joe and Mabel's shelter in the Italian embassy. The next morning we returned to the Davies Street house where Mother said her good-byes. Father went alone with the four of us in a taxi to the American Embassy. At the embassy Father shook my hand and told me I was now in charge of my two sisters and younger brother. He kissed the girls and Malcolm, and told us that we must stay together and pull as a team, the Barlow team." (He repeated these instructions two months later, in a letter written November 15: 'Keep bright and cheerful all of you; pull together in one team.")

As he was leaving us, my father turned to take a last look

at his four children. When he did so a sudden premonition flashed into my mind: I thought I would never see him again. As I looked at his retreating figure I had a hollow feeling in the pit of my stomach. There were tears in Sue's eyes; Malcolm started to cry, but Sheila and I took Father's departure more stoically.

"After Father left us, we went into a big room which had letters hung all around it. We went to the 'B' section, where there were about fifteen other children. We waited for about an hour, and then were introduced to the woman who would be in charge of us. After that, the buses came and we all climbed in. We had a police escort to Euston Station. On the platform we saw a German pilot surrounded by guards on his way to internment."

Anthony Bailey mentions he, too, "saw some captured German airmen under guard at Euston Station." I recall that the German pilots looked as though they could have posed for one of Hitler's propaganda posters, with their blond hair and handsome Nordic features.

The passing crowd looked at them without comment, and even seemed a little embarrassed by their own curiosity. There was no sign of hostility toward these prisoners of war. Perhaps the realization that the Germans were holding captured British and Allied prisoners of war at the same time tempered the reaction of the adults in the crowd. They were aware that the 51st Highland Division had been forced to surrender in France on June 12th, and eight thousand Scotsmen passed into German hands.

When we boarded the train we had first class carriages, and had a really comfortable trip. My letter to my former headmaster makes no mention of the fact that our train to Liverpool was bombed sixteen times. Anthony Bailey does not mention it in his account either. The bombings were reported in the September 30, 1940 *Montreal Gazette* after our escort mentioned them to the Canadian reporters. I do recall that the train stopped dead on the track several times on the way to Liverpool, and that we were instructed to pull down the window blinds to prevent flying glass from causing injuries. It is nice to know that our escort told the Canadian reporters we took the sixteen bombings "bravely."

Continuing my letter to my former headmaster, I wrote, "When we arrived at Liverpool, the air raid siren greeted us, so we had to go down into the station air raid shelter, which was very crowded and hot. When it was all over, we drove to a school where we stayed until the ship came in. We had quite an exciting time there. One night we were all down in the cellar when we heard a whistling bomb coming down. The next minute the ceiling of the cellar was in flames. Next morning we found that the kitchen had been hit. We got no meals until the afternoon, but we did not feel like eating as it was the day we were to go aboard the ship. The buses took us through Liverpool that afternoon, and the place looked like a wreck. There were several vessels in the harbor of different sizes, and we had quite an argument as to which one was ours. We were very disappointed when it turned out to be the smallest ship of the lot. We went aboard our ship, *The Antonia,* and were shown to our cabins after the officers looked over our passports. We were lucky and managed to get one cabin for Malcolm and me, and one for Sue and Sheila. Malcolm did nothing else but ask questions all day long. The cabins were small, and when Malcolm began to spray comics around, there wasn't much room. We sailed at midnight, and it was a very dark night. We no sooner got underway when German bombers came over and tried to bomb the ship. A tug, which was pulling us, was hit, blowing it out of the water. This is not an authentic report as I slept all through it and did not hear a sound. I slept like a log, and when I woke I dressed Malcolm and we rushed on deck. We were just passing Scotland and could see the coastline. We were very excited and spent a wonderful day exploring the ship. The food was very good, and we acted up to the proverb, 'Eat, sleep and be merry!'"

Anthony Bailey did recall the German bombing of our escorting tugboat. "Liverpool was being raided on the evening we left. German bombers buzzed through loose clouds pockmarked by tiny dark ack-ack bursts. A bomb fell in the harbor close by the *Antonia*, sending cascades of Mersey water over one of the tugs that was chevying us out of dock. We wore life jackets and carried our gas masks in their little cardboard boxes on cords hung around our necks – tight-fitting rubbery masks to which were attached a sort of black cylindrical can with a filter in it. We were glad, once at sea, to be able to stow our gas masks in our cabins, though the bulky life jackets had to be carried around with us for the rest of the voyage."[1]

Our group was comprised mostly of children from poor families. As before, at Stone House, once again we had trouble understanding the Cockney accents of some of the children. This did not keep us from exploring the ship with them, which would probably not have been the case in pre-war days.

Anthony Bailey notes our ship was "The *Antonia* ... one of Cunard's popular 'A' liners ... which in peacetime made the Liverpool-Montreal run, and offered cabin-class passengers accommodations which looked like comfortable bedrooms on shore. (There was no first class.)"[2] What exploring of the ship we did was done mostly by Sheila and Malcolm; Sue and I were too seasick to leave our bunks. I remember feeling somewhat better after a few days at sea, and decided to go look for Malcolm. I finally found him in a children's playroom in the bowels of the ship. He was on a wooden hobby horse happily rocking in one direction, while the ship rocked in the opposite direction. One look at him and I felt queasy all over again. I just made it back to the cabin in time. It was several more days in my bunk before I felt well enough to venture forth again.

Our escorts did their best to keep us from getting homesick. Anthony Bailey describes lifeboat drills twice a day, and morning sing-alongs on the poop deck. "The women who were escorting us led us in songs that spanned the Atlantic: 'Swanee River' and 'I Dream of Jeannie' from one side, and 'A Long Way to Tipperary' and 'D'Ye Ken John Peel' from the other. Presumably this singing wasn't just energetic exercise for the lungs and larynx but was to take our minds off periscopes and torpedoes and mummy and daddy."[3] For the first five or six days we were in convoy with some fifty ships, the sight of which tended to keep our minds off ourselves.

Two exciting incidents happened while we were crossing the stormy, gray Atlantic. One was the sighting of icebergs after we left the protection of the convoy. Fortunately they were floating majestically well away from the path of our ship. I knew about the *Titanic*; perhaps I was the "older boy" mentioned in Bailey's book who "told us cheerfully about the *Titanic*."[4]

The second incident was reported in the *Montreal Gazette* of September 30, 1940. One day the ship's alarm bells sounded, and we were directed to report to our lifeboat stations immediately. What looked like a submarine had been

following the ship since the *Antonia* had broken away from
the convoy. While we waited by the lifeboats in our orange
life jackets, the "submarine" surfaced. It turned out to be a
playful whale, much to the relief of the ship's officers and
our women escorts. Like the other children, I was thrilled to
see a real live whale. I gave little thought to the danger we
would have faced if the whale had turned out to have been a
German submarine.

The possibility that the *Antonia* could be sunk by a German submarine was not far fetched. The day after we left
London for Liverpool, the British ship *City of Benares* was
torpedoed after nightfall, in rough weather, 600 miles out
from England. According to Bailey, "Among 406 passengers, 98 were English children aged between five and fifteen. Of the passengers who survived, 13 were children.
Some were killed at once by the explosion of the torpedo.
Some drowned when the lifeboats foundered. Others died
of exposure before ships picked them up. In one lifeboat
containing 40 adults and six small boys, the boys sang 'Roll
Out the Barrel' as the boat was lowered over the side. Then,
missed by rescue ships, they sailed eastward for eight days.
Meals were half a biscuit and a fraction of sardine. Soon
after food and water ran out, they were spotted by a flying
boat [a plane with pontoons]; it radioed a warship which
rescued them."[5] The ship's fate shocked the civilized world.
This ship was the last ship to leave England with evacuees
aboard; it departed from Liverpool the day after our own
ship, the *Antonia*.

The most enjoyable part of the voyage for me was when
we reached the calm, clear waters of the St. Lawrence River.
The sun was shining, and the New World was wrapped in a
lush, green mantle. From the deck of the *Antonia*, we could

64   see neat, small farms dotting the riverbanks. Off in the distance were rolling, wooded hills. On Saturday September 28, 1940, the four of us, along with 112 other evacuee children, docked safely at Montreal, Canada. The crossing of the Atlantic had taken eleven days.

CHAPTER NINE

$\mathcal{W}$hen we disembarked from the *Antonia* at
Montreal, we were met by reporters eager to take photographs of the "little heroes," as we were called in the *Montreal Gazette*, and to interview both us and our escorts. Like other evacuee children who had reached Canada before us, we were more than willing to perform the wartime gesture of "thumbs up" to demonstrate we were not downcast. A reporter took a photograph of Sue and me, probably because we were one of three sets of twins in our group.

The reporters found us "not talkative on the subject of the bombings ... They [the children] all agreed that to be bombed was most frightening, but they didn't want to dwell on the unpleasant subject." The most extended comment came from Kenneth Wright, age 14: "Of course it's very frightening, but it's good to see our planes knocking the Germans from the skies." The reporters claimed to have found us "polite, cheerful, and full of life."

Miss Nancy Tresawna, the 29-year-old London tennis professional who served as chief escort for our group, told reporters of the repeated bombings of the evacuation train enroute to Liverpool and aboard the ship. "The most remarkable thing," she said, "is that not only were none of the children hurt—the train was not struck—but not one of them, up to the time we left England, had suffered a casualty in his immediate family or among his acquaintances."

In addition to one woman escort for each group of 15 children, our group included a physician, Dr. Ian B. MacKay of London, whose task was to "guard the health of the youngsters." He said, "No nervous cases, or anything like that. Bombing does not have as much effect on children as you would think. They quickly get back to normal once they are away from it."

Anthony Bailey's book confirms the doctor's remarks. "In Montreal we ate huge quantities of ice cream and heard a rumor that the ship which had moved up to take our place in the convoy (destination New York) had been sunk the day after we went off."[1] That rumor was correct: the *City of Benares* was attacked and sunk the same day after our ship left Liverpool, September 17th.

When our ship landed in Montreal, Uncle Caldwell Johnston and his wife Etoile met us on the dock. They had arranged for us to visit their house, where two of us would stay, and the other two would be hosted just down the street.

After visiting the Johnston home we had a nice picnic in a park and then were returned to our ship with plans for the Johnstons to pick us up with our bags the next morning. However, arrangements had already been made without our knowledge to send the four of us to New York City, along with 114 other English children. It seems that because we had American visas, the Canadian government would not permit us to remain in Canada. The fact that we were under the auspices of the U.S. Committee for Care of European Children probably also entered into the decision to send us all to New York.

The train ride from Montreal to New York City was made in day coaches, which were different in design and comfort from the first class carriages I had traveled on in England. We were fascinated to find that on American trains the backs of the seats could be moved, so that passengers could face each other or not—by choice. We were given box lunches on the train. One of the children told a reporter, "When they gave us our lunches on the train we were all very surprised. The lunches were in little boxes, just like those used for gas masks at home, and we wondered why we should be getting gas masks in America."

As the train drew near New York City after dark, we were enchanted to see so many bright lights. It was in startling contrast to the "blacked out" London and Liverpool we had left behind.

It was dark when our group arrived in buses at the Gould Foundation in The Bronx. The massive brick building loomed up before us, rather cold and forbidding. The *New York Times* reported that, in a group of 77 English children taken to the Gould Foundation on August 26th, "one child plucked a reporter's arm and in a steady voice, but with despair in his eyes, asked, 'Are we just going to an institution?'"

I felt the same way myself. The homes we had thought we were going to in Montreal seemed very far from New York City. England was still father away. The only consolation was that the four of us were still together.

Consul Caldwell Johnston and his wife Etoile.

CHAPTER TEN

*A*rriving at the Gould Foundation after dark on September 29, 1940, unsure as to what was going to happen to the four of us, I experienced the first bout of homesickness since we had left England. Up to this time I had been too involved looking after my younger brother and two sisters to give much thought to home.

However, I soon cheered up at the thought of new worlds to explore. By daylight the institutional look of the Gould Foundation became less threatening, although the building did seem huge to my 12-year-old eyes. The American staff did their best to make us feel at home. It helped that we spoke English, and our accents seemed to delight Americans. Shortly after our arrival at the Gould Foundation, two celebrities made a visit to cheer us up. One was Douglas Fairbanks, Jr., and the other was Charlie Chaplin. Since no birthday party in England was a success unless Charlie Chaplin films were shown, the four of us eagerly crowded around him. Without his bowler hat and Hitler mustache, he did not look like the Charlie Chaplin we were familiar with. However, when he did his bun dance with two forks, and his famous "Little Tramp" walk, we knew at once that he was authentic.

Front entrance, Muncy Farms.

Henry Gibson Brock and Margaret Burgwin Brock.

Four English Children Will Arrive Tonight to Be Guests Of Mrs. Brock at Muncy Farms

Four English children, members of one family, evacuated from their home near the North Sea coast months ago, will arrive at Muncy Farms, Hall's Station, tonight, to be the guests of Mrs. Henry G. Brock.

The evacues are Brian and Susan Barlow, 12-year-old twins, their sister Sheila, 10, and their brother, Malcolm, 5.

They are the children of a prominent English business and professional man, an engineer.

Their home is a Overdeban, Woodbridge, near Ipswich in Suffolk, one of England's southeastern counties. This is but a few miles inland from the coastline over which German planes are now passing each day and night on their raiding flights, the Suffolk Coast being directly across the North Sea from Holland.

The home of Mrs. Brock, where the children will be guests, is noted locally as the oldest habitation in Lycoming County, incorporated in it being the dwelling of Samuel Wallis, who settled there in 1769.

Article from Williamsport Sun, a Pennsylvania newspaper, November 3, 1940.

Left to right: Sue, Sheila, Malcolm, Brian at Muncy Farms, November 1940, the day after their arrival. The dog, Circus joined them in the picture.

FORM II-B

STATE OF
PENNSYLVANIA } ss.:

COUNTY OF
LYCOMING }

I, HENRY G BROCK, , residing at
(NAME)

R. J #2. , MUNCY , PENN⁰ ,
(STREET) (CITY) (STATE)

have been advised by the United States Committee for the Care of European Children, Inc., a corporation not for profit approved by the Attorney General of the United States and acting in compliance with the order of the Commissioner of Immigration and Naturalization and the Attorney General, dated July 13th, 1940, as follows:

(1) That said Corporation intends to take such steps as may be necessary to enable a child (or children), seeking to be safe from the dangers of war, to secure asylum and refuge in the United States on
☐ a visitor's visa;
☐ an immigration

(2) That such child (or children) will be placed in a home selected by a Child Care agency acting as agent for said Corporation, there to be cared for and supported in accordance with the standards, present and future, of the Children's Bureau of the United States Department of Labor, and that the care of such child (or children) will be at all times subject to the supervision of and termination by said Corporation or its duly designated agent; and

(3) That the said Corporation is seeking to obtain similar undertakings from other persons in the United States in respect to other such children.

In consideration of the taking of the steps aforesaid by said Corporation, and in consideration of its obtaining similar undertakings from other persons as aforesaid, and in consideration of the giving by said Corporation of appropriate assurances to the proper governmental authorities that said child (or children) will not be permitted to become a public charge, I undertake

to pay to said Corporation, as and for the support of said child (or children) and on account of various and sundry charges and expenses of said Corporation in connection with the reception, transportation in the United States, and placement of said child (or children), the cost of maintaining its supervisory service, the sum of $138.00 for each said child (or children) upon the execution of this agreement and

upon notification to me by said Corporation that said child (or children) has arrived in the United States, the further sum of $ FULL CARE payable

Subscribed and sworn to before me
this ___ day of ____ 1940

Robt K. Reeder,
ROBERT K. REEDER, Notary Public
My Commission Expires Jan. 14, 1941

(SEAL)

(SIGNED) Henry Brock

The affidavit, signed by Henry Brock in July 1940, to accept evacuated children under the aegis of the U.S. Committee for the Care of European Children.

To pass the time at the Gould Foundation, I took to reading the local Bronx newspaper and became especially curious about the World's Fair. One afternoon, without telling a soul, I decided to go see the Fair for myself. I hailed a taxi cruising past the Gould Foundation and in my English accent asked to be taken to the World's Fair. The cab driver immediately began to ask personal questions about my English background and reaction to the London blitz. In return he told me all about his own family in a Brooklyn-ese accent I found difficult to understand. Just as I was beginning to worry about how to pay the fare shown on the meter, the cab driver turned off the meter and told me I was his guest. He insisted on paying my way into the Fair and accompanied me, showing me what he could in an hour's time. Then he drove me back to the Gould Foundation, refusing my proffer of money. From that day on, I was taken with the friendliness and generosity shown to strangers by the ordinary American.

No one was aware of my secret adventure. I didn't even mention it to my two sisters or my younger brother, because I was afraid that they would be upset at not having been included. My guilty conscience was eased a few days later when the Gould Foundation arranged to take all the English children under its care to the World's Fair. On my second visit, I recall riding in moving armchairs through the General Motors exhibit. I think it was called "World of the Future." The four of us did a radio broadcast from the Fair but ours was not included in the British broadcast to the disappointment of my Mother who was listening for it.

On October 4, the Gould Foundation doctors gave the four of us physical examinations. Sue, Sheila and I tested positive on the tuberculin test, which was to cause a problem later. The milk we drank in England was not pasteurized which was probably the reason we tested positive. Malcolm tested negative.

Shortly after our arrival at the Gould Foundation, our names, ages, and interests had been put on a list and sent to the Williamsport, Pennsylvania, Committee for the U.S. Committee for Care of European Children. I was said to like outdoor games, Sue domestic needlework, Sheila acting, but Malcolm's likes were left blank. Our religion was listed as Church of England; father's occupation "highly skilled engineer;" financial status of our family "well-to-do." On October 18, the Williamsport Committee contacted Mrs. Henry Brock, recently widowed, and informed her that her home would soon be reviewed for its suitability for placement of the four of us.

One day near the end of October, the foundation officials told me that a visitor was coming to see us that afternoon. I don't recall that any explanation for the visit was given. Mrs. Brock's name meant nothing to me. When the time came, we were ushered into a small reception room and introduced to Mrs. Brock and her late husband's aunt, Miss Gibson. We were startled by their appearance: both were dressed entirely in black. I did not realize they were wearing mourning clothes, and thought the women must be nuns. I don't remember what we chatted about, but I was aware that we were being looked over for some unknown reason. The next day I was asked if we would be willing to live with Mrs. Brock for the duration of the war. It was explained that she was willing to take in one large family. If we didn't accept her offer we four might have to be separated. American families were applying for no more than two children. Finally I said we would go with Mrs. Brock providing we could re-

74   turn to the Gould Foundation if we were unhappy with her. The foundation official breathed a sigh of relief. Our parents, of course knew nothing about my decision—made at the age of 12.*

Mrs. Brock was recovering from surgery on an abscessed wound in her hip, so she was too weak to make a second trip to the Gould Foundation to pick us up. Instead, she sent an old friend, Mrs. Josephine Gorham, widow of a former farm manager, to bring us by train to the Muncy station. Just as we had arrived at the Gould Foundation after dark, we also arrived at Muncy Farms after dark. The date was November 3, 1940.

---

*   Years later, my sister Sheila would recall that momentous visit of Mrs. Brock and her sister-in-law to the Gould Foundation. She said Mrs. Brock looked "small, thin, sweet and patient." Five-year-old Malcolm had a different first impression. Looking at their formal black clothing, he whispered to his older sister, "They're witches!" His eyes grew round as he gazed at the two women. Sheila said Mrs. Brock fell in love with him on the spot. She said Malcolm was one reason she agreed to take all four of us: she "just couldn't leave that big-eyed little boy behind."

CHAPTER ELEVEN

*A*s we drove into Muncy Farms, the headlights of the car allowed us to see the huge elm trees that surrounded the house. The largest tree pre-dated Columbus' discovery of the Americas. The headlights also revealed a large, stately house built of fieldstone, with the exterior woodwork painted a gleaming white. There was a blaze of lights to welcome us.

We did not enter the house by the handsome colonial front door with its hand-blown glass fan light, but—as was the custom—we used the door which opened directly into the library. This room was in the oldest part of the house, which had been built in 1769, and now made up the mid-section of the house. To the left of the library was an elegant three-story wing, built in 1808. To the right was the service wing, added in 1926 after the Brocks tore down a Victorian-style wing that did not harmonize with the colonial design of the rest of the house.

A fire burned brightly on the library hearth. The fireplace was paneled in chestnut wood, with a seascape painting set in a panel above it. Two windows flanked the fireplace and looked out on a stone-paved courtyard. On the other three walls of the library were books, from floor to ceiling, bound in fine leather. On the side with the entrance door, the bookshelves were separated by three windows which looked out on the front circle of lawn and elm trees.

The library, a large room with an oak-beamed ceiling, was furnished in the style of an English country house. An oriental rug in soft pinks covered the floor. Across from the fireplace was an original davenport sofa covered in a sturdy plum-colored fabric. Chairs and another sofa were covered in faded prints. An oil portrait of one of Mr. Brock's ancestors hung above a massive oak partners' desk. At the other end of the room stood a Steinway grand piano. Heads of mountain sheep hung above the door to the 1808 wing and above the door to the dining room. Despite its size, the library had a comfortable and informal look to it.

Five dogs of different breeds jumped off chairs to greet us eagerly. Mrs. Brock rose from the sofa across from the fireplace and welcomed us warmly. I was glad to see she was no longer dressed in black, as she had been when we first saw her at the Gould Foundation. She wore a pearl-gray dress, set off by the soft lustre of a pearl necklace. She was of average height and very thin. Her gray hair was parted in the middle and drawn back in a soft wave on each side. She instantly put us at ease by asking us questions about the train ride from New York City. When it was my turn to answer, I immediately felt that I had her undivided attention. When I said something that amused her, her eyes would crinkle up and she would laugh with unaffected enjoyment. I thought she was wonderful from that first evening on.

Mrs. Brock had arranged to serve lamb for supper, as she thought we would be more familiar with mutton than something American like hot dogs or hamburgers. She had planned the entire meal to be as "English" as possible. I think we even had trifle for dessert. She needn't have worried. At our ages, we were always hungry, and would have done justice to any typically American meal.

Realizing that we must be tired from our long train ride and from all the excitement of arriving at our new home, Mrs. Brock showed us to our bedrooms not long after supper. She had chosen for us the two bedrooms directly above the library, as they were the closest bedrooms to her own. Malcolm and I shared one bedroom, and Sue and Sheila the other. A connecting bathroom separated the two bedrooms. Both bedrooms had fireplaces in one corner. Later we were to discover that every room in the house had a fireplace. When she said good night, Mrs. Brock told us not to hesitate to come to her room if we needed anything during the night. I slept very soundly that first night in my new American home.

I remember waking up the next morning and dashing to the bedroom window to look outside. Below us was a steep bank going down to a small stream, and off in the distance was tree-covered Bald Eagle Mountain. With great excitement Malcolm and I got dressed. Sue and Sheila heard us and asked us to wait for them, but we didn't. We took the stairs down to the entrance hall with its crystal chandelier and enormous Irish breakfront filled with fine china. By trying various doors we found our way into the library. Soon Sue and Sheila joined us.

We discovered a tennis ball that belonged to the dogs, and were tossing it to each other when suddenly a strange couple entered the library. They were old friends of Mrs. Brock and had arrived from Philadelphia after we had gone to bed. Aunt Josie Molten told us years later that the four of us instantly drew together and politely inspected them. Then in a clipped English accent, I asked them if they cared to play. Not wanting to turn me down, they agreed to toss the tennis ball with us. When Mrs. Brock came down to breakfast a short time later, she was startled to find her guests and the four of us tossing a tennis ball in the library. I think she thought her best friend and her husband should have known better than to toss a tennis ball in the library, as two valuable American Indian pottery lamps on the table behind the sofa were in danger of being broken. However, her guests became our instant friends, and we were eventually to look upon them as an aunt and uncle.

After being served breakfast by a staff of four, we explored our new home. The house had a curious history, and the arrival of four young English children to stay there in 1940 gave it an ironic twist in light of a 1940 discovery in England. The original builder of the house, Samuel Wallis, was one of the largest landowners in Pennsylvania at the time of the American Revolution. He was a friend of many of the American patriots, like Judge James Wilson, a signer of the Declaration of Independence, and was thought to be a firm supporter of the Revolution. However, documents discovered in 1940 in England showed him to have been a secret Loyalist and a paid British spy. In his book, *Secret History of the American Revolution*, Carl Van Doren writes, "There can be little doubt that 'The Gentleman in Philadelphia' was sly Samuel Wallis. As there can be no doubt that Wallis was [Benedict] Arnold's agent and sent secret intelligence to the British, neither can there be that he (if he was 'The Gentleman') had no scruple about making any money he could out of shipping the British Army of Occupation food with which to carry on the War. But in Philadelphia Wallis went on expertly pretending to be a Whig. So long as Congress should be in power he would stand well with the patriots. If the British forces should put the rebellion down, then he could prove that he had long been a useful Loyalist."[1]

Wallis carried out his plan so successfully that, as Van Doren wrote, he was "untouched by suspicion, [and] stayed quiet and safe in Philadelphia till 1782, when he went back to his stone house (Muncy Farms) on the West Branch of the Susquehanna River. There besides increasing his estate to about 8,000 acres, he devoted himself to trading in land, particularly as a representative of the Holland Land Company of Amsterdam." Judge James Wilson of Philadelphia was one of his associates in the Holland Land Company.

The final chapters of the Samuel Wallis story are related in *Homes and Heritage of the West Branch Valley*, published by the Williamsport Junior League in 1986. "Soon Wallis's financial affairs became complicated as he overextended himself in land purchases. He made an effort to secure the payment of a large amount of money owed him by Judge Wilson. Wallis pressed the Judge one evening to sign a paper whereby the entire amount was to be paid in cash. Wilson, however, did not affix his signature, giving the excuse that he was tired and would sign the next morning. Wallis consented to the request, and when morning came, Wilson was found dead in his bed of an overdose of laudanum, an opium derivative.

"Broken in spirit because his entire fortune was now endangered, Wallis began a journey to Philadelphia. While en route, he stopped at an inn and was lodged in a room whose previous occupant had died of yellow fever just the day before. Unfortunately for Wallis, the bed linen had not been changed, nor the room cleaned. He contracted the disease and died a few days later in Philadelphia.

"Without Wallis's management, his financial affairs could

not be untangled, and his widow died nearly penniless. The great stone house and four thousand acres were sold at sheriff's sale to Henry Drinker, of Philadelphia. He in turn sold it to Robert Coleman, of Lebanon, who gave it to his daughter, Elizabeth, on the occasion of her marriage to Charles Hall. The house remained in the immediate Hall family until one of the Halls used it as collateral to borrow money, which he unfortunately lost. After this incident, it passed to the Brock family, who were cousins of the Halls. It was Mr. and Mrs. Henry G. Brock who were responsible for restoring the house to the grandeur and elegance of the days when the spy, Samuel Wallis, came in from the cold."[2]

The day after our arrival at Muncy Farms a *Williamsport Sun* reporter was sent to take photographs of the four of us and to interview Mrs. Brock. One photograph was of the four of us standing at the base of one of the huge elm trees at the front of the house. The oldest of the five dogs is shown with us. Another scene had us playing a mock game of croquet.

Over the next few days we explored our new home. We learned that Muncy Farms consisted of some 500 acres of fields and woodlands. The farming was done by an elderly farmer and his middle-aged son, employed by the Brocks since the 1920s. The son and his wife had twins, a boy and a girl, who were a little younger than Sue and me. We soon became good friends with the twins and included them in all our games. We discovered there was a dairy herd of some twenty cows, mostly Guernseys, which provided fresh milk and butter for our table. I remember that the milk was so creamy it would barely pour out of the pitcher. Eating dry cereal for breakfast became something I eagerly looked forward to each morning. In summer, the milk was used to make ice cream with either fresh strawberries or peaches. The ice cream was churned by hand, and the four of us got to take turns cranking the handle. This homemade ice cream was glorious stuff, far creamier and better tasting than the ice cream we had eaten back in England. It tasted quite a bit like Devonshire cream. We were thrilled to find in the main barn—a magnificent structure with handhewn beams—two Percheron-type horses named Bert and Nell. They were the pride of the old farmer, who had never really taken to tractors. Occasionally Bert and Nell would be used to plough or haul the hay wagon. The old farmer controlled them by voice commands. We were fascinated to watch them being shod. The old farmer was too frail to lift up their feet any more, so he had trained them to put their hooves on a wooden stand for shoeing. We would have spent more time patting Bert and Nell, but we quickly discovered that the old farmer didn't like children playing in his barns.

Muncy Farms was a "working" farm. All the corn, hay and straw needed for the dairy herd and the other farm animals was raised on the farm. Vegetables were raised for our table by a gardener. We could eat all the smoked ham, sausage, eggs and chicken we wanted, and could drink as much milk as we liked. After the rationing we had experienced in England, this seemed to be too good to be true. The one stricture Mrs. Brock insisted on, was that you must eat a little of each thing served at the dining room table or else you would not get to eat dessert. As dessert was often homemade pies and other delights, I found myself trying new dishes, some of them American, like corn pudding. Sheila, on the other hand, got highly skilled at hiding on her plate dishes she didn't like. The cook found out I didn't like corn on the cob, so would cut off the kernels for me, ignoring Mrs. Brock's instructions not to spoil us.

Nearer the house, we discovered an *en-tout-cas* tennis court and an Olympic-sized swimming pool. We all learned to swim in the pool at Muncy Farms. Having grown up on the North Sea, which is cold and has strong undertows, none of us could swim when we arrived in the States. Although Orwell Park had a huge swimming pool (built by my father), I don't recall ever swimming in it.

Up until mid-November, the only communication we had received from our parents was a telegram: "All letters received. Writing today. Love to you all. Mummie and Daddy Barlow." But finally, on November 15, I received a letter from my father, addressed to the Gould Foundation in New York. It said, "We had a cable from a Mrs. Brock, Muncy, Pennsylvania. We cannot write as we do not know her address. Letters from America keep crossing our letters from the Johnstons. I have been waiting to hear for weeks." Two days later he wrote to Sue, "Now remember, all of you, keep smiling, laugh, be bright and pleasant. Learn to like your new parents. Be good!" Father had learned by that time that we were not living in Montreal with his friend, Caldwell Johnston. However, he was obviously not aware that Mr. Brock had died before we arrived at Muncy Farms. All he knew was that we had been given shelter somewhere in Pennsylvania and were together. His four youngest children were safe at last.

The safety of his wife and Derrick, were still a matter of concern.

CHAPTER TWELVE

*W*e had only been at Muncy Farms a few days when
I sensed that Mrs. Brock had not only opened her home to
the four of us, but also her heart. She had longed for children of her own, but, sadly, could never carry a pregnancy
to full term. Her one regret in an otherwise extremely happy
marriage was that she had been unable to have a son to carry
on the Brock name.

Mother's first letter to "My Dear Mrs. Brock", was dated
January 8, 1941. "I am so glad Malcolm found his way to
your heart. He is a funny little boy; everyone seems to love
him. Wherever we go, Malcolm makes friends with everyone. Please do not be worried that the children are reserved
with you. They are always a bit like that with me. Sue is never
demonstrative. She very rarely becomes affectionate even with
me, and hates me to make any fuss over her. Sue is a tremendous thinker, and often spends hours with a book, or just
sitting thinking things out. Brian is always happy-go-lucky,
and is not so brainy as Sue, although I think he is brighten-
ing up a bit now. Sheila is quite a tomboy, and is always saying how she wishes she was a boy. She is much more
affectionate than the others, and always ready to do anything
she is asked."

Mother described our interests. "Sheila is very fond of all sports, and is a very good runner. She won several prizes at school. Both Sue and Sheila are very keen on tennis, and were getting quite good last summer. They used to play in local children's tennis tournaments at Thorpeness three times a week in the summer holidays. They both had lessons with the Professional, who was very impressed with Sheila, and said Sue would be reasonably good, but it was more difficult for her, being left-handed. Brian did not play much, as he preferred to play cricket at the club. He was becoming quite a good cricketer. A friend of mine, who was a well-known cricketer and played for England, is a clergyman who used to come to Thorpeness every summer. He took Brian in hand and gave him some coaching. All the children have longed to be able to swim. I have tried very hard to teach them. Sue is a bit nervous, but Sheila was beginning to swim a little bit. Brian can swim fairly well. Malcolm was very brave in the water until a big wave knocked him down and nearly drowned him. Since then he has been a bit frightened."

Mrs. Brock must have asked about giving us a weekly allowance, because Mother wrote back, "As regards their pocket money, I used to give them all one shilling a week each. I found them very good with money, and they always saved some of it. Sue is quite a miser; Brian very generous. On their birthdays and Christmas I used to give them extra. They have all got bank money boxes, and they were very good in putting some of their money in. I now put it in for them each week."

About bedtimes: "Malcolm usually went to bed about 6:30 p.m. and later in the summer, the others about 7:30 p.m. and also later in the summer time. They have never any of them rested during the day, as I found they slept better at night without it. I believe the people in charge of the children had quite a battle with Malcolm while they were waiting for the ship at Liverpool. He had a great objection to resting in the afternoon."

Mother concluded with a description of our life in England: "I had two nurses with the children when they were tiny. Only one when Malcolm was a baby. She left me to go to India to be married when Malcolm was 18 months old. Since then I have not had one. I tried various governesses, but they were not a success, so sent three of the children to school. My housemaid was very fond of Malcolm, so we looked after him between us. When he became four years old, he demanded to go to school with the others, so they used to take him with them in the morning, then bring him home to lunch. Sue and Sheila went back in the afternoon; Brian was at boarding school. Malcolm loved being at school. He joined in the games with the older boys, and they were marvelous to him."

How to handle our health reports from the Gould Foundation in New York was the first problem that faced Mrs. Brock. Because Sue, Sheila and I had tested positive on the tuberculin test, Mrs. Brock wrote to the U.S. Committee for the care of European Children for guidance as this committee was their legal guardian while they were in the United States. She discovered by chance, that the local caseworker for the Children's Aid Society was about to send a report to the Barlow parents and intended to refer to the children's tuberculosis susceptibility and x-ray pictures. Mrs. Brock was somewhat alarmed because she did not feel this question should be handled by the agency before she was able to take the matter up with the family herself. This question of health is, of course, a grave matter, and while the parents should be notified she felt with a little more thought and care it could be done in such a way as not to alarm them. Mrs. Brock wrote "Please understand I am not complaining about the Agency, and I realize that it is probably over-anxiety on their part to do the right thing that has created this situation. At the same time, this involves a principle that will continue during the period of their visit with me, and I would like very much to understand just how your Committee wishes us to handle such questions.

"Another thing about which I feel very strongly is the possible concern of these parents when they receive a letter on the heading of a social service organization. To the average Englishman, children in care of a social service agency would immediately connote lower class or 'problem' children. I had felt that all reports would go through on the heading of your Committee, in whose care these parents feel the children are placed, so that they would not feel that there has been a shifting of responsibility or a change in methods beyond which they had been told to expect before sending the children."

On November 29, Mrs. Brock was informed that the U.S. Committee had written the Children's Aid Society suggesting they talk with her "in detail about the plans which you have in mind for letting the parents know of the children's physical condition, which would seem to be a very kind and thoughtful way of approaching the problem."

Mrs. Brock's suggestion that she write our parents directly evidently prevailed, because in her January 8, 1941 letter Mother wrote, "I must say I am very surprised to hear the doctor's report on Sue and Sheila. There has never been any sign of anything like that [tuberculosis] in either of our families. Anyhow, we are not a bit worried about it, as I know they could not be in better hands than yours. We think you have been absolutely marvelous to them, and cannot express our gratitude enough. They did have a rough time in London, but I am sure they will soon forget all that. The mere fact that they have all put on weight seems to me to be the best sign."

On the same date, Mother also wrote to us: "I hope you are all eating lots of the lovely food you get over there, because I want to see you all well and fat. If you had been here, you would not have had half such nice things. We are very strictly rationed now, but we get plenty of variety to eat, eked out with our shooting. But you are all much better off being out there, so you must eat lots to please me."

Mother's first letter to Mrs. Brock concluded, "My husband is always saying when this war is over, if we have anything left, that we shall come and live in America or Canada. I am sure the children will never want to come back to England. Well, again, very many thanks for all your kindness, and a very Happy New Year to you. Yours very sincerely, Violet Barlow."

Thus was forged the first link between two women who had not known of the existence of each other before the war brought their lives together.

On March 12, 1941 Mother wrote to the four of us. "I do think your Aunt Peggy looks nice in the snap. I am looking forward to the day when I can meet Mrs. Brock. Perhaps now that America is going to help us with supplies, that day will not be very far off." She was referring to the fact that on December 17, 1940, President Roosevelt had given a press conference outlining a scheme, which he called Lend-Lease, to give aid to Britain. His argument was that, "if a neighbor's house is on fire it is only sensible to lend him a hose to stop

88   the fire spreading to your own house, and that it would be
       stupid to think of asking for payment in such circumstances."
       On January 10, 1941, the Lend-Lease Bill[1] was introduced
       to Congress. There was considerable opposition. But finally
       on March 11, 1941, the Lend-Lease bill was signed into law.

CHAPTER THIRTEEN

"*J*ust received a letter from Brian, written from your new home," wrote Mother on December 1, 1940. "What fun you must be having on a farm. You have often told me you would like to live on a farm."

Like other English parents who had sent their children to safety overseas, Mother and Father were constantly worried that we might misbehave. Most letters contained admonitions to "be good." Mother told us, "Mind you try and help Mrs. Brock as much as you can, and be good." Father wrote, "You must learn to respect them (your new foster parents) and treat them as if they were your father and mother. Obey every request." It is clear that when he wrote that letter, Father did not yet know Mrs. Brock was a widow.

The admonitions were not really necessary. With my strict childhood training in polite manners, I was more likely to be concerned with the question asked by an eleven-year-old English boy upon his arrival in New York City, "Will they think I'm a sissy? Last summer my American cousin said English boys were sissy because they had quiet voices and were polite."

The American woman who had been the boy's escort to the U.S. explained the politeness of English children in an article written for the *New York Times*: "Remember that if the politeness of an English boy or girl annoys you, it is second nature to them. They are not 'putting it on;" they are taught it almost before anything else. If ever you are tempted to say 'sissy' to an English boy because his voice is lower, or his words seem to be more carefully chosen, will you remember this: anything from seven to fifteen years ago England was full of gently-spoken, polite boys like that. Today the skies are full of those same boys, now grown to be hard, keen, brave men whose hourly deeds of heroism are one of the great epics of our time. Day after day, night after night, the seas are patrolled by men who not so long ago were just like the boys you will soon have as your guests."[1] This American woman had evidently not come into contact with children like our evacuees from the East End of London!

Although Father and Mother never expressed any concern in their letters that Mrs. Brock might spoil the four of us, other English parents tried to communicate their expectations. The *New York Times* magazine printed a letter sent by an English father to the host family. "My dear friends, I have, of course, not the faintest idea what you are like ... You, for your part, will realize what effort of will it has needed to send our son away like this ... We are, and shall continue to be, grateful for the kindness you American people have shown in organizing for the withdrawal of our children from this dirty and painful business, but we cannot help realizing that it may be for one year or even two or more. These are vital years in a child's life, and Michael being 11 years old on September 30, we feel we shall now lose that interesting period of 11-14. He will, at times, be a nuisance and get into trouble.

We hope you will be firm as we should be. He is a handsome little chap, but that is to his disadvantage. People will say, 'oh, what a lovely boy,' and that is no good for any child.

"He has been bathed and in bed at what we consider a proper hour, always 8 o'clock, during the last two years. Like all boys, he hates washing and teeth cleaning, keeping nails neat, etc. He is not a big eater and until recently we always had to coax him. He will eat corn flakes and milk at any time and all the time, avoids eating bread, drinks milk freely. He has always had 3 pence per week pocket money, not more on principle, and I always made sure he had some money to avoid any temptation. His school reports have been mediocre and could all have been good or very good but for that boyish attitude—laziness, play before work." The father's letter continues with a few more details, such as giving the names of friends who would arrange for Michael's return to England "in the event of our being killed."[2]

Like other English parents of evacuated children, our father felt it necessary to justify his decision. He wrote me, "Always remember the reason we allowed you all to go to America was this part of the world has gone mad, and a mad dog [Hitler] has been let loose in our civilization, and his brain works for destruction."

English parents who sent their children overseas in 1940 paid a heavy price. Malcolm worshiped our father, and Father pined especially for him. Mother accepted our separation from her more readily, perhaps because she had her first son, Derrick, still in England, whereas Father had given up all his children. Unlike Father, Mother was confident that the four of us would return to England someday. Also, Father kept bottled up his deep sense of loss at our departure.

Mother was able to express her affection for us much more openly in her letters than she had ever done in person during our childhood.

My parents shared the concern of other English parents that their overseas children would forget their English heritage, and—even worse—no longer speak or act in the English manner. On November 17, 1940, Father wrote me, "Always be proud of your name, Bohun Barlow [all four of us had Bohun as our middle name]; it dates back to 1066 when your ancestors arrived from France." The *New York Times* wrote about a Christmas 1940 broadcast in which fourteen English children spoke to their families in England over a radio network. The article mentioned one mother in Leeds who told her son he "talked like an American" because he said being in Canada was "OK."

It came as a surprise to the four of us whenever our parents' letters mentioned that they seriously considered emigrating to the U.S. after the war "if we have any money left by then." Over the next couple of years, they continued to talk about living in America after the war. Such talk did not please me, because I looked forward to the day the war would be over and I could return to England. The King had no more loyal subject in the Colonies than me.

CHAPTER FOURTEEN

$\mathcal{A}$lthough the war was beginning to seem very far away to the four of us settling in at Muncy Farms, it was an everyday presence for the family we had left behind in England. Some time after we left, our parents relinquished the Davies Street house in London and returned to Woodbridge in Suffolk. There they rented yet another house, and attempted to resume the rural way of life they were accustomed to. Mother could still write in October 1940 about "going shooting," but it was not the same as in pre-war days. For the first time, our father was without a gun dog of his own. Likewise, Mother could still write about playing golf but several of her favorite courses were closed because of the war. And when our parents went to Ipswich to shop, now they rode a bus. Their two Rolls Royce cars had been sold when war broke out because they could not get enough petrol to run them.

Even though this latest Woodbridge house was much smaller than Stone House, our parents still thought it necessary to employ servants, which was still possible to do in late1940. They took on a cook and a gardener, and a "daily" to do the cleaning. This allowed them to continue to invite friends for a "country stay." In December they invited Joe and Mabel, the caretakers at the Italian Embassy in London who had offered us shelter during the Blitz, to come for a weekend.

When our parents returned to rural Suffolk from London they thought they would be out of reach of German bombers, but the fall of France in June had given the Germans nearby air bases from which to attack England, and Suffolk was right on the path of the incoming German planes. On December 1, Mother wrote, "Since I last wrote you, we had quite a bit of excitement as we had a big air battle right over the garden. The Italian and German planes came over, and one was brought down on the golf links, and the newspapers said 15 more were downed in the sea off where we used to live. Then one Sunday morning at breakfast time, another lot came over and I saw them fighting overhead. I saw our people shoot down one; then a German shot him down, and the English pilot landed unhurt in the garden of a friend of ours. Then we shot the other German down. After that they all went out to sea as hard as they could go. Lately, we have heard the planes going to bomb London, going over here at night in great numbers. Occasionally they drop something on the way, but nothing very near us at present. The other morning I was looking out of the bedroom window and saw a German Dornier flying quite low towards the house. The guns fired at him, and he turned off and flew over the town. Then he tried to bomb a station in the country a few miles away. He missed the station and got some cottages and injured a few people."

Father also described the German air raids. "There is not much to tell you except every night soon after it gets dark, the German planes fly up the River Deben, and when they are over our house they turn left for London or right for the northern towns—Liverpool, Birmingham, Glasgow—which they bomb every night. We have had lots of bombs all round Woodbridge, some as near as 150 yards from our house. At night the sky is a blaze of searchlights trying to find the German planes in the darkness. When the German planes come over the house, the vibration shakes all the plates and cups and saucers on the table."

Although rationing had gone into effect in January 1940, Mother never complained about it. She, like others, accepted it as necessary. Bacon, butter and sugar had been on the ration list since January 8. On January 11, the government announced that Fridays were to be meatless days, and that no beef, mutton or veal would be sold on Mondays or Tuesdays. To supplement her vegetable garden, Mother invested in four hens.

At first, after her return to Suffolk, Mother found time heavy on her hands. On October 31, she wrote, "I still haven't found very much to do here yet, so have been making woolly clothes for some of the children who have been bombed out of London." From this small beginning was to grow a clothing depot run out of her garage. In December, she wrote, "I have been very busy making children's and baby clothes for some of the people who have lost their homes in London and are now living in the surrounding villages. The clothing depot is going strong. I have given out over 100 different clothes in ten days. I have just received a few things from the American Red Cross, which were very welcome, as everyone has given all the clothes they can around here. Every day we get mothers and children arriving from London, and as I am very short of children's things, I have to work very hard to make them some. I started this depot after I had sent the clothes you all left behind to London."

Father's 1940 letters do not mention whatever war work he was involved in at the time. Not until he sent me an article he had written for the *Eastbourne Courier* in 1943 [the headline read "Reconstruction Means Progress"] did I learn about a project he had been working on long before 1940. "In June 1930 I was reconstructing and preserving some old Roman underground buildings, situated in a small east coast seaside town. They were in a perfect state of preservation, built below ground in solid clay. Above ground on top of these buildings, I constructed a large, ornamental lake, with six concealed water fountains, which reached a height of twenty feet, creating a pleasing spectacle, and big improvement on what was ugly waste ground.

"The Roman underground building below I made into an air raid shelter for three hundred people, with coal fires; the chimneys were disguised in the form of old ruins. Facing the sea I constructed concealed machine gun emplacements, again in the form of old ruins. This was the first air raid shelter built in the country and became a target for those who ridiculed the idea of war.

"Local interest in the shelter from people with large families of children caused me to offer my services free to construct another underground shelter with hospital and first aid posts, for two thousand people, under the hill of clay. Among the permanent residents of the area were millionaires. The local golf course cost an enormous sum of money to build. My proposed public air raid shelter, including the hospital, would have cost less than one-fourth the money expended on the golf course. But the shelter project was turned down—excuse: owing to cost. The Mayor made a public speech, boasting the town had the cheapest Air Raid Protection Service in the country—one extra fireman at £3 per week. When war broke out, in the first raid on the town, over one hundred bombs were dropped."

By the end of 1940, his current engineering projects having been completed, Father began a letter writing campaign to locate a new wartime project which would use his engineering talents.

As 1940 came to a close, my family in England remained undaunted by the privations on the home front and by the perils from the German bombs. They faced with equanimity the possibility of an invasion by Hitler's armies, flush from their victories on the Continent. On November 17, Father wrote Sue, "In England we are having a very hot time, and it will last a long time, perhaps many years. You need not fear. We shall win by gradually wearing the Germans down, until they are unable to carry on. Then their troubles will increase day by day."

CHAPTER FIFTEEN

*E*xcitement built day by day, as the four of us prepared for our first Christmas in America. Christmas cards arrived at Muncy Farms by the dozens, and we put them up on the library shelves. By the time Christmas day arrived, the cards decorated three walls of the library. We helped put up green fir ropes to frame the huge fireplace, and draped them over the oil paintings. Red ribbon bows were tied around the necks of the two mounted mountain sheep heads. The most exciting event for us was the selection and cutting down of a live Christmas tree in the woods on the farm. We all opted for the biggest tree we could find, and when it was set up in the east wing hall, its top reached above the second-floor landing. We found it a very satisfactory Christmas tree!

On Christmas Eve, Mrs. Brock held her annual neighborhood party. Parents were encouraged to bring all their children, no matter how young. Drinks and sandwiches were served, and then a carol sing took place around the grand piano in the library. After the caroling, the party ended so that parents could put their young children to bed, assemble new toys, and attend late night church services.

After the party, the four of us were sent to bed. We were each given a stocking to hang at the foot of the bed, and told that Santa Claus visited only "good" children who went promptly to sleep. While we slept, Mrs. Brock and the staff decorated the Christmas tree in the hall. It was adorned with hundreds of lights and fancy balls, some dating back to Victorian times. Under the tree were placed brightly-wrapped presents for each of us.

The next morning, when we saw the tree, we were enchanted by its magnificence. We had awoken to find our stockings full of presents. Mrs. Brock heard our delighted comments and told us to bring our stockings to her bedroom. While she sat in her big double bed, we tore the wrappings off the stocking presents. In the toe of each stocking was the traditional tangerine.

Breakfast was a hurried affair because we were not allowed to open the presents under the tree until we had eaten something. Mrs. Brock's big gifts to us that first Christmas were skis and skates. An ice rink had been made on the lawn in front of the house, and we spent most of Christmas day learning to skate. Despite the many falls, it was lots of fun. We also tried out our skis in a field with a gully near the main barn.

My gift to Mrs. Brock that year was a lamp I had made with the help of the chauffeur. It was made out of the hub of a wagon wheel I had found near one of the barns. I painted it red, but because the wood was so dry, most of the paint was absorbed, giving the lamp quite an attractive antique look. I bought the lamp fixture with my 75 cents per week allowance from Mrs. Brock. I had to give her the lamp without a shade, as I could not afford one. She was delighted with it, although it cost her a pretty penny to have a custom lampshade made for it. To this day, that lamp sits on a table in the library.

Mrs. Brock was unusual in her willingness to display the

gifts the four of us gave her over the years, although in retrospect some of them were "little horrors." I once gave her a garish Spanish galleon, and it sat for years on the grand piano. Malcolm gave her an ashtray he had won at a local fair. It was made of plaster, and the orange paint on the lion was half on the animal and half on the blue base. She kept it on her bedside table for years.

In England, Christmas of 1940 was a far cry from those in previous years. Mother was worried that her Christmas presents to us would not reach us in time. On December 1st, she wrote that she had been obliged to send our packages at the beginning of November, and that they had to be sent to Montreal, as she had not known where we were going to be. As it turned out, we still had not received her parcel by early February; she wrote on February 6, 1941, "What a shame you have not got the Christmas parcel. I spent £12 getting you some really nice things." The Christmas package eventually reached us some time in mid-February, and on February 21, Mother wrote, "So glad you have got the Christmas presents at last. I really had begun to think they had been sunk. I am sorry the glass was broken in the clock. I wonder how that happened, as when it is zipped up, the case is supposed to protect it. I have almost forgotten what I sent you now. How did Malcolm like his carthorse? I thought it was rather nice. As those things took so long, I don't suppose Sheila got her presents in time for her birthday. Well, Sheila darling, how does it feel to be eleven now?"

Despite the war, in 1940 in England it was still possible to shop for Christmas. Mother wrote that she and Derrick had gone shopping in Ipswich in their new car. "It was quite a job to get Derrick's large feet into my little Austin 7, especially as we had some parcels as well. I bought Derrick a watch for as he wanted one when he gets into the Air Force. I got him a really good one. We bought Daddy his usual socks."

Father sent Malcolm a special letter on December 22nd. "Daddy's Boy—In three days from now it will be Christmas Day. Do you remember the nice old Christmases at Stone House, when Malcolm used to feed the goldfish? Do you remember little Robin Red Breast and poor little bunny rabbit with the blue face and pink ears?" He illustrated his letter with drawings of the goldfish pond, the robin, the rabbit, and a drawing of Malcolm Barlow.

Mother's letter added an amusing note. "Daddy bought a goose in town the other day, and brought it home for the cook to pluck. You would have laughed if you could have seen us all having a go at it. The kitchen looked like a snow-storm. We were all smothered in white down, in our hair, in

Drawings included in one of my father's letters to Malcolm.

our clothes. In the end we had to give it to the gardener to finish plucking. We told Daddy if he buys another with feathers on, we shall make him pluck it."

On Christmas Day, our parents listened to the radio, because, as Mother explained, "we heard some of the children from America were going to speak at ten thirty in the morning. When the programme came on, we got quite excited because they said the first recordings were of twins. However, it turned out to be girl twins. We listened to the whole programme, but no luck. In the afternoon there was another programme broadcast from America, but we knew you would not be on that, as it was parents talking to their children in America, and we had not put in an application, as we thought there would be so many we probably should not have a chance. Also it meant spending a night in London, which we were not very keen to do. Perhaps one of these days we shall hear over the radio the records you made when you were in New York."

On January 1, 1941, Mother wrote, "We had a very quiet Christmas, just the three of us, and we did not even have a turkey. They were so expensive." Our parents had hoped to have Joe and Mabel come from London to spend Christmas, but Joe was on fire duty on Boxing Day, so they could not come. "However," Mother wrote, "we all had two nights free of air raids."

Mother reported receiving three letters from us about our first Christmas in America. On January 30, she wrote, "What a lovely Christmas you have all had. Wish I had been there to see you all. Never mind; perhaps we shall all be together next Christmas. As usual, the siren has just gone. It always goes when I write you. The guns have been going, and I heard machine guns in the distance."

CHAPTER SIXTEEN

*O*ur older brother, Derrick was seventeen when the four of us left England. Because he was older, we had grown up convinced that he had always lived a more glamorous life. We were quite sure of it when Father wrote Malcolm on December 22, 1940, "Derrick is home for Christmas and in a month's time will join the Royal Air Force and will soon be flying Spitfires over Germany."

Mother never failed to keep the four of us posted about his activities. She and Derrick had always enjoyed a close relationship and often did things together like tennis, golf, and theatre-going. On December 21, 1940 Mother wrote, "Derrick came home a week ago, and has now joined the Home Guard until he goes into the Air Force next month. He looks very fine in his khaki uniform. He brought it back from school with him, as he was a Sergeant in the O.T.C. Two or three nights a week he goes to lectures and drills, which he quite enjoys." Mother finished writing this letter the next day and told us, "Derrick is just off to a practice manoeuvre with the Home Guard. I expect he will find it very cold, as it is bitter out today."

In *The Home Front*, Arthur Marwick writes, "Winston Churchill first used the name 'Home Guard' in a broadcast of 14 July, and this became the formal title of the new organization on 23 July 1940. On 6 August 1940 came the so-called 'Magna Carta of the Home Guard,' which began the process of properly integrating it into the Army. In November the 'provisional' character of the Home Guard was given 'more permanent shape;' it was not to have commissioned officers, NCOs, and a fixed organization ... The functions of the Home Guard were both very real, since parachutists and a seaward invasion were genuinely expected, and unreal, since the invasion did not in fact materialize, and since some of the Guard's activities seemed rather remote from the true realities of war. It is in a way ironical that the Home Guard is often said to have been at its period of greatest importance during the time when an invasion was a possibility, although it was never called upon to deal with such an invasion, whereas later, when it performed many other valuable tasks, such as aircraft-spotting, guarding of bomb sites, and so on, it was held to have passed its period of glory. In British social history, the real importance of the Home Guard was the sense which it gave to many citizens, who also retained their normal civilian employment, of complete involvement in all aspects of the war effort."[1]

When the Home Guard got its start as the Local Defense Volunteers, "neither arms nor uniforms were forthcoming, so that the LDV often presented a disconcertingly amateurish appearance," according to Marwick. "It is probably for this reason that some of the earliest pictures of LDVs were suppressed by the censor." However, in a January 16, 1941 letter, Mother could write, "Derrick is doing a lot of training with the Home Guard now, and looks taller than 6 ft. in his uniform, now that he has got it all complete. I think he quite enjoys it, although he is longing to get into the R.A.F. soon."

Mother's letters gave us glimpses of the war. On January 8, 1941: "We have had quite a busy day yesterday in the way of raid warnings, but I only saw one German plane, and that one was in a hurry to get out to sea again." On January 16: "Well, darlings, we are still quite alright. We had several Alerts last night, and heard lots of gun fire in the distance, and some bombs dropping." On January 30: "Last night's raid was the first in 10 days. We heard the planes going over here until the 'all clear' went about 10 p.m. Also some of our planes were off to bomb Germany, which is always a delight to us to think they are getting a good dose as well. We have been very lucky here at present, as we have only heard bombs dropping in the distance with lots of gun fire. Anyhow we are all ready for anything. I have had heaps of sand put in various spots round the house, and when Derrick and I go out at night to see the planes go over, we nearly always fall over the sand that is put there in case we get any fire bombs. At present the Germans' chief form of amusement seems to be to machine gun the passenger trains and people working in the fields."

On February 6: "We have had lots of Alerts here lately. In fact, the Germans seem to be taking quite an interest in this part of the world lately. However, they have not dropped anything very near. We hear the guns and the bombs, and I saw one machine-gunning the town as it passed over the other morning. There was one shot down off here the day before yesterday. We saw our planes coming back doing the Victory roll, which usually tells us they have shot a plane down." On February 13: "I started to write a letter to you yesterday, but some big guns somewhere on the coast made so much noise all day, I could not get on with it, so I have started again now. We seem to have had quite a lot of aeroplanes about here this last week, and have seen several bombs dropping near [censored]. When Derrick and I came back from the pictures the other night, we could see some German planes quite clearly in the moonlight, crossing the moon. We went to Ipswich on Monday to do some shopping and of course had several alerts, but I managed to do everything I wanted. Never forget, darlings, that you are all very lucky to be in America out of all this. As soon as everything is over, and we have put paid to Hitler, then we will all be together again." The last letter in February: "We have had lots of bangs round here lately. They seem rather fond of East Anglia these days, but nothing very near. The S—s had a German plane quite low over the house this week. Of course, Peter, a neighbor wanted to have a shot at it, but it was out of sight too quickly. There is one just gone over the house now, but I expect the fighters will get him before he gets back to the coast.

"I am having quite a job to write this letter, as there is so much excitement going on outside. I have to stop now and then to have a look. A plane was not far away a little while ago, when all the guns opened up on it and some funny things they call 'flaming onions' went up in the sky. They looked rather like the red balls on a string we used to put on our Christmas tree. I expect you have read about the 'onions' in your *Continental Daily Mirror*." [This was a newspaper Mother had sent to us]. "Our pilots, when they go over Germany, sometimes say when they come back they run into them. One or two large flares were dropped near here a few minutes ago. They light up the place so much, you could read a newspaper. In fact, we thought a bomb had fallen on the town, but it had not."

During the early months of 1941, Derrick considered various military options open to him. On January 30 Mother wrote, "Now that the new Act is out for calling up men from 18-40, Derrick is off on Saturday to join the Air Force. He may have to go soon after he has signed on. When he gets into his uniform, he says he will send you a photo." On February 6, Mother reported: "Derrick has been to London to see about joining up, and is going back again on Saturday. He cannot make up his mind whether to join the R.A.F. or a regiment." On February 13, "Derrick has gone off to London again, and has now decided not to join the Air Force, but is going into the Army in a Home Defense Unit in a few days. He has to serve as a Private for three or four months, and then hopes to go to an Officers' Training Unit to become an officer." On February 27: "I wonder what Derrick thinks of the Army. He joined up two days ago, and I see by the papers where he is stationed he has been able to see lots of air flights. I do not suppose he will get leave for some time yet." The next day: "Today is Derrick's birthday (his 18th), and I have just heard on the wireless that there has been an air raid at the place at which he is stationed. I don't call that a very nice birthday present, do you?" Later we learned that Derrick had volunteered for the 70th Battalion, The Buffs, an Infantry unit. It was half comprised of civilian prisoners released to serve in the army to fight Hitler. They proved to be so incorrigible they were returned to prison. For a new 18-year-old recruit, it was a startling experience to be among such tough men.

Derrick never wrote to us himself, but Mother's letters told us what his Army training was like. On March 12: "I have had several letters from Derrick, and he seems to enjoy it although he is working very hard. He says he has been very stiff after the route marches with full equipment, but he is getting used to it now. Last week he sent me some chocolate, as we cannot get any here. I sent him some socks I had knitted for him, and a large tin with two cakes in it. He made me laugh, as he says he has to do his own mending and darning now, and if he had known what a long time socks took to darn, he would never have worn his socks into such holes for me to darn. However, now I am going to knit him several pairs, then he can send his others home, and I will darn them for him … You all ought to be proud to think you have a big brother fighting for you over here now." On March 27: "I had a letter from Derrick yesterday, and he had passed two tests on a Bren gun. He was very pleased with himself, as he has only been in the Army three weeks, and most of the others had had more than ten weeks training. He was the only one in his squad to pass the second test, so you can imagine how thrilled he was."

Mother often mentioned the German air raids. On March 12, "We have not had quite so many Alerts for the last day or two. A few days ago we had eight Alerts. We got to the state when we did not know whether it was Alert or All Clear, so we went to bed and hoped for the best … I am afraid Joe and Mabel [in London] had a very bad raid the other night. It was all round their district. I haven't heard from them, but hope they are alright." On March 19: "Last night was a dreadful night. German planes were attacking a town on the East Coast and they passed over the house in one continuous stream until six o'clock in the morning. Several bombs were dropped, but we are still alright. You are very lucky to be in America." On March 26: "We had great excitement here a few days ago. At six in the morning there was a terrific bang that shifted my bed, and I looked out of the window and saw a German plane diving and machine-gunning a house a little way away. Then he flew off towards the coast. I believe our fighters got him. Anyhow he dropped some bombs about [censored] a half mile away, but did not do a lot of damage. We thought we were in for a big raid, but the fighters soon drove them away. It was quite an excitement while it lasted." Father also wrote about the same incident: "A few mornings back a shell from one of our guns burst over the house just before daybreak. We shot at a German bomber who had lost his way, and got him down. Sometimes we cannot get any sleep all the week. The air raid sirens go continuously all day and all night."

Derrick's goal was still to become an officer, but it was not smooth sailing for him, despite his college background. On April 30, 1941 Mother wrote, "Derrick has got into his Officers' Cadet Training Unit Platoon, and has to do three months there before he goes to training camp, so I expect in a few months time he will be an Officer. He is thrilled with himself."

German air raids continued throughout April and May of 1941. On April 11 Mother wrote, "We are all feeling a bit tired at the moment, as we have been up till early morning lately. There have been so many planes about, we thought it safer to be dressed. However, we are still quite alright." She sounded a more upbeat note on April 18: "So Malcolm wants to know if we are winning the war in England. Well I certainly think we are here, as they haven't bombed us out yet. And everywhere, all over the country, everyone is standing up to the raids marvelously. Joe and Mabel have had a very bad time lately, as they got bombed both times in the London blitz. The first time a bomb blast blew out all the windows, and the next day some incendiaries set the roof on fire. Joe went up and hacked the roof away and promptly fell through, but luckily did not hurt himself. It is in all the papers how the American Embassy went to help them put out the fire. We rang Mabel up, and they are quite alright, but they say they have an awful lot of mess to clear up. Mabel said when Joe and the Americans came downstairs, with their tin hats on, they only wanted banjos and they could have performed on the beach as black minstrels ... We have had quite a bit round here lately, but nothing very near, although we have heard the familiar 'scream' like we did in London, remember?" On May 18: "We nearly had all our windows cracked the other night, and I managed to dodge a bit of shrapnel by falling down on the ground. Otherwise we are fine. The nightingales have been singing so beautifully every night in the woods opposite, and do not seem to mind the gun fire a bit." By May 25: "We have had a very peaceful time lately. In fact, it seems quite funny if we do happen to hear a siren."

In April 1941 the town of Woodbridge, Suffolk, held a War Weapons Week. Mother described it in an April 18 letter: "We have got a War Weapons Week here, and in two days they passed the amount set for the whole week. Yesterday the pipers played through the streets. They did look marvelous all in their peacetime uniforms. We have lots of war weapons on show in the various shops, and one huge bomb, the picture of which I expect you saw in the paper some time ago. It stands 11 ft. 6 inches, and the placards round here call it Hitler's mistake. You can go and look at it, and then put pennies in the box for war weapons. The fire brigade gave a display in the Park, so we are having quite an exciting week." On April 24: "Woodbridge has just finished the War Weapons Week, and aimed at getting £30,000 and succeeded in getting £79,000, which wasn't too bad, was it?"

Despite the air raids, by June 1941 the Germans gave

up the air war over Britain. Recognizing the futility of bombing England, the German air strength was transferred to the Eastern Front. Germany attacked Russia on June 22, 1941. Now the planes flying over my parents' Woodbridge house were British. "We hear lots of gunfire in the distance, but that is all. Also, now to our great joy, we see crowds of our planes going out to bomb France and Germany several times a day, as you will have read in the papers. We count them all going out, and then again when they come home. Even Daddy gets a kick out of it."

A change in Army regulations dashed Derrick's immediate hopes for an officer's commission. On July 20, 1941, Mother wrote: "Poor Derrick is very disappointed as a new Army order has just been issued, which does not allow Privates to go to an Officers Training Unit, so now he will have to try and become an NCO by getting a stripe." On July 27, she told us, "I heard from Derrick yesterday, and now that the new orders that only men with stripes could go to the Officers Training Unit, and as he was due to go at any moment if that order had not come in, it made him feel very fed up. So when men were asked to volunteer to be trained as observers and pilots in the R.A.F. he put his name down, and is now waiting to hear the results."

While waiting for his transfer to come through, Derrick worked on getting himself a stripe. On September 2, Mother wrote: "He has now finished his Army training, so has been learning to drive cars and lorries. He can now ride a motor bike, and has passed his tests as a Dispatch Rider, so is very thrilled." The next news from Mother was that Derrick had been promoted. On October 26: "Don't forget to put Lance Corporal Steedman now that Derrick has got one stripe." On November 30: "Derrick is now attached to the Motor

Transport, and seems to be dashing all over the place with cars and lorries. Now that he can drive he loves it." Her last letter in November told us: "Derrick is still waiting to be called for the R.A.F. and getting rather tired of the wait. He has been playing Rugger for his regiment, and hopes to come to London on a Saturday to play for one of the big clubs."

News arrived in September 1941 which had Sue and Sheila agog. Mother wrote, "I pull Derrick's leg a lot. He has a girl friend in the A.T.S. She drives staff cars, and is stationed near him. Now he goes to dances every week." Shortly after, Mother sent us a photo of Derrick's girl friend. She was striking in her uniform. However, nothing came of his first romance, much to the disappointment of my two sisters.

From time to time in 1941 Derrick would get short leaves from the Army. Sometimes he made it home to Woodbridge, Suffolk, but on other leaves he would meet Mother in London. On December 25, she wrote: "Derrick arrived up on Monday, and we went to a cinema and saw Joan Fontaine and Cary Grant in *Suspicion*—very good. The next day he took me to lunch at his Club. On Monday we have taken seats for *Gangway*, a sort of revue with Bebe Daniels and Ben Lyon in it. Then he goes back to his regiment. He goes back on the coast soon, so I suppose he will have an exciting time like last year."

After the Germans' attention became focused on Russia in June, Mother's letters indicated that air raids in her area had become quite infrequent. On July 6: "The German planes still come and pay us an occasional visit in the distance, just to remind us that they are about." On July 27: "We have not had any excitement around here for some time. I expect the nights are too light." On September 2: "We have had a few raids round here, but nothing very much. The moon is ris-

ing again so we may get some shortly. I do not seem to have $\qquad$
very much news for you this time. We more or less do the
same thing every day."

The military provided a dash of color in the drab wartime lives of the English. Mother's September 2 letter told
us, "We have had quite a lot of excitement lately watching
the Army manoeuvres going on. It was such fun to see Tanks
dashing about. The planes all joined in as well."

CHAPTER SEVENTEEN

$\mathcal{T}$he "Americanization" of the four of us began in 1941. It was not intentional on Mrs. Brock's part. Her goal was to return us to our parents as little changed as possible. To this end, she did not encourage us to lose our English accents, change our English manners, or diminish our English love of King and Country. However, the erosion of our "Englishness" was swift and unstoppable.

Even before our arrival at Muncy Farms, Mrs. Brock had looked into schooling for the four of us. As there were no private schools in the area, she decided to send the three oldest of us to the public school in Muncy. This required her to pay tuition. For grades 1-6 the tuition was $3 per month per pupil; for grades 7-12 the tuition was $6.50 per month per pupil. Malcolm was to go to nursery school in Muncy for part of the day.

I remember well my first day in the 6th grade of an American public school. Mrs. Brock had outfitted me in new clothes, so that I would be dressed like the other boys. It seemed strange to go off to school in long trousers, rather than the grey flannel shorts, grey flannel shirt and grey knee socks which was the uniform for my English school. It also seemed strange to be going to school as a day student, not a boarder. The principal took me to my first class of the day. I was surprised to find that my teacher was a woman. In England, all my teachers had been males. I was equally surprised to find there were both boys and girls in the class. Since the age of seven, I had only been in classes with other boys. The teacher put me at a desk in front of her own. She told the class I had come to America to escape the German bombing in England. Probably for the first time in her teaching career, you could have heard a pin drop in the classroom.

The other students were intrigued by the sudden appearance of a 12-year-old English boy in their school, especially one who lived on the Brock farm. At the end of the first class, several girls offered to show me the way to my next class. We arrived in the classroom before the teacher, an event which caused me to make my only gaffe of the day. When the teacher—another woman—entered the classroom, I stood up, as I had always done in England. My classmates looked at me in astonishment. The teacher was equally nonplussed. Rather sheepishly, I took my seat amidst giggles from the back of the room.

Mrs. Brock had arranged for us to eat a hot lunch each day at the home of a Muncy resident, Mrs. Rogers, who lived only a short walk from the school. She was a very friendly person with a son near our age. Her lunches introduced us to such American food as hot dogs, hamburgers, coleslaw, jellied salads, and peanut butter sandwiches. As I was always hungry, I had no trouble eating American food. I thought American ice cream was far superior to the Walls ice cream I had always eaten in England.

Our parents took a great interest in our American schooling. After a trial period, the three of us were moved to higher grades. Mother wrote on March 19, "I am so glad to hear you are all going to be moved up at school. I was very interested in your reports, although I found them a little hard to understand as they are so different from the English ones." Letters constantly urged us to work hard in school. My father wrote me on May 31, 1941: "I hope you all continue to work very hard at school. You must really try and do your very best, because your life in the future will now depend upon your efforts at school. Do not waste any time. Work and work must be your motto. The world has changed. Everything is different."

At the end of the school day, each of us pursued our interests. I spent much of my time hunting and fishing on the farm. Fordyce, the son of a former farm manager, gave me a fishing rod. Fordyce also took Sue and me along when he went deer hunting that fall. I was eager to have a gun and started to save for one out of the allowance given us by Mrs. Brock. Mother wrote, "What fun for you, Brian, when you have enough money for that gun. I wish I could help towards it, but I am not allowed to send you money. Never mind, I expect you will get it one day." And later, "Will you please tell Mrs. Brock that Daddy says you can have a gun. He has written to her about it, but we thought we would put it in again in case the letter gets lost." A month later, she wrote, "Daddy bought me a .22 rifle automatic. I suppose the same type as you are going to have. He seemed to think I had better have one in case we move into the country and any stray Germans come around. I wonder which of us will be the first to chalk up a win, you or I?"

In the meantime, I practiced with my Red Ryder BB gun, which almost cost me the chance to own a .22 rifle. Mrs. Brock was not pleased when the gardener told her that I had shot out all the outside lights of the garage (the bulbs made an irresistible "pop"), and killed a red cardinal, which she told me was against the law. However, eventually she did allow me to purchase a .22 with my savings.

In April 1941 Sue joined the Girl Scouts and I joined the Boy Scouts. Mother wrote "Sue, darling, fancy you as a Girl Guide. How are the 'Bundles for Britain' getting on? I hear, Brian, you are joining the Scouts. Mind you both get a nice lot of badges. I expect they wear them on their arms as they do in England, don't they? Over here the Girl Guides are doing marvelous work as messengers in the A.R.P. service, and lots of jobs in the villages." At eleven, Sheila was too young to join the Girl Scouts, so she and Malcolm looked after a menagerie of animals that included rabbits, chickens, and ducks.

While we were busy settling in at the farm and at school, Mrs. Brock's health took a turn for the worst. Prior to our arrival, she had been plagued with a series of abscesses on her hip. After weeks of draining, the abscess would slowly heal over, only to start festering again. In March 1941 Mrs. Brock had to go to the hospital once again to have an operation on her hip. After the operation, she returned to the farm with a trained nurse who was to live with us for more than a year.

After she returned from the hospital, our mother wrote to us, "You must all have missed Aunt Peggy when she was in the hospital. I am so glad she is so much better. So glad you call her Aunt Peggy now. It sounds so much more friendly, after her being so good to you. After all, she is being much more to you all than even an aunt. You must remember she is taking my place while you are over there. I think she spoils you all."

Aunt Peggy had been told by the hospital doctors that

they could do nothing more for her, other than to suggest that she spend the coming winter in a warm climate in the hope that continuous sunshine might in some way help the healing process. She took their advice and began to make plans to take the four of us, two of her staff, and the trained nurse to Tucson, Arizona in the fall. We were to spend the winter months there, attending local schools, and living in a rented house.

In the meantime, she covered up her constant pain and discomfort in our presence, although she was forced to spend most days in bed. She was always ready to hear about our activities and to laugh at the funny situations we got ourselves into. One day, just after she had returned from the hospital, we came to her bedroom to tell her we had caught a fish for supper. Thinking it was the usual tiny sunfish we usually caught, Aunt Peggy asked if we thought one fish would be enough. "Oh yes," we told her. "This fish was so big it took all of us to haul it out of the stream by its tail." It turned out that what we were about to cook for her supper was a "sewer carp," which had come upstream with others to spawn.

We took one trip to Philadelphia, partly to shop for clothing to replace the clothes we had outgrown, but also to see Mr. Brock's aunt, Miss Gibson. It was Miss Gibson who had accompanied Aunt Peggy to the Gould Foundation to meet us for the first time. Miss Gibson lived on the last big estate left in Wynnewood, Pennsylvania. Her home was a Victorian turreted mansion which her father had built as a summer home because as a young girl she had always wanted to live in a castle. After the deaths of her parents, Miss Gibson had added to the house a magnificent marble ballroom that was used for occasional dances and for charity events. We loved to play in the ballroom because up in a balcony was an organ which could play paper tapes of classical music. We would take turns pumping away at the organ, filling the ballroom with music.

The four of us thoroughly enjoyed our visits with Miss Gibson—we were to end up calling her Aunt May—because she had a gentleness about her which endeared her to all, but especially to children. With children she shared an innocent delight in the world around her. She loved to see others enjoying themselves, and delighted in occasions that called for festive decorations. Near the end of her life, she kept her Christmas tree up into the summer months so she could continue to enjoy the decorations. I remember once she took us all to an afternoon movie. She enjoyed it as much as we did, so she decided right then and there that we should all go see another movie. Aunt Peggy couldn't imagine what was keeping us from returning on time for supper.

On our first visit to Miss Gibson, Malcolm came down with acute appendicitis. He had to have an emergency appendectomy at the Presbyterian Hospital in Philadelphia. Mother wrote, "Well, my naughty little Malcolm seems to have been distinguishing himself. Fancy getting into the hospital. I expect you were all quite worried about him. Now Brian and Sue, don't you get ill. Otherwise, Aunt Peggy will think you are a dreadful lot of children to have."

Mother had reason to be concerned about our health in 1941. Sheila had been sick in bed for a week in April. At that time, Mother wrote, "I was sorry to hear you had been so ill, Sheila darling. That is not like you. You are always the strong one of the family. Anyhow I am glad you are getting better now. I hear you were very good in bed, which I was pleased to hear. You must always be good; if you are ill it makes a lot of worry for Aunt Peggy." Mother's admonition not to get sick did no good, because in August both Sue and I had to have our tonsils removed. Fortunately there were no complications, and with a trained nurse in the house, we both made a speedy recovery.

In the summer of 1941 Aunt Peggy sent the three oldest of us to camp. Sue and Sheila went to the YWCA Pioneer Day Camp for two weeks. A photograph in the *Williamsport Sun*, dated July 9, shows Sue and Sheila with some other girls hemming "clothing for unfortunate children in the warring countries." Sheila is described as "a refugee from England" and "an industrious worker," which she never let the rest of us forget.

I went to Camp Cory on a lake in New York State for two weeks. My first postcard said, "I am having a swell time. The whole camp is putting a circus on this Saturday. We are putting up a sideshow in which you hang Hitler." The next week I wrote Aunt Peggy, "We made $11 profit from our sideshow." And then, in what was to become a standard closing for my letters, "Will you send me another $1 in case I need it? I have 85 cents left out of the other $1. I have not been doing any swimming lately as I have poison ivy on my feet. There are such a lot of other things to do I have not missed it much." I caught poison ivy every time I went near it, and was sometimes forced to spend a week in bed because of it. Mother wrote on August 19, "How is the poison ivy? You seem to excel in catching that. Hope you passed the swimming tests alright in spite of it. Did you get to know the English boy in the next cabin? Hearing all this has made Daddy and me quite determined to come out to you there, whenever this war is over and we are allowed to travel. We are saving every penny we can, so as to be able to make a home out there. You would all find it very dull in England after the free outdoor life you have led in America." By this time my "Americanization" had progressed to the point where I thought Mother might have a point.

Mother's August letter concluded, "Lots of love, darlings, and I miss you a lot, but we must finish off this war before we shall see you again. It gives me lots of happiness to know you are safe out there. I should be much more worried if you were here. So, darlings, learn all you can, so that you can all become really useful in the world, and make a name for yourselves."

On September 20, 1941, as required each year around the anniversary of our arrival in America, Aunt Peggy notified the Immigration and Naturalization Service in Washington D. C. that the four of us were to accompany her to Tucson, Arizona, on September 24. She bought a new station wagon for the trip because there had to be room for two of us; Mickey, the housekeeper; the cook, Vivian, who did the housework and served in the dining room; and the chauffeur. Since Aunt Peggy's chauffeur had just left to enter some other profession, Miss Gibson lent one of her chauffeurs to drive us West. The station wagon was very smart looking, with its real wood side panels and its maroon color. Aunt Peggy was to travel to Arizona by train, accompanied by her nurse, Malcolm, and Sheila.

The trip had been planned so that there would be adequate time for us to see the sights along the way. However, the chauffeur, a genial Irishman, had other ideas. He had made a bet with another chauffeur that he could reach Tucson in record time. Nothing would induce him to stop along the way to see any sights. It was all Mickey could do to get him to stop for meals. He was a superb driver, and the result was that we reached Tucson several days ahead of schedule.

The owner of the house Aunt Peggy had rented had not yet cleaned, nor vacated it. The swimming pool was empty and in the process of being cleaned. The owner hurriedly vacated the house, and Mickey and Vivian did their best to put it in order before Aunt Peggy arrived. Fortunately for the chauffeur, he had already left by train to return east before Aunt Peggy reached Tucson.

It was the first time any of us in the station wagon had seen the West. We were dazzled by the vast vistas, the desert cacti, and the rugged beauty of the Catalina Mountains to the west of Tucson. Our rented house was just off Speedway Road, which in 1941 was on the edge of the desert. We were delighted to discover a "Western" riding stable only a few blocks from the rented house. We were also impressed by the friendliness of Westerners. The same afternoon we arrived in Tucson, an old friend of Aunt Peggy's invited us to accompany her to a party at a friend's house. Guests at the party immediately extended invitations to us to join them in various activities.

I remember well the party that afternoon because it was the first time I had met a real, live Native American. He was a striking-looking middle-aged man who was married to a wealthy Boston society woman. Later Aunt Peggy told me it had been fashionable in the 1920s for Eastern society women to marry so-called "Indian chiefs." He was dressed in a dark green velvet Navajo shirt adorned with silver buttons. Around his neck was a magnificent silver squash-blossom necklace. His face remained without expression all evening, and he made no effort to talk to any of the guests. He spent the afternoon and evening pouring down one drink after another. By the time we left he was very drunk. Having grown up on Western films in which "Indians" gave away everything they owned in return for "firewater." I was fascinated by this Native American guest that day.

During the winter months in Arizona, Aunt Peggy was forced to spend most of her time in bed. The large abscess on her hip refused to heal. She asked Vivian to take charge of us, so Vivian and the four of us did many things together. We all learned to ride "western style," and Vivian always got a lot of attention from the cowboy instructor. On October 26, Mother wrote from London: "I hear you have started to learn to ride. Do you like it? I should like a snap of you in your cowboy things. I expect you look fine in them. How lovely for Malcolm on his horse, being able to do everything himself. I expect he gets very excited. What sort of horse has he got? Write and tell me all about your horses, and what you wear to ride in. Shall look forward to seeing some snaps of you all on your horses."

In Tucson we were all sent to different private schools. Aunt Peggy did not want comparisons among the four of us to be made by teachers. She was also interested in picking schools which would meet our individual needs. I was enrolled in the Russell Ranch School for Boys as a boarder. This school was located fifteen miles west of Tucson, on the other side of the Catalina Mountains. The school took only fifteen boys, all placed at various grade levels. Each boy had his own horse to ride and care for. My horse was a gentle strawberry roan, rather unimaginatively named "Strawberry." I soon became very attached to him.

In a report to the Lycoming County Children's Aid Society back in Pennsylvania, in December 1941, Aunt Peggy reported, "Brian lost a few pounds due to the emotional disturbance of coming out here and adjusting himself to a new school, I think, but he has gained these back and looks and seems hale and hearty." Tactfully, she didn't mention that tests had revealed my academic skills were below the independent school median for eighth graders.

The assistant headmaster at The Russell Ranch School wrote Aunt Peggy in November, "I am very anxious to find the solution to Brian's needs for he is a boy I thoroughly enjoy and appreciate. There are so many qualities which are constantly manifested in our social and community life, and in these Brian excels. His straightforwardness, honesty, even temperament, and unselfish cooperation make him loved and respected by both Masters and boys. These qualities make us all the more eager to help him and to develop habits and trainings comparable to his other characteristics." Because in some classes I was the only student, and in others there were only two or three of us, I soon improved in the subjects that interested me. Subjects I didn't like—such as math—thwarted efforts of even the most patient teacher to teach them to me. When schoolwork did not go well, I always had "Strawberry" to console me, so I was very happy at The Russell Ranch School, even though I was one of only four boarders that year.

My twin, Susan, was enrolled in the Potter School as a day pupil. The school prided itself on being a copy of a fashionable Eastern girls' prep school. Mr. and Mrs. Potter, who ran the school, were an elegant couple. I think Mrs. Potter came from the South; she was the first woman I had seen to carry a parasol when out in the sun. I remember that Sue had to wear an Eastern riding habit and use a flat saddle, unlike the rest of us who rode with a Western saddle. Aunt Peggy's report on Sue included mention that she, too, had lost weight, "due to the many changes of the last year," and in a later report, she stated that "her art teacher says she shows talent far above the average."

Sheila went to the Thomas School, also as a day pupil. Aunt Peggy's report on Sheila said, "Sheila is doing well in her classes, is in the sixth grade, and is leading her class in all subjects. I hope before the winter is out that she can be advanced into the seventh grade, where I feel she really belongs." A subsequent report mentioned she had been moved into seventh grade and continued to be "at the top of her class in all subjects. Sheila is very active, plays tennis better than any child in school, and out-rides even those who have been riding several years. I have, therefore, taken her out of riding at school and am allowing her to ride twice a week with an older and more advanced group."

Malcolm was sent to the Pueblo School, a private day school for young children. Aunt Peggy's report to the Children's Aid Society said Malcolm was in first grade and had "progressed very well, has finished three primers in reading and now has a reading vocabulary way above the average six-year-old. His reports at school are good, and the teachers tell me he is well-liked and has more friends than any child in school of his age. He is a dear child, with an alert mind, who enjoys everything and everybody."

CHAPTER EIGHTEEN

*W*hereas 1941 was an exciting year for the four of us in America, for our parents it was to end up as a disaster, although it didn't start out that way. Unlike many in England, in the first part of 1941 my parents were able to maintain their pre-war style of living. But this was not to last, and by the end of 1941 the Woodbridge house would be closed under distressing circumstances.

Food was mentioned frequently in the 1941 letters we received from home. Father wrote on March 27, "Thank your lucky stars none of you are here in England, because with your enormous appetites you would all be hungry from morning till night. We cannot buy food. Your Daddy weighs 18 stone.[1] Try and picture me with a ration of meat per week one shilling's worth, and then only when available. Both you and Malcolm would eat my meat ration at one meal." Mother added, "You would laugh. You know how Daddy likes cheese. Well, now we are rationed to one ounce for each person per week, and I have great difficulty keeping my eye on my little piece when he is about." In *The Home Front*, Arthur Marwick writes, "By mid-1941, some weekly rations amounted to no more than what in a respectable pre-war household would have been thought sufficient for a single helping: a shilling's worth of meat [about eight ounces], one ounce of cheese, four ounces of bacon or ham, eight ounces of fats (including no more than two ounces of butter), two ounces of jam or marmalade."[2]

Because they had a large garden, Mother was able to supplement their meager rations with the help of the gardener, Marsh. Despite an unusually dry summer, Mother reported on June 30, "This week I have put in 70 tomato plants, so we ought to have plenty later on, besides another 20 in the greenhouse which are now in flower. We had our first peas and strawberries today. Do you remember what a lot we had in London last summer? They do not taste so nice as we get no cream now. I bottled 21 bottles of gooseberries from the garden this week, so we shall be able to live on those if we do not get anything else. I am afraid this year we are going to have no apples or pears or cherries, as the weather has been so dry. All the fruit and even the leaves have fallen off the fruit trees." On July 15, she wrote, "I have been very busy this week picking the red currants—an awful job. I wish you had been here to do it for me. I made quite a nice little bit of jam, and bottled the rest. I still have black currants to bottle, but now we have had our first rain for months I have got to wait for them to dry a bit more. I am going to have a shot at bottling peas and tomatoes. I am hoping we shall have plenty of tomatoes soon." And on August 11, "We have been getting some mushrooms off the lawn and in the field, which we have enjoyed, as it makes such a nice change for lunch."

Mother's five chickens did their best to supplement the food ration, and provided much fuel for her letters. She was either pleased with them, or very much annoyed with them, depending on whether or not they were laying the much-prized eggs. At times she found their behavior amusing. On March 12, she wrote, "My chickens are doing fine. In fact, they are getting so tame they will arrive in the kitchen every morning to see what their food is. This has only happened since I bought the lovely cock. He leads them all over the place. I have to sometimes fetch him back from the drive. He is very funny. When the other cock on the farm begins to crow, he gets up as high as possible and crows for all he is worth. While we are having breakfast, he comes to the window and sits on the sill and looks in, and of course Daddy spoils him by feeding him." On June 9, she reported, "My chickens are behaving very badly now, and I only get one egg a day now. Yesterday one of them laid a tiny egg, just the size of a pigeon's egg. Daddy said it must have read of rationing in the newspaper." Father wrote Malcolm, "We have some new fowls—Indian Game Birds—and don't they fight. One is so clever she picks up a stick and hits the cockerel on the head with it if he crows too much. Maybe she thinks he is a German."

Shooting also helped to fill their larder. January 1: "We have been out to do a little shooting, and walked for miles on Saturday and only got a hare, but anyhow it will be very useful to eke out the meat ration." January 8: "Daddy and Derrick went shooting the other day, and got several wild duck and a hare, which we are having for lunch tomorrow. Derrick managed to shoot some pigeons. He was thrilled." However, despite their efforts to supplement their food ration, Father wrote on August 13: "The food question is very difficult. Our larder these days is always empty, not like when you used to go in and help yourselves to rows of pastries, cakes, jam, and marmalade. All those days are gone, and we are rationed so much per person per week. When that is gone, there is no more."

Because of the food shortage, we were surprised when Mother wrote on January 16: "Derrick and I are always laughing at Daddy, as since he came back from London, he has put on so much weight the buttons on his suit keep bursting. We try to drag him out for a long walk every day, but he soon gets fed up with it." On February 12: "We have sold

Horace Victor Barlow with his dogs. The black labrador is his gun dog, Slick.

130   the little Austin car. Daddy is getting so fat, we nearly needed a tin opener to get in and out of such a small car. Now we have one nearly as big as the Rolls. It is an 18-80 H.P. Wolseley—all black and chromium, very smart. We cannot use it very much, as we only get eight gallons of petrol a month, but it gets us into Ipswich now and again."

In March 1941 came the first clear indication that my parents' pre-war style of living was over. Mother reported that they were losing both Marsh, the gardener, and Estelle, the part-time cook/maid. "We shall probably lose Marsh soon as he comes under the new scheme for getting workers for the factories. Estelle was down here the other day, and she comes under the scheme as well. She is thinking about going in the A.T.S." Estelle was the first to leave. By September, Marsh, too, was gone. Mother told us that if she and our father eventually came under the same scheme, she had decided to "volunteer to drive cars."

Both our parents tried to offer their services to aid the war effort, but surprisingly they were rebuffed. On March 27, Mother wrote, "Daddy is still trying to get something, but has not been lucky yet. I expect when Hitler starts [the German invasion of England] then we shall both be wanted. I tried three times to drive an ambulance, but although they are short of drivers here, they are so grand that unless you have lived in the neighborhood for a lifetime, there is no hope. They made me feel so fed up that when it was hinted the other day that they could not find drivers and that they might take me, I refused. I shall get something when things begin to get serious."

Father's inability to find a war job drove him into a frenzy of letter writing. It soon became an obsession with him to the point where his letters to the four of us in America grew fewer and fewer. Mother sometimes had to write us in long-hand, because Father's secretary was using the typewriter. She took rejection less harshly than he did, because for the time being she was busy making clothes "for the children who get bombed out in the big cities. Since you left I have knitted 122 different children's garments for bombed out children, not counting the things I made for you and Derrick. I still have some wool left, but when that comes to an end I shall have to get wool for the Forces from one of the organizations. If wool comes under rationing, it will stop my knitting which is rather a pity, as I had made such a lot of nice clothes."

From time to time in 1941 it looked as if Father might land a job, even if it did not require his engineering expertise. On March 19, Mother wrote, "You may hear of Daddy and I on a barge later on. We have volunteered to run one on the canals. The Ministry of Transport advertised for members of yacht clubs who could run barges. As they are very similar to our Dutchman [sailboat], Daddy and I thought we might be of some use. We heard that our application was being looked into, so I may be able to tell you more about it another time." But sadly, an April 11 letter told us, "All our hopes of going on a barge have been dashed, as after asking for women as well as men, the Ministry of Transport now decided not to employ women, so Daddy is no longer interested, as we wanted to go together. Now we shall have to think up some other job."

Frustrated, our parents considered moving to Scotland in April. The combination of a prospect of a job there for Father, and a new government order rekindled their earlier interest in Scotland. In February, Mother wrote, "Daddy has probably got a job up there, and I expect I shall find plenty to do, as I may take some children who have been bombed out to look after."

In April, Mother wrote, "We hope to fix something up soon to move, as an order has gone out in towns around here that people who have no business to keep them in the district should move if they can, in case of invasion. So as we haven't [a business], we thought we ought to. If we get the house we are after, we shall be miles in the mountains with plenty of fishing and shooting, but some way from a town, and no electric light. Anyhow I don't suppose it will be too bad. We hope to be able to help with some of the evacuated children, as an American association has several houses full of them up there."

The move to Scotland turned out to be more complicated than they had anticipated. "We have been having quite a business to get the furniture on the way. We shall have to go through London to go north by the night rail, so I shall be able to see Mabel and perhaps Joe. I hope we shall not get any raids on the way up in the train. We thought it would be better to go by night, as we leave in the evening and get there the next morning. The house is in the mountains, so there is plenty of shooting, in fact 6,000 acres, which would suit Brian, and plenty of lochs for fishing. We are having frightful excitement over the chickens, as we want to take them with us and we do not know how to do it. I may have to take them in a coop on the train with us. I hope they behave themselves. I expect the cock will crow all the way." The billiard table from Stone House also complicated the move. "We are trying very hard to get rid of the billiard table, as it is such a heavy thing to cart about and we shall have no room big enough in Scotland for it. I gave it to Sir Malcolm Campbell, but unfortunately some of his house has been taken over, so he cannot do with it. Yesterday I offered it to an aerodrome, but they already had two, so now we are looking round for somewhere to store it."

But after all this, the move to Scotland was not to be. Much to our surprise, Mother wrote on May 18, "We are not going to Scotland after all. We found the house had not been lived in for years, so we are going to stay here." Father was bitterly disappointed, and was later to accuse Mother of having never intended to move to Scotland right from the start.

Father was very frustrated over his inability to find a job, and his health began to deteriorate. He became badly depressed. Mother was unable to give him support. She had always been very afraid of any illness. (Our Aunt Cecile, Father's sister, once observed to Aunt Peggy, "The children were never nursed through illness at home. They went to a nursing home, where Violet would go and see them—loaded with gifts—daily.") On May 18, Mother wrote, "Daddy has been doing a lot of moaning and groaning this week, as he has had lumbago badly. Derrick and I could not help laughing at him. He is better now." A week later: "Daddy has been in bed for ages, on and off, as he has had an attack of lumbago, and has been full of grunts and groans. He is still in bed this morning. He says he would be in an awful mess if the Germans decided to invade now." June 1: "Daddy is still not very well. He has been in bed all the week, unable to move with sciatica, but he is up again now and just able to crawl about."

Life for our parents had become steadily more drab by the middle of 1941. Father wrote Sheila on June 1: "There is nothing nice here now. Half the shops are closed, and it is very difficult to get sufficient food. We are unable to buy it.

So please do not get homesick." Mother wrote on June 17, "Now that the rationing of clothes has come in, I have given up wearing stockings, except when I go into town, and my legs have gotten very sunburnt. I shall find it very difficult to send you very much in the parcels now, as the only things not rationed seem to be games and books."

For Father in 1941, his only source of amusement was to go to the cinema with Mother. Mother mentions a surprisingly long list of films they saw together in 1941: a Mickey Mouse one called *Tugboat Mickey*, a Laurel and Hardy film called *Beau Chumps, Saps at Sea*, ("even Daddy laughed at it"), *Pinocchio*, Charlie Chaplin's *The Great Dictator, 20 Mule Team, Neutral Port*, a Dead End Kids film, *Waterloo Bridge, Brigham Young, The Northwest Mounted, Mark of Zorro, They Knew What They Wanted, Thief of Baghdad, Seven Sinners, The Bad Man from Wyoming, Brother Orchid, Balalaika, Swanee River, Cavalcade of Variety, Spring Meeting, Bad Man, Major Barbara, Boys Town*—a March of Time film, *America Speaks, 20,000 Men a Year, Invisible Woman, Mexican Spitfire, Lady Hamilton*, and *49th Parallel*. Many of these movies I had seen in America. Mother wrote me, "We always seem to see the same pictures, don't we?"

During the summer of 1941, Mother continued to play tennis and golf. "Last Saturday I had some very good tennis and played with a pal of Derrick's single for an hour and a half, and we could not beat each other. We got nine all, and then gave it up, as everyone else had finished tea." In August: "I am going with a friend to Framlinham to play in a charity tennis tournament. She and I have great hopes of doing well in it." In September: "I have been playing a little golf lately. The weather has been so lovely and warm. I may to go a golf meeting in aid of the Air Raid Distress Fund in a fortnight's time if I can get a partner. It is being held outside of London."

After Father's health improved, the hunt for a smaller house continued. In July Mother wrote, "We had an idea we should like to find a smaller house, and have tried to find one on the Norfolk Broads somewhere, but there does not seem to be anything." In August they again briefly considered looking for a house in Scotland. They even considered renting Edgehill, the large house near Ipswich where Sheila had been born. But by August 9, Mother wrote, "Daddy has some hopes of getting a job at the moment, so is away. If he gets it, we shall shut down the Woodbridge house, and then I shall look round for something to do. All our ideas of living in Scotland are off."

Disaster loomed. When Father returned to the Woodbridge house later in August, Mother was not there. She had left him. Mother's letters from September on to the end of the year made no mention of Father. Once I wrote to her and asked her what Daddy was doing. On December 20, she replied, "Darlings, now that I am away from home I have no idea what Daddy is doing. I haven't seen him for three months. I don't think he is doing anything."

Her reply puzzled me, especially as we had not received any letters from our father. It would not be until many years later that I would learn the true explanation about what had happened. When going through Aunt Peggy's files, I found a letter written in 1944 by Aunt Cecile describing the situation. "My brother telephoned me here at the factory to tell me Violet had left him. He said he was ill—alone. Could I go to him at once? I told our managing director, Mr. Quilter, who has been a personal friend of my brother's for twenty years. He was troubled as I was, told me to have a month's compassionate leave, and go to my brother. I found my brother, who had obviously had a stroke, living alone in the house. All maids gone; been called up for factories. All blinds down. I got a doctor in; he could not sleep. I had to keep with him all the time. He would not go to bed before two in the morning, then would come and sit on my bed to talk of Violet, of the children—saying over and over, 'I shall never see my little Malcolm again.' I could not console him.

"At the end of more than three months, he was definitely better. The furniture was stored, and he decided to go and live at his club in London. My brother, who was never demonstrative, left me with the pantechnicons, the moving men, the house to clean—everything to do. He stumblingly muttered thanks to me for saving his life and his reason. Stood silent, and said he was taking his suitcase to the station. I knew that he had gone for good, and that he could not say good-bye."

We children never saw this letter to Aunt Peggy. She elected not to show it to us, although she did save it in her files, and that is where I found it, many years later.

CHAPTER NINETEEN

$\mathcal{I}$n the last months of 1941, all of Mother's letters were sent from London. She made no mention in those letters that she had left Father, nor did she ever mention the matter in subsequent letters. Baffled, I wrote Aunt Peggy from the Russell Ranch School, "Have you had a letter from our father yet? It has been quite a long time since I have heard from him."

We sent Mother a food parcel. She wrote in return, "It was sweet of you all to send the food parcel. I could not think where it had come from. Don't spend your money on any more, darlings, as we get heaps of food over here, and now that I am in the Services, I really do not need it, so put the money to something for yourselves."

Mother wrote about her war work. November 3: "Have been very busy, as I have been driving a private car for one of the Red Cross officials, and have been to all sorts of interesting places. In the newspapers, when you get them, you will see a photo of the Queen at the Free French hospital. Well, I was there and stood quite near the Queen. She looked so lovely in a lovely shade of mauve, frock and coat and hat to match. The French General de Gaulle was with her, and also Admiral Muselier. The

French sailors formed a Guard of Honor, and looked so quaint with their large berets with big red pom-poms on the top. The local Girl Guides were allowed to come, and lined up on the drive. When the Queen was leaving, she came over and talked to all of them.

"The hospital was in a lovely park and the trees were marvelous shades of red and gold. I have been living in the country for the last week while I have been on this job. The weather has been much colder, and we had quite heavy sleet showers one day. Another day I went to a lovely country place in Hertford, and then came back to London in the black-out, and what a job it was. When I got on the outskirts, all the roads looked alike, and it was very dark.

"I had Sunday off, so I went to play golf at a club near London, which was rather nice, as I sit down so much driving. It is lovely to get a walk in the country air. Played quite well.

"We had our first air raid warning since July on Saturday. I had just got into bed when the warning went. I cursed like anything, as I was on duty, so had to get up and dress. Tonight I am off duty until 10:30 p.m. and then on Fire Watch duty all night. I have got very thin with all this tearing about, and lost 4 stone in 3 months. I only weigh 9 stone now."

In November 1941 Mother took part in a Remembrance Sunday parade, which she described to us: "Yesterday was Remembrance Sunday in England, and there were church parades of the Forces all over England to different churches. In the afternoon, we marched with the Pioneers to church. It was a terrific effort, as we had been drilled by a Sergeant Major for weeks. When we arrived at the starting point, to our horror we discovered their drill was quite different to ours. However, we followed them in all they did and the result was quite good. We were headed by a brass band. Quite a lot of people lined the pavements to see us go by. Really, once we got over our fright of being the only women to march with hundreds of men, we quite enjoyed it.

"I now live in a ladies club with all the other drivers. I certainly miss all the lovely eggs our chickens used to lay, and am very sad that all my tins of jam and marmalade that I had since before the war are in store, so I cannot get at them. When I was at home, we got heaps of things that now I am in billets we don't get.

"Some weeks we go out showing off how the ambulances work, as there are several different types. We have what is called a mobile unit, which has several different types of ambulances, an X-ray unit, and a canteen. We go to various parts of London and show the public what their pennies that are collected each week are spent on.

"I spent all day in Trafalgar Square last week and have had the most awful cold ever since. In fact, I lost my voice for two days, but am recovering now. I had a lovely trip last week to Oxfordshire to collect an ambulance, and the country looked so lovely. All the trees were just beginning to change color and there were miles of beech trees on the way down, all a lovely bronze color.

"Tell Aunt Peggy I still am very grateful for all she is doing for you, and I have just posted a letter to her, but I hope she will not be angry with me for not writing often, as I really have very little time. The few hours I have off are usually taken up with cleaning my shoulder plates and mending."

A November 26, 1941 letter shows no slowing in the pace of Mother's activities. "I have again been away to Scotland, so have not been able to write, and since then have been delivering ambulances at several places on the West Coast. Still haven't had time to have the photo taken. All the London shops shut at 4 p.m. now, so I find it very difficult to do anything about it.

"We have been driving big chassis lately. They are the engine and framework of the car before the body is put on. A very cold job, as there is no windscreen and you just sit on a board nailed across and can see the road underneath you. After two trips on them, I very nearly had to take my meals off the mantelpiece, I was so sore.

"I had some lovely butter in a tin given me last week from Canada. A friend of mine, whose son is in the Navy, has just come back from Canada, and brought me some. I saw Mrs. L— again when I was in Scotland. Her son was on the *Ark Royal* when it was sunk, but is alright and coming on leave." The *Ark Royal* was one of two aircraft carriers attacked in the Mediterranean by German U-boats. Within 25 miles of Gibraltar, it was hit once and badly damaged. A fire broke out, and the *Ark Royal* had to be abandoned and left to sink.

Mother mentioned Christmas in her November 26 letter. "Only a month now and it will be Christmas. Fancy, that is the second Christmas you have spent in America. I wonder what sort of fun you will have this year. Some of the London stores are looking lovely with the Christmas gifts, and the toy departments look quite cheery. I wonder if my Christmas parcel has arrived yet. Hope it will be all complete this time."

December turned out to be a fateful month both for the four of us in Arizona, and our parents in England. At the Russell Ranch School, the boys were expected to go to church on Sundays. Dr. Russell was an ordained Presbyterian minister, although I never saw him wear a clerical collar. Some

Sundays we would ride out to the foothills of the Catalina Mountains, where Dr. Russell would read the service in front of a large wooden cross. Behind the weathered cross towered majestic Cathedral Rock. At 13, I liked this kind of church-going best. During the service, we could hear the horses chomping the grass and nickering softly to each other.

Thus, on December 7, 1941, I was attending church in Oracle, Arizona, where Dr. Russell had been asked to preach. As we drove back to school after the service, we heard over the car radio the news that Japan had attacked Pearl Harbor. The next day we listened to President Roosevelt tell Congress that the attack was "a date which will live in infamy". At the age of 13, I heard a country declare war for the second time.

Some Sundays I would attend St. Philip's in the Hills, Tucson. This was the first church I had seen with a picture window behind the altar. The window framed the rugged Catalina Mountains. One guest preacher made enough of an impression on me for me to write Aunt Peggy, "The last two Sundays Father F— has preached. It's a wonder he hasn't broken his neck the way he throws himself around in the pulpit. He has this technique: he goes along in a whispering voice and then comes an emphatic part of his sermon, and he does acrobatic stunts in the pulpit. It makes the sermon very interesting."

Some time in December we received a photograph of Mother in her Red Cross uniform. Then she told us, "I have finished my job with the Red Cross and am now going to drive for an aircraft factory. The hours are rather long, but at least I shall feel I am really doing my bit. I do not start until Derrick goes back from leave. Have now got to find somewhere to live near the factory."

The next letter said, "Have been offered a permanent

job in the Red Cross in Norfolk, but it will not be ready for a week or two. If I do not take it, I may switch to the W.A.A.Fs."

Mother wrote on Christmas Day: "Today I have been with all my friends in the Red Cross, and we had a big party. All the tables had small Christmas trees on them, all decorated. We had crackers, a lovely turkey, and two enormous Christmas puddings, which the Warden of the club set alight. We drew the curtains, so it looked quite pretty, all on fire. After lunch we all felt rather full up, so we slept, and then listened to the King's speech.

"Then came an enormous tea, which we could hardly face, and a really large Christmas cake, iced with little Christmas trees all around it. After tea we had a treasure hunt, which kept us busy for three quarters of an hour. I helped do the clues and hide them. Then I came back to my hotel and ate another Christmas dinner alone. Now I really feel I shall not need another meal for a week. I had several nice Christmas presents from my friends in the Red Cross, handkerchiefs, flowers, scent, etc. I listened to President Roosevelt lighting the Christmas tree, and heard our Prime Minister speak. Yesterday I sent you all a cablegram for the New Year. Hope you got it alright."

Mother's last letter to us in 1941 told us, "I had a small food parcel arrive a few days ago, and thought it was from you, darlings. Then I discovered Montreal on the label and found it came from the Johnstons. I thoroughly enjoyed the bars of chocolate in it, as it is very difficult to get now and I really cannot stand in a queue for it. The tins of paste, etc., that were in it I gave to the girls in the Red Cross billet. They thoroughly enjoyed them. I wonder when your parcel will come. I am longing to see what you have sent."

Our Christmas package never reached Mother. That was

one disappointment. The other was that there was no snow in Arizona, and Christmas without snow was a let-down. We decided we liked Christmas at Muncy Farms best.

I never learned how Father spent Christmas day of 1941, because no word came from him. Later I learned he had been in London defending himself against a divorce action filed by our Mother. The suit was dismissed. Mother agreed to return to Father. On January 7, 1942, she wrote, "Today Daddy and I have been to Eastbourne. We have taken a little flat there near the sea." The news did not surprise us because we did not know they had separated.

On January 31, 1942, Father wrote Sheila, "Mummy is very happy in our new home." This was uncharacteristic of him because his letters as a rule contained no mention of the private side of his life. His reserve about private matters was not uncommon to English people. His sister once wrote Aunt Peggy, "I am beginning to wonder if this reserve and our silences are not in very truth as much an integral part of the English make-up as folk of other countries apparently think. We guard our privacy of mind as well as action, more than anything else in our lives. Perhaps it would occasionally be better if we raised the barriers sometimes."

CHAPTER TWENTY

$\mathcal{M}$other's reconciliation with Father got 1942 off to a good start for them. Our parents were pleased with the new apartment in Eastbourne, a seaside town in which they had lived earlier. Mother wrote on January 7: "It is very modern, on the third floor. Out of some of the windows we can see the Downs. It has four small bedrooms and two larger sitting rooms, a kitchen, all electric, stove and Frigidaire and central heating. We have got some of the large furniture in, but it so fills the flat up we have got to sell some of it and get some smaller. When I have got it all straight, I shall be back on my job again."

Father wrote Sue: "Pearl Court is a magnificent block of flats with views over the Sussex Downs and only a few hundred yards off the sea. Eastbourne is a nice town with plenty of good shops. When we lived here before, you and Brian were little tots, and I remember still you crawling under the gate-leg table to get out of the way of Brian. Mummy has lots of friends here. Your grandfather and grandmother (on Mother's side) lived here many years, and Mummy went to school here at Eastbourne."

And Mother wrote to me: "Sheila was born in Eastbourne, but you and Sue were too small to remember what

Eastbourne looks like, although you used to cause great excitement on the Front in your double pram."

As he had always done in the past, Father made all the arrangements for the move from Woodbridge, Suffolk, to Eastbourne. "It was a dreadful business for your Dad," he wrote Sheila on January 31, "getting all the furniture from Woodbridge to Eastbourne. I had to do all the packing at Woodbridge, and then unpack here. I have been working night and day for nearly six weeks. We are busy with the 'black out', fitting all windows with pelmets and side screens to stop all light showing. Every night we have to pull the curtains and make sure no light even from a little crack shows. The police fine offenders, and second offense people are sent to prison."

Our parents had to replace some kitchen items. Mother wrote on February 20, "Daddy and I were in London last Monday. I had to buy some things for the kitchen, as all ours were stolen. I only had one saucepan left. Anything in that line is very difficult to get now. After searching all over London, I managed to get one saucepan.

"We are practically straight in the flat now, and Daddy is quite an expert cook when he is there. We were quite excited yesterday as a friend gave us a rabbit from his farm. We had not seen one since we left Stone House. You remember how grand Daddy was and would never eat them. Well, he will now, and was quite thrilled about it when I was cooking it last night. Also we managed to get some herring, another thing we have not seen since we left the East coast."

Rationing continued to be a problem to be reckoned with in 1942. Father wrote Sue in January, "Thank your lucky stars you are out of England. Life here is very far from pleasant, and shopping becomes more difficult every day.

146   We are rationed, and all clothes, food, etc., can only be obtained with coupons. Everybody gets the same amount, regardless of size or weight. Your Dad lost 5 stone [70 pounds] in weight in six weeks during his illness and all my clothes hung on me like big bags. I did look a sight!" Mother wrote that Daddy had used some of his clothing coupons to buy her a pair of sheepskin-lined boots for the cold weather.

Father's spirits were greatly buoyed by Mother's companionship. She wrote us on January 7, "Daddy is much better now and hopes to get a job soon," and on January 17: "Daddy and I have been very gay lately and been to quite a lot of theatres. Some of them were very funny." She even got Father to take walks with her; on February 20, she wrote, "When Daddy is in Eastbourne, I make him come for long walks, and he is beginning to enjoy them." In April, she told us, "Daddy and I have been going three miles into the country on Sundays and having a picnic tea. Do you remember how he always said he hated picnics or tea in the garden? Well, now he thoroughly enjoys it."

Father began to write me at the Russell Ranch School once more. As before, he gave me his views on the war: "The War will last a long time now, owing to the success of Japan in catching the American Navy asleep. If the American Navy had won the first battle with Japan, the War would have been over this year. Everything now depends on Russia. Your Dad knew Russia would fight Germany; also they would in the end defeat the German Army. Caldwell Johnston will confirm. Like all Americans, he did not believe the great progress Russia has made during the last ten years. I wrote 2 ½ years ago, the only people who could and would save the British Empire would be the Russians, with their huge army and huge reserves of manpower. Today I am not so sure they haven't also saved America. What England and America are getting today we have asked for—the penalty of not keeping a big Army, Navy, and Air Force, and teaching other nations how to make and use machinery to make guns and ammunition to destroy us. All the *talk* in the world will not alter anything—only action. The Germans do not obey any civilized rules of warfare. They have become a nation of killers, reverting back to the law of the jungle like wild animals. They have been de-civilized by the Nazi doctrine." After praising Churchill as "a great man," Father instructed me to "tell the American people Hitler is no fool—also a great man, a son of the Devil, right out of hell."

Father wrote my twin sister that same day, "Do not worry about us or the War. Germany will be defeated. We are always talking and thinking about you, Brian, Sheila, and Malcolm. We look forward to the day when we shall all meet once more. Won't it be a wonderful day! Cheerio!"

Derrick turned 19 in February 1942. Both our parents sent news of him in letters; Father on January 31: "Derrick is still in the Army. I hope to get him transferred to the R.A.F. He is stationed at Dover, Kent, and has a front seat with plenty of excitement." Mother on February 5: "Derrick cannot get his transfer to the R.A.F. now, as there are no more allowed from the Army. So now he is talking of going into either Tanks or being a Commando (one of those men who go on the raids to Norway. You have read about them in the papers, I expect.) Anyhow, when he is finally settled I will tell you all about him. At present, he is still in The Buffs and is a Lance Corporal in the Motor Transport Section. He is quite good on a motorbike now. He has just been in hospital a week with a chill, but is alright now. He hopes to come here on 48 hours leave the week after next. He has been in the Army a year next week and has grown so big—6 ft. 2 inches—and very heavy as well."

Mother realized the four of us were growing up too. "When you write to me, tell me how big you all are now," she wrote on January 17, "as I have no idea of your sizes. Now that I have some clothing coupons for you, I could send you something nice instead of toys, but you must send me your correct measurements."

Anxious to return to her wartime job as a driver, Mother wrote on February 5, "As soon as we get really straight in about another week, I hope to join the Women's Transport here, if there is anything doing. If not, I shall have to go back to London and come down here when I can." Father told us on March 7, "Your Mum is on A.R.P. and drives my car." Another letter from Mother said, "At the moment I have a perfectly foul cold. I had a slight one and then had to sleep all night in an empty flat on my A.R.P. work and in spite of eight blankets, I was frozen all night, so now am sneezing and coughing as well. Hope I get rid of it before the day after tomorrow, as I am on duty all night again. I have got my Civil Defence uniform now, which is quite nice. A navy blue battledress top, like the Army wear, with C.D. and Eastbourne in a golden yellow on the pocket, and either skirt or trousers—it just depends what sort of job we have to do. Then a very thick navy blue coat with two rows of silver buttons and a blue beret with a silver A.R.P. badge on it. I have to dash out with the car every time a siren blows."

During the first part of 1942, the English were constantly on the alert, once again anticipating a German invasion, just as they had been in 1940. "We get far more alerts down here (Eastbourne)," Mother wrote on February 5, "than we did in London, but we haven't seen anything." Father wrote

Sheila a month later, "Any day in England we expect invasion by the Germans, but do not worry. Your Dad, as you know, never misses and every German he puts his eyes on, it will mean one crack of the rifle and another German will be in the next world. Nobody here is frightened. We all hope they come. It will be rare sport and lots of excitement and fun. Remember, the Bohun Barlows arrived in England in year 1066, and our family crest proves we have fought in every war and won our laurels."

The next day, Mother wrote, "There was a practice with the guns here one night, and everyone thought the Germans had arrived. We got quite excited about it, especially as we could hear a lot of planes overhead, but they were ours going out on a job. Derrick has volunteered for the Commandos, of whom you have read in the American papers, I expect, and failing that, [he has volunteered] to pilot a glider for troop carrying. He should hear very soon now for which he has been accepted.

"It was Derrick's birthday on February 28. I sent him some money as he wanted an electric iron to press his trousers and a wireless set. The wireless set I could not buy, so we managed to fix one up for him from two other sets we cannot use, as they are American, and there are no valves for them over here. However, it works, so now he will be alright. I hope he is coming on seven days leave in two weeks time, and after that he may be stationed near us, so we may see more of him."

Eastbourne held a fund raising event to buy war weapons. Mother wrote on March 8, "The Warship Week begins here on March 21, and Eastbourne is trying to get £300,000 to build a ship. There are all sorts of schemes to raise money—concerts, bridge parties, and a boxing tournament. We—

the Civil Defence Services—are going on parade with some of the Army in procession." A later letter said, "Eastbourne was trying to get £300,000, and by Friday—with another day to go—they had got over £450,000. At one big hall here was an exhibition by all the Defence Forces. There were mines and guns displayed by the Navy. All the boys under 16, who are the Air Cadets, had made wonderful model planes of both English and German planes, and they demonstrated them flying. All the girls from the Council schools had a marvelous display of knitted comforts for the troops. The Council boys had carved lots of naval ships out of wood, and some of them were really excellent. Someone lent thousands of lead soldiers of all sorts of regiments, and they were all lined up on a long table. Then there was a stall of lovely soft pullovers and mittens, etc., all made from combings of dogs' hair. Some of the things made from the hair of a light brown Pomeranian were lovely and soft. Then there was a big naval gun in the park outside the hall, so that everyone could see what they looked like. There were concerts and dances, a darts championship, and the Army Boxing Championships as well as football matches. Down at our A.R.P. depot we tried to raise more money than other depots by buying Savings Certificates."

Despite our father's brave words, and our mother's enthusiasm for fund raising activities, war news in the first part of 1942 was far from encouraging to those in England. On March 7, Father told Sue, "We are having bad news, and nobody knows what the future holds. Do not worry. Your Dad will look after your Mother."

By "bad news", probably he had in mind the news from North Africa. By the end of February 1942, the German General Rommel had recovered almost all of the ground so dearly won by the British at the end of 1941. The Rommel magic had become legend even among British troops. Father might also have had in mind that the Germans seemed to be winning the Battle of the Atlantic. In the first seven months of 1942, German submarines sank an appalling total of 681 Allied ships, at small cost to their own navy.

CHAPTER TWENTY–ONE

Shortly after the beginning of 1942, Aunt Peggy heard about a doctor in Tucson who had a reputation for cures in difficult cases. Some in the community considered him a quack, but Aunt Peggy decided she had nothing to lose and went to see him. He told her he suspected the infection in her hip was due to an abscessed tooth and suggested a thorough dental check-up. Sure enough, an abscess was found in the gum under a molar. Next the doctor told her she was starving to death because she was not getting enough nutrition from eating three meals a day. He told her to eat small meals six or seven times a day. In addition, he gave her some foul-smelling and foul-tasting powder to mix with orange juice or milk. Aunt Peggy followed his regimen and gradually her health improved. The large abscess on her hip began to heal, this time for good. Soon she decided she was strong enough to venture out with the four of us for the first time since her arrival in Tucson.

She elected to go with us to the rodeo. We watched cowboys ride broncos and rope steers most of the afternoon—a thrilling sight to us. As we were leaving the rodeo grounds, we spotted an amusement park area. We all tried various rides, with Aunt Peggy watching from the ground. Finally we begged her to go on just one ride with us. She said she would if we could find a ride that was not strenuous. We passed a ride called the Caterpillar, which was moving very slowly around a track somewhat like a miniature roller coaster. Aunt Peggy thought she could handle that ride, so she bought tickets for us all. We climbed into one of the open cars that made up the Caterpillar's body. With that, a bar snapped over our laps, a hood closed over us so we were in complete darkness, and the Caterpillar took off like a rocket, corkscrewing around the track. At times we were almost upside down. Aunt Peggy's pearl necklace broke and beads shot in every direction. After what seemed like hours, the ride finally came to a halt and the roof snapped open, the sudden bright sunshine making it almost impossible to see. All five of us staggered out of the Caterpillar, Aunt Peggy ashen. Fortunately by the time we got home, she had recovered enough to laugh at her poor choice of a ride. (We managed to recover most of her pearls.)

Mother commented, "I expect you all enjoyed the rodeo. What fun to see a real one. I saw one many years ago over here. There was one brought especially from America, and everybody was thrilled to see the cowboys ride." (January 7) Mother must have seen the famous Buffalo Bill Cody.

My 1942 letters to my parents from the Russell Ranch School were chiefly about my roan horse, Strawberry. I told them about our daily rides on the various working cattle ranches adjacent to the school. The school newspaper, *Russell Ranch Rattler*, informed its readers in an April issue, "Brian Barlow does not have a real hobby, but he reads a lot about horses and worries about his horse, Strawberry, so much that you might call that a hobby." Mother wrote on March 29, "I think your horse, Strawberry, looks a beautiful horse. I should love to see it." (I thought the "it" for my gelding was a bit unnecessary.) "You all look very nice riding. I am so glad you like it, Brian dear, as it will always be a useful accomplishment." I asked Mother why we had not had horses at Stone House. "I expect the reason we did not have any horses at Stone House was because riding in England is not so nice as in America. Here there are so few places to ride, as there are so many rabbit holes, which makes it dangerous. Also, horses are very expensive over here."

Now that America was at war, even our daily rides took on a warlike tone. Over the Easter vacation eight boys from the school spent the time at the Carr Canyon Ranch, managed by Capt. J. H. Healy, a retired Cavalry officer. An April issue of *Rattler* reported, "On several occasions we had cavalry drill, ably conducted by Captain Healy, which was one of the most enjoyable things we did while staying there. The Captain also instructed us in the effective use of rifles, pistols, and revolvers. We shot at a target several yards away and recorded our scores, which were very meager." Earlier the entire student body had attended a gymkhana at the 14th Cavalry Base as guests of Lt. I. G. Hayes. Cavalry drill formation, a personal explanation of the new Garand rifle, and a horse jumping exhibition were highlights of the morning's activities. The *Rattler* reported, "During the visit, Harry T—, the school's aeronautical authority, was given the 'privilege' of donning a new gas mask."

America's entry into the war brought changes in the life of the school. In the April 1942 issue of *Rattler*, Dr. Russell told the parents, "Each morning after chapel service our boys listen to a fifteen minute broadcast, and frequently at 4:45 p.m. they follow *Around the World Survey*. An hour is devoted each week to a discussion of outstanding events and trends of the day with special articles presented. Each month there is a quiz, following the method of the old-fashioned spelling bee. Allen D—, devotee of the *New York Times*, to date holds leading honors. Brian Barlow, our English boy, has been most helpful in narrating actual experiences in wartime England and in interpreting to us the viewpoint of our Allies." (Mostly I passed on comments from Father's letters.)

In 1942, Tucson became a center for aircraft production. The school found it increasingly difficult to keep "help" as the factories paid much higher wages and encouraged women to join the production line. We boys were asked to do chores around the school. Mother wrote, "Brian dear, how did you get on with the meal you told me you had to cook for the school? I hope you were able to eat it." A new plan for "maintaining neat rooms and general order in the school was instituted the second semester," according to the April *Rattler*. An "adjutant system" was organized on a quasi-military basis. "Every day one of the faculty members acts as 'Officer of the Day' with the boys alternating as adjutant. The cardinal aspect of this system is that it teaches the boys a sense of responsibility and at the same time keeps general decorum. The adjutant must also see that the flag is up in the morning and down at night." There were four inspections of the boys' rooms by the adjutant each day. Needless to say, at the age of 13, I entered into the "military" life with great enthusiasm. Once again, as I had in England, I found that war made life much more exciting for schoolboys.

Visitors to the school now often had something to do with the war effort. The *Rattler* reported, "Miss Antonia Bell's talk on Britain at war was informal and informative and brightened by a sharp sense of humor." Miss Bell was a "very

British young lady touring the Country in the interests of the English Speaking Union."

America's being at war did not at first cause a cut in supplies of gasoline for the school's two station wagons. We continued to attend cultural events in Tucson. The April *Rattler* reported, "The entire school went to hear Marian Anderson's superb concert at the University Auditorium. Miss Anderson had what was reported as the largest audience ever to be assembled under one roof in Tucson, and the boys felt that she certainly deserved it." Miss Anderson had earlier been refused permission by the Daughters of the American Revolution to sing in their hall in Washington D. C., Eleanor Roosevelt, wife of the President, had resigned from the D.A.R. over the incident.

At the end of the school year, we all returned to Muncy Farms for the summer. Aunt Peggy was in better health than she had been for the past several years. We arrived back at Muncy Farms in far less state than had been the case at our fall departure for Arizona in a brand new station wagon. The Arizona sun had dried out the canvas roof so that it now leaked like a sieve. Pedestrians were somewhat startled to see us with umbrellas up inside the vehicle whenever it rained. The wood panels had been so scoured by blowing desert sand that no varnish remained on them. Because of the war, it was no longer possible to buy a replacement vehicle.

CHAPTER TWENTY–TWO

*D*errick's long-awaited transfer to the Royal Air Force came through at last in March 1942. Mother wrote on March 29: "Derrick came home on leave last week, but was recalled as his transfer to Gliders came through. He is now in training as a glider pilot. I expect you read all about the Air Force Regiment in the papers I send you every week. He was very excited about it all."

The Glider Training Course was rigorous, and we followed Derrick's progress through it in Mother's weekly letters. "Derrick seems to be getting on alright now. Do write him as he is not able to get leave at present, so loves getting letters. He is at present training to get his 'Wings'. It will be quite a thrill when he does. We are all going up in the world, as Derrick has now been made a full Corporal and has left his training centre now, having completed his hard training like the Commandos have to do. Now he is at flying school in the Midlands and went for his first flight last Wednesday. I have not heard how he got on. He told me to hold my thumbs for him to bring him luck. He says he loves being in Gliders much better than the Army. He has already completed 6 hours of dual flying. Derrick has now passed his solo flying and can now fly a plane. The last letter I had from him he was going up with an instructor to do aerobatics. He said at first it seemed awful, but he enjoys it now. He is still working for his navigation, etc., and will be about another 5 weeks. Then he hopes to have passed and put his 'Wings' up before he goes to his final course."

Finally, on November 15, Father wrote to Sue, "Derrick is in the Gliders and can fly any plane. He has got his Wings up. Looks very smart, I am told. When he gets leave his mother stays with him in London." In December 1942, Derrick passed his final course with an "above average assessment" and was appointed Sergeant—1st Pilot.

Beginning in March, 1942, Mother threw herself into supporting the war effort with her usual single-mindedness and enthusiasm. On March 29, "I have been quite busy with the ARP, as I have to sleep all night at the depot every 4th night and in my spare time I am doing some work with the Red Cross." A May 20 letter told us, "I am now an Officer in the Red Cross and wear a red and white band round my hat and gold stars on my shoulders. I am what is called an Assistant Commandant and have a detachment of 80–100 people."

In great detail Mother described her work for the Red Cross. "My Display Week for the Red Cross went off quite well. [The next sentence was cut out by the censor]. Anyhow the three concerts went off well. At one of the concerts, 50 children from a dancing school performed. Some of them were only three. They were all in fancy dress and one small girl of three was dressed as a Dutch girl and looked very sweet; a small boy of five was dressed as a toy soldier and he sang and danced beautifully. There was one very pretty scene of Toytown, and they were all dressed as different toys. Some of the older girls did tap dancing. One of the teachers was dressed as a clown with a white face and funny red streaks. The other big concert was given by the Police Station and was excellent. They were very funny and some of them sang and one played a saw. I had to attend whist drives and dances and all sorts of things like that, and tell the people what the pennies we collect all year round are spent on."

With a friend (another Red Cross officer) Mother also formed a Youth Detachment of girls between the ages of 12 and 17. "We are going to teach them First Aid and Nursing. As a sideline, we do book binding, which is great fun. We are covering all the books for the hospitals in nice gay coverings, chiefly from wallpapers, but still it is quite fun. All this week I have been very busy giving First Aid and Home Nursing demonstrations and have not been in one night before 10:30 p.m. This afternoon, I had to go about five miles out to give classes in a village and coming back—I had a friend with me, so we had taken some sandwiches with us—we ate them in a wood at the side of the road, which was absolutely blue—like a carpet with bluebells. So we picked big bunches and left them at the hospital as we came by for the Children's Ward. They were so pleased with them. I am hoping to find time very shortly to go and work a few days a week in the Children's Ward. In my next letter I will write and tell you all what I am doing with my Youth Squad. We are going for a picnic in two weeks' time, if all is quiet here. We are also going to have some films and lantern slides. In our detachment of the Youth Squad we have adopted a Prisoner-of-War, who has no one to send him parcels. He is a Spaniard fighting with the Allies and as he can read and write English, we get letters from him, and one of the girls takes it in turn to write to him. We send him a big parcel of useful things every three months. This week I have been busy buying the things he has asked for in his letters. The girls are always getting up concerts or something like that to raise money to pay for his parcels. We also have two Englishmen, who come from Sussex, to whom we send books and parcels."

The last letter in 1942 to give details about Mother's Red Cross work was dated June 26. "I have been very busy lately with the Red Cross, as we have had two more parades since I last wrote. I will send you the photos of the parade the Duke of Kent inspected. Since then we have been to another parade for the United Nations. It was held in the big cricket ground here and we had a church service. Most of the various services and organizations were represented. Last Saturday I went to a lovely little village called Chiddingly. Most of the houses were very old and all the gardens were blazing with flowers. We had a Red Cross competition in the grounds of a lovely old house, very like Stone House. We were all dressed in indoor uniforms with caps and aprons. All my detachment wear light blue frocks. I wear a scarlet one with a white collar and cuffs, a white apron with a red cross on it and a large white cap with a red cross on the front. There were eight supposed casualties and they were very realistic, all made up to look as if they had been bombed, and lots of ox blood all over the place. We had a team of five and had to render First Aid to them all and were allowed twenty minutes. There were four teams and I regret to say we were third. Unfortunately, the night before the competition I had to release three of my best people, as there was some sort of Home Guard exercise, so they had to be at their First Aid posts. However we all enjoyed it. It was a lovely day, very hot, and we had a gorgeous tea."

That same June 26 letter contained the news that "the new call-up notices are out and I have to register on August 8, so I may have to do some other full time job of work. If things improve by September, I may get a little Red Cross petrol for essential jobs. I get awfully tired walking about, as I have so much to do and get no petrol for the car." Mother did manage to buy a new bicycle after waiting for six months. "I feel just like a child with a new toy. Daddy gave mine away at Woodbridge while I was in the Transport, and it has been impossible to buy one."

For my Father, 1942 was not a good year. Once again, he found himself alone much of the time, as Mother channeled her energies into her Red Cross work. As far as Father's job prospects were concerned, 1942 was no better than 1941 had been. On March 29 Mother wrote, "Daddy is off to London tomorrow and has hopes of getting a job at last." But, once again, no job offer materialized. He wrote Sue on November 15, "Your Dad has tried to get in all the different Services: Navy, Army, Air Force, Engineers, but I am refused—too old. Your Dad is 55 years. The Army is getting rid of men (Officers) even under the age of 50 years. Only last week I applied again—my twentieth application. I have volunteered to go abroad to Russia, Africa, anywhere, but it is a young man's war. How your Dad wishes he was in America or Canada. I tried so hard to get to Canada. I volunteered to serve on a ship as stoker, cook or Engineer, but it was impossible owing to regulations."

None of Father's plans that year worked out. Once again he tried to get Mother to consider moving to Scotland. On June 26 she wrote us, "Daddy and I have just written about a tiny house in Scotland again. It is on the seashore and has some shooting. Just in case we have to move from here." Father confirmed the news in a July 7 letter. "It is quite possible we shall leave here and move to Scotland. It is one of the regrets of our lives we did not go there a year ago. We were very foolish. Our next move will be the seventh since the war." On September 28, Father wrote Aunt Peggy, "We received your very long descriptive and nice letter. The reason we have not replied is we have been in Scotland, where we rented a house for the duration. Our life has been hectic in more ways than one. It is very difficult to write any news. My wife is very happy. We both are."

The trip to Scotland buoyed Father's spirits, but his hopes of keeping Mother close at hand were quickly dashed. Mother decided against living in Scotland, although she never told us that herself. In a letter dated December 9, Father explained, "We obtained Military Permits to live in Scotland, where few people are allowed to go—it is a forbidden area or Defence area. When we arrived at Oban, a new order came in about petrol and fewer motor buses. With the result that—if we had gone to Rahoy—every time we wanted to come into Oban, it would have meant a ten-mile walk to the ferry steamer. It was a great disappointment, because I was looking forward to shooting wild deer, grouse, and masses of wild fowl—geese, wild duck, etc. Your Mother would have spent her time fishing for salmon, sea trout and pike in the lochs, like she did at Oulton Broad."

When Mother refused to stay in Scotland, Father wrote Sue, "We are now returning from Scotland back to Eastbourne. Where we shall live is very uncertain. It seems impossible to find a house all over England. Everywhere is full up. How we miss our lovely home, Stone House, Aldringham."

After their return from Scotland, Mother spent "whole weeks in London," according to Father. He suffered in silence, doing his best to assess what the future held. He wavered between optimism and pessimism. On September 28, he wrote me, "Civilization is going to be very tough. Everybody will have to work. Make up your mind to be a master man, which means become your own boss." On November 8 came more advice: "Listen to your Dad's advice. When at school get down to it; work hard at your lessons. Forget play until the holidays. There is a wonderful new world coming for you with unlimited chances to make your way—obtain a good business position, provided you take every advantage of your school days." Three days later, Father wrote his old American friend Consul Caldwell Johnston, "Keep your eye on the children. I doubt whether they will ever see England again. Everything is different. We shall be as poor as church mice for a long time after the war, and will the pot boil."

Father's brief burst of optimism had been sparked by news of General Montgomery's victory over Rommel at El Alamein, and the news that the Allies had invaded French North Africa under General Eisenhower. On November 8 he wrote, "The war news is great and it won't last much longer." The encouraging war news inspired Father to write a newspaper article for the *Eastbourne Courier*, which took up most of page four of the December 11, 1942 issue. Ever the engineer, he outlined his vision for Eastbourne in the post-war period. "Instead of hundreds of old obsolete houses which now exist, picture twenty huge buildings with every modern appliance and comfort with perfect hygiene. Artistically planned and positioned, they would stand in beautiful grounds and gardens, with large open spaces for children's playing grounds, model yacht ponds, miniature cycle and push-car tracks for the children, tennis courts. Suitable buildings could be provided for inclement weather, for spacious large indoor nurseries, again with indoor gardens. My plan

164   would mean work for 100,000 men, skilled and unskilled, the moment the war stops, and with it local prosperity to suppliers of materials, and the housing of workmen would bring benefit to room-letters and local tradesmen." To dream about doing a project on this scale was now my Father's only source of happiness.

Derrick Crombie-Steedman, captain of Glider 170, standing top center, and his crew.

Aunt Cecile Bunn in uniform, ca. 1942. She was the only sister of the author's father.

Violet Layman Barlow, the author's mother, in Red Cross uniform, ca. 1942.

CHAPTER TWENTY–THREE

*A*fter the desert landscape of Tucson, in the summer of 1942 Muncy Farms looked as green as Ireland. We were all glad to be back home. Aunt Peggy wrote to the assistant headmaster of the Russell Ranch School, "We are settling down at last and enjoying being at home again. I especially am glad to be back with good health, for life is becoming more complicated every minute with the shortage of labor and gas and oil rationing, etc. It takes more time and strength to manage a farm and four children, and I am glad to be in better shape to try my best at it."

We spent much of that summer helping the farmer bring in the hay for the dairy herd, working in the vegetable garden, and keeping the flowerbeds around the house presentable. Aunt Peggy no longer had a chauffeur/gardener; he had left for a job in a war industry factory. So Mickey, the housekeeper, took over management of the vegetable garden, which continued to supply our table with an abundance of fresh vegetables—peas, beans, lettuce, tomatoes, squash, and my favorite, asparagus. The four of us took turns churning ice cream with peaches or strawberries out of the rich milk sent over from the farm each morning.

We swam all summer long in the pool, and that summer Malcolm learned to swim. On June 26, Mother wrote, "Can you swim the length of the pool yet, Malcolm darling? Now you are getting such a big boy—nearly seven— you ought to be able to write me a little note soon and tell me all about your friends." We all played tennis on the court at the farm, and Aunt Peggy gave Sheila tennis lessons at a club in Williamsport. She won a local tennis tournament that summer.

In July, Sue and I turned 14. A letter from Mother arrived ahead of our birthday. "I do hope, Brian and Sue, you have a perfectly lovely birthday. Isn't it a shame I cannot be at your parties. Just think of it, both 14. You will soon be grown up." To me, Mother wrote, "Mind you always remember you are the oldest boy of the family now that Derrick is not with you, and that you look after the rest of them." It was a memorable birthday for me because Aunt Peggy gave me a horse of my own. He was a gray gelding named Prince. Prince had been kept in a stable in the town of Muncy. The stable door opened onto a dirt road which led to the wire rope factory nearby. Workmen used the road to get to the plant. As they passed the stable, they would stop to pat Prince and talk to him. They would also feed him something out of their lunch pails. In this way Prince got very fond of apple pie and cake icing. He also got to enjoy being around people. At the farm no matter where he was in the pasture, as soon as he spotted visitors, he would come galloping over to visit with them.

I rode him sometimes twice a day all that summer, and we explored every corner of the farm. The stable work was my responsibility, and I curried Prince until he shone like an Arabian show horse. I tried to teach him to jump, but after trying it he decided it was too much work, so I had to drop that idea. I did manage to train him for driving. Every visitor that summer found himself in the buggy for a drive around the farm. Prince got so he would count the number of people in the buggy, and if he thought it was excessive, he would flatly refuse to move. I would have to ask some of the people to get out; Prince would check again, and if satisfied, he would happily trot off. Father wrote me on July 7, "I pity your horse; it looks like it is having a very busy time with every friend and all of you riding it. Remember horses like a rest sometimes. Don't treat such a wonderful present as a piece of machinery."

In July the four of us had to make our annual "Application to Extend Time of Temporary Stay" to the U.S. Department of Justice because our temporary permits expired on August 8. The extension was granted. Later in the year we were sent Alien Registration cards and told to keep them with us at all times.

The summer of 1942 also sticks in my memory because I had an emergency appendectomy. We had been to see a movie in Muncy and, as was our custom, after the film we ended up in the ice cream parlor. I spent my week's allowance on a huge banana split. Having some allowance left over, I then insisted on buying a large milkshake, so the banana split would have some company. At that point, Aunt Peggy said to me, "If you get sick, don't come to me." I had no sooner gotten into bed when sharp pains began. At two in the morning, I could stand the pain no longer, so I knocked timidly on Aunt Peggy's bedroom door. She immediately put me in her bed and called Dr. Rankin, the old country doctor, who was in his seventies. He had come out of retirement because of the shortage of doctors due to the war. He took one look at me, said my appendix was about to burst, and arranged to have me admitted to the Williamsport Hospital, where he removed my appendix. I carry a seven-inch scar to this day.

Father wrote Aunt Peggy on September 28, "You are truly wonderful with our children, getting them through all their illnesses. What a trial they have been to you. Your love and kindness to them is quite beyond me to thank you in words." The same day Father wrote to me, "Delighted with your bright and cheerful letter. You are lucky to get rid of your appendix." Mother, too, wrote Aunt Peggy, "I was so delighted to receive your last letter and to hear that Brian is OK. I really must apologize for the bad behavior of both the boys having appendicitis. Perhaps the whole family will now be alright." Father wrote Malcolm, "Every morning and night your Mummy and Dad talk about you, Susan, Brian and Sheila. We wonder what you are all doing. We picture you swimming, diving, fishing, and helping Aunt Peggy. Always be kind to Aunt Peggy. Do everything she asks you."

Near the end of that summer Aunt Peggy recognized that she would be unable to stay at Muncy Farms over the winter months. Her heating oil allotment was not enough to run the three furnaces required to heat the house. Also, because she had refused an X card for gas for the car (as a farm owner, she was entitled to an unlimited supply of gasoline), it would now be possible to go to market in Muncy only once a week, if that. Fortunately, Aunt May Gibson offered her the use of an empty servant's house in Wynnewood. The house was not large, so Aunt Peggy planned to take with her as staff only Mickey, the housekeeper, and Vivian, who was to look after Malcolm, Sue and Sheila.

She made different arrangements for our schooling over the winter months. To my joy, I was to return for a second

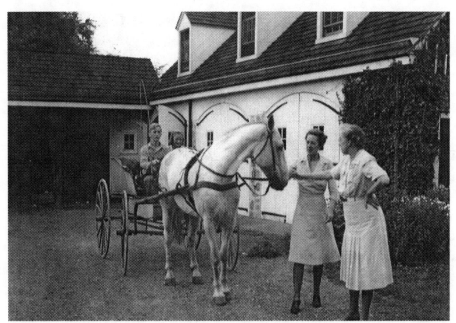

Left to right: Brian and Sheila in the cart; Prince, the horse; Aunt Peggy and Aunt Jo Gorham at Muncy Farms.

Brian begins training Prince to pull a cart.

year to the Russell Ranch School. During the summer she had written the assistant headmaster, "As I wrote Dr. Russell, I am extremely grateful for what you all did for Brian. He still has a long way to go, of course, but since we have come home I have noticed a great change from this time a year ago. He shows more sense of responsibility, more repose, both physical and mental, and altogether seems to have gained many of the things that seem essential before scholastic achievement can come. That is why I am so anxious that he should go back to you." She ignored the comment made by the headmaster of Episcopal Academy, a private school, where she had decided to send Malcolm as a day student: "I note on the form that the Russell Ranch School charges $1,200 for the fourteen-year-old brother. This seems an outrageous price under all conditions. If other schools in the East are making special arrangements [for child war evacuees], I think you are justified in asking them to consider similar assistance." The fact was that the Russell Ranch School was too small to offer financial assistance to any child.

The headmaster of Episcopal Academy did offer a discount for Malcolm. "If Malcolm comes to our E Form, the tuition is $225. Malcolm will be billed for $125 and such incidentals as luncheons, books, transportation, etc. We have a dozen of these English boys at The Academy; some of them have been over here for two years. We took the stand at the outset that we would give them all half rates and have tried to collect some funds toward this purpose. Of course, we had contemplated that the war would not last indefinitely when the arrangement was made. People have been very good in helping us."

Sue and Sheila were to attend the Agnes Irwin School, a

private school in Wynnewood. Miss Gibson had been in its first class. The headmistress wrote Aunt Peggy, "The scholarship committee was glad to help out with your two charges next year and will give them half-tuition scholarships. For Susan this will amount to $225, and for Sheila it will amount to either $165 or $215 depending whether she is able to enter the seventh grade or must go on with the sixth. It will be very pleasant indeed next year having them in the school and having you as a neighbor."

On September 7 Aunt Peggy notified the British Consul General in Philadelphia and the U. S. Committee for the Care of European Children of her winter address in Wynnewood, but said, "In May I expect to return to the above address [Muncy Farms] for the summer months." His Majesty's Vice Consul replied, "Your close cooperation is much appreciated." For some unknown reason, his stationery had a wide black border.

The big day finally arrived for me to head west for another year at the Russell Ranch School. I was to take the train by myself to Chicago, and then meet up with Dr. Russell and the other boys for the rest of the journey to Tucson. Before my departure Aunt Peggy gave me an impressive lecture about "living within my means." She suggested that I write down all my expenditures and in that way I would be able to quickly spot the extravagant ones. I immediately vowed to end my extravagant ways. I dutifully started listing all my expenditures, and soon Aunt Peggy's files were full of my lists on odd scraps of paper. However, I can honestly say that I never found even a single expenditure that was not entirely justifiable. Once or twice I did consider cutting back on my generous tips, but *noblesse oblige* overruled that idea.

After my arrival at school, I sent off to Aunt Peggy the following account: "Saturday: I spent 50¢ on Reader's Digest and a pillow. It rained until we got to Chicago. The car I got into had a whole section to myself, but at Pittsburgh they took my car off and so I had to sit up all night.

"Sunday: I spent $3.58. Checked suitcase 10¢ because I had a two-hour wait. Sundae 18¢ and a funny book 10¢. I tipped a porter 10¢ at Union Station. Dinner $1.50 plus 20¢ tip. Supper $1.50 plus 15¢ tip. It was a hot and muggy day.

"Monday: I spent $2.87 on: breakfast 75¢ plus 10¢ tip. Coca Cola 10¢. Supper $1.12 plus 20¢ tip. Lunch 50¢ plus 10¢ tip. Spent the day in Dr. Russell's car.

"There are five new boys. I am rooming with a new boy named P— from New York. He seems all right. There is great improvement in the school, but as we have to write Sunday I will tell you then. Strawberry recognized me, and I will have to use a lot of will power to not take him. Tell the doctor to write a letter as quick as he can as we start riding Thursday. It is terribly hot here. Love, Brian."

Aunt Peggy had been worried about my train trip west and the two-hour layover I would have in Chicago. She suggested that I take a taxi to the Blackstone Hotel and pass the time by getting a haircut. I did so, and found the elegant Blackstone to be my kind of hotel. The barbershop was all marble and glass. The barbers were all elderly gentlemen—at least to my fourteen-year-old eyes—never failing to call even their youngest customers "Sir." I loved the careful attention, the hot face towels, and best of all the Bay Rum lotion. I chose the Bay Rum from a large array of bottles because my father always smelled faintly of Bay Rum. The barber doused me liberally with the Bay Rum. On the way out, I ran across the men's room and was delighted to discover that it, too, had a supply of Bay Rum. I gave myself another shot before taking a taxi to the other side of Chicago from which the trains to the west departed.

Taking a train west in the 1940s was a glamorous experience even in wartime. A red carpet was unrolled on the platform for those boarding one of the "crack" trains to the west coast. The food was marvelous, and fortunately I knew about finger bowls from home. Dr. Russell usually booked roomettes for the boys, but Aunt Peggy had objected that a roomette was an unnecessary expense, so Dr. Russell had booked me a Pullman berth. Some other parents got wind of this, so they, too, insisted on Pullman berths for their boys. Thus that year three of us traveled to Tucson in Pullman berths. Much to our delight, we found we were free of Dr. Russell's supervision, as his roomette was quite a distance from the Pullman cars. Needless to say we had a glorious time exploring the train. We especially enjoyed talking to the soldiers on board.

When I wasn't apologizing to Aunt Peggy for not writing, I did my best to keep her informed about my activities. Some samples: "This summer in Arizona was the driest summer they have had in 60 years and there is no grass for the horses, so we have to feed them hay, which is very expensive. Flaxen (my horse) is in fine shape and is looking better than he did last year. It feels fine being on a horse again. I wonder how Prince is? One of the horses ate too much hay and died of colic. I hope it doesn't happen to Flaxen."

"We still go to church every Sunday, but Dr. Russell said we will use our chapel in a few weeks. Thank goodness! Going [to other churches in Tucson] at 35 mph is awful slow."

"Worked like a slave all week and was able to go on the

pack trip. We went to the same place as last year about 12 miles from the school. Seven boys and Mr. and Mrs. S— and Earl [the cowboy] went along. It was a lot of fun though none of us slept much. We managed to keep a fire going all night, so it was warmer than last year. I think last year we had more fun because there were all older boys so we could do more. Maybe going to the same place took a lot out of it. During the night Earl shot a rattlesnake. It was just a small one about 3 ½ feet long. It is wonderful riding Flaxen as everybody says he is a very pretty horse and all the other boys are very envious of me. I am pretty pleased with myself at the moment as the other person in my class in French has been getting 75 all week, while I have been getting 45. We took a test at the end of this week and I got 75 and the other boy got 45. I don't see how I did. Hope I can keep it up."

"My cellmate jumped off his desk and onto his bed and broke it, so he is not in my room now but will come back as soon as the bed is fixed. I broke the water jug yesterday. P.S. Still sorry I forgot your birthday. If you need another horse I will bring Flaxen. I don't like Flaxen as much as I do Prince."

"We have changed roommates and I have Walter B—. I am lucky as I don't have to look after a little guy again. There are two new boys. Sorry this is written in such a hurry but I don't eat unless it is done. Tucson is crowded with soldiers. The shops are not half as interesting as last year."

"We had to do our Christmas shopping a week ago. I bought all the presents I wanted, as I was afraid to let it go as Dr. Russell told us we would not have another chance to get in before the gas rationing. This is what I bought. For Susan, a natural colored wooden horse. Price $2.50. It was the only thing I thought Sue might like. For Sheila, a silver bracelet and a silver horse. Price $2.50. It is quite a nice set as the horse goes with the bracelet. For Malcolm, two Vaquero ties, one red, other green. Price $2.00. For Mickey [our house-keeper] a silver horse bracelet. Price $1.00. And a present for you. I spent $8.00, not counting your present. Could you make one of my Christmas presents some money, please."

"For Sue's information the Potter School came to church last Sunday and they have quite a few new girls. Silvia B— is back and she has her hair up. Isn't that the girl who got good hands at the horse show? The only other girl I clearly re-membered was a girl who wears glasses and has a long nose. She had her hat on backwards. There were a few more I think I saw last year. They all still wear lipstick and it looks awful. This is the longest letter I have written this term."

"I agree with you when you say I spend more than I have but because of gas rationing we hardly ever get to town and when we do we overdo it. Anyhow, I had a lot of fun buying the Christmas presents and I hope everybody will be satisfied. It's wonderful to hear that you are able to work and it doesn't hurt you any more. Wait till this sum-mer and then you can really be able to play with us. Won-der how Prince is? Glad to hear the girls are doing all right."

"The play, which was put on last night, was a great success and we made over two dollars for the Red Cross. The play was *Midsummer Night's Dream* and I was Snout. I was very much pleased when I was admired for my smell. The reason was that in the second scene I had to be sheet white, and the only thing we could think of was powder, so I was drowned in Mrs. Russell's lavender powder. Earl shot and butchered the hog today and she must have weighed at least 350 lbs. A ter-rific animal and for table talk she has the most insides of any animal I have ever seen. Which, come to think of it, is only as big as the rabbit's insides that I skinned at Stone House. Now to get down to business and answer your questions about my clothes and other things. All my clothes are in good shape except the below. These are what I need. 4 pairs of Levis as all but one pair is too small. 4 brown everyday shirts. The last lot are just beginning to wear. It would help if I had two more white shirts as the laundry is awful hard on them. And me and the laundry together don't leave much shirt. I probably will need another pair of shoes before the term is out. Would or could you make me some sweaters for this summer and fall. Mine are all decorated with holes. Two more pairs of frontier pants would help as now [when I dress up] I have to wear my gray trousers. Also my white trousers are about six inches too short and can't be let down. And when I get back another pair of corduroy pants would help. What shall I do with the clothes that don't fit me?"

"Dear Sue and Malcolm, Hope you had a good time at Christmas. Thanks a lot for the book. I have not read it yet because it is hard enough to get into the bathroom after lights in ordinary times but around Christmas it's impossible because everybody wants to read their new books. It looks very good and I will try and read it soon. Love, Brian."

"Dear Sheila, Hope you had a good Christmas. I had a swell time. [I spent it at school with other boys who lived too far away to go home for Christmas.] Thanks a lot for the pencil. It is a honey. You have good taste and at my rate of eating up a pencil in every two days it will not only come in very handy but will save me or Aunt Peggy some money. I've forgotten who is paying for pencils, but I think it is me so I say again thanks for the swell pencil. Love, Brian."

A large Christmas card with an English hunting scene on it reached me in Tucson from Father. He sent it from the

Royal Aero Club in London. There was no message, but it was signed in his own handwriting, "from Dad. Xmas 1942."

On January 5, 1943, I wrote Aunt Peggy about how I had spent Christmas Day. "Got up with my usual love of bed at eight o'clock and went over to the main building with Mr. R—. Had breakfast and then the big moment came. There was a stampede for the presents. For lunch we had turkey, mashed potatoes, peas, and for dessert, plum pudding. Listened to a program on the radio that night."

1942 was coming to an end.

December 31, 1942

On the Eastern Front: Troops of the Soviet Fifth Shock Army, driving southwest from Nizhne Chirskaya, expel the Germans from Tormosin. The German Army Detachment Hollidt can do little to halt such strong attacks.

Guadalcanal: After a fierce battle with American troops in the Pacific, the Japanese High Command decides to evacuate the island. The orders are issued on 4 January, 1943.

Libya: A Free French force under the command of General Leclerc advances from Chad into the South Fezzan. They will continue to move north and join up with the British Eighth Army during January 1943.

CHAPTER TWENTY–FOUR

"*V*iolet has gone again," were Father's words in a tele-
phone call to his sister on Christmas Day 1942. In a letter
written two years later [1944] Aunt Cecile told Aunt Peggy
about this time in her brother's life. "From this time he once
more began to write me about his sorrows. Letters came more
quickly than I could reply. They finally took on a despairing
tone, and I—oh! How I tried to cheer him, to make him
keep a grip on his courage. I talked to Mr. Q — who tried to
persuade him to come here and see him. I tried, too." But
Father would not leave the Eastbourne flat.

For the second time, Mother had her London law firm
file divorce proceedings against Father. The first time he had
hired a solicitor to defend himself, and the suit had been
found without merit by the judge. This time Father had no
money left to employ King's Counsel before a Judge in Private Chambers. He had no recourse this time.

According to Aunt Cecile's 1944 letter, Father was more
worried about his children than himself. He was convinced
that Mother would never make a home for us. "He alter-
nately asked me to look after them [but the Woodbridge
home was rented, and he had no home for them to come
to], and then wanted you [Aunt Peg] to keep them, as he

180 felt you loved them and had been so wonderful to them. I assured him that the moment the children had definitely and legally passed from his care, he would regret it and fret. And at that stage I felt the children would feel it a hurtful action to be given away, however much they loved you."

Completely unaware of what was happening with my parents in England, I anticipated that 1943 was going to be the best year so far in America. I was very content at the Russell Ranch School and my schoolwork was showing improvement. Father wrote me, "We [perhaps the 'we' indicated he still hoped for a second reconciliation with our mother, or else he was reluctant to admit the separation to his 14-year-old son] are so glad you are happy at your school. Work hard at school—your lessons will become easy if you get down to it. Make friends and remember to keep an address book with all names, dates (year) and addresses. In years to come you will find your whole life career made up by and with the people you know, especially your schoolmates. If you want to train your mind, get a small daily diary and keep it up to date. It will interest you and your Mother when you meet."

Father's early 1943 letters revealed obliquely his concerns and, viewed with hindsight, they sound like a farewell. "Your Dad never forgets you or Susan, Sheila and Malcolm, and while I live you can always depend on me to look after your interests and your future happiness. Be sure and write to your Mother every week—nice short letters. So many get lost in transit. If you write each week some must get through."

This particular letter—January 17th—ran to eight legal-sized pages, and contained both a great deal of personal and business advice. "Do not do anything you are likely to be ashamed of—keep the name BARLOW clean, and do not break the laws of any country, whatever the inducement offered. Your name and liberty are worth more than a mountain of gold. At school you will be taught about legal contract laws, but lessons in school at your age do not impress upon your mind the serious part they will play in your life in the future. Coming from your Father, who is trying to give you the benefit of his 35 years experience, so that you can avoid the traps and pitfalls that exist for the unwary and uneducated, may make more of an impression ...

"This letter is written also for another purpose, to impress upon you the necessity to really work hard at school—make it your number one objective. Then your school and masters will be proud of you, and if they see you are trying hard, it will give them encouragement to help you. Play and sport may seem important, but the future is very uncertain for everybody in every country owing to the war, because the whole business structure and fabric has been destroyed, broken up, disorganized. When the war stops, there may be chaos. Only those with learning and education will be able to reconstruct and rebuild the business of the world. Your future job in life entirely depends on yourself and what you learn at school. Plan your life ahead; safeguard your future by saving every penny. Strive to get one thousand pounds in your bank. When you have succeeded, it will bring you confidence and stability and happiness—freedom from worry. Always think of rainy days ahead. Nobody goes through the world without trouble and adversity. Keep your temper; refuse to quarrel. Only fools quarrel and make enemies. Laugh and the world will laugh with you. Remember, keep your troubles in your own circle. Other people have their own." The letter concluded with, "Nothing else, except remember the BARLOW TEAM, which means unity and strength."

Conditions were also chaotic in the early months of 1943 for Aunt Peggy. At home in Wynnewood my two sisters and younger brother were passing measles, chicken pox, mumps, and whooping cough back and forth. Things got so bad that Aunt Peggy hired back the trained nurse who had looked after her when we first arrived at Muncy Farms.

On January 15, 1943, I wrote Aunt Peggy, "Sorry to hear that you may have mumps and that it has hindered you a lot. You must feel like I did when I missed a pass and broke my ankle. Also you don't have the consolation I did when I had mumps, because when I had them the rest of the school did, and it is funny to see everybody with round faces. Also I hardly noticed mine. Anyway, I hope you don't have mumps." Another January letter commented, "From reading the first paragraph I see that you have been terribly busy this last week. You do more in one week than other people in weeks. Hope Sheila is all right. You ought to teach Sue how to look after colds and give you a rest." In February I wrote, "I hope Malcolm doesn't have the measles!" In March I wrote, "Hope you don't have measles, chicken pox or whooping cough. In the next letter I get from you I expect to hear that you have hit Sue and Malcolm hard over the head. I wouldn't blame you, because they couldn't have done worse if they tried. Your troubles certainly all come at once. Hope your teeth don't hurt too much." By the end of March, I was still sending Aunt Peggy sympathy: "Sorry to hear you are having such an awful time. I hope it will get better soon. I suppose now Sue, Sheila and Malcolm will keep changing their troubles. I must say, I am glad I'm not there, but maybe if I was I could do the marketing, etc."

Life was chaotic for Father and Aunt Peggy, but it was

exciting for me. I was enjoying observing new places and people. Because I was too far away to go home for winter vacation that year, Aunt Peggy paid extra to send me to a dude ranch near the Mexican border. In a January 15 letter I told Aunt Peggy all about it. "We went down to Kenyon Ranch after eating lunch at the Old Pueblo Club. It took about an hour to get there. And as you have been down there, you know that it is pretty rough country. Well, Kenyon Ranch is right opposite to the town, or rather village, of Tubac, which we were informed was the second oldest town in the U.S. The ranch stands up on a knoll about a mile from the road, and is surrounded by mountains. The ranch is made up of lots of little houses and the main ranch, where the dining room and library are, stands in the center. It is quite an artistic place. All the walks are of loose gravel and all the buildings blend into one. I mean that they are all the same color and nearly the same design. Mr. and Mrs. Allen are the owners of the ranch, and they are very nice people. For the first few days I roomed with a new boy by the name of Jim T——. His father is in charge of getting the Japanese into internment camps for American Japanese. Later in the week I moved over to where the rest of the boys were, which was another house just for the boys.

I wrote to Aunt Peg, "We had a swell time. Rode twice a day, and they had a small burro by the name of 'Heelitrop', which we rode every day. 'Heelitrop' means 'flower of the desert', and he was the funniest thing you could think of. I had a nice but fiery little horse, and whenever I wanted to stop, he'd shoot out his front feet and stop from a lope to nothing. It pretty nearly dislodged my backbone, and Flaxen, my horse at the Russell Ranch School, seems like air compared to him. We had one swell ride which was up to the top of the Tumacacori Mountains, which are about as high as the ones around Tucson, but are not as steep or rough. We went up to a place called Smugglers' Notch, which is, as I understand, where all the cattle were rustled across the Mexican border. It has quite a history and a good many outlaws were shot bringing cattle across. There we had a picnic lunch and then we had a 40-minute climb to the top. It was hard climbing, but worth it. From up there you could see the Mexican border."

No western ranch was complete without genuine cowboys, and the Kenyon Ranch did not disappoint us. "There were two cowboys, one called Slatts, the foreman, and the other called Jim. They were both very nice, but everybody liked Jim the best. Probably because he had been in quite a few rodeos and was the one we always went with."

At the age of 14, I could not write letters home without mentioning food. "The meals and beds were swell, and I took full advantage of the bed, never getting up before nine. The way they ate at that place you'd think there wasn't a war on, or even rationing. You could eat as much butter and meat, and drink as much coffee as you wanted. I don't see how they did it, but they did."

Father would have been pleased to know I had begun to notice what people were up against in the "real world." In January I wrote Aunt Peggy, "I think I told you that Mr. S— was fired. I don't think anybody misses him, because he had an awful temper and swore so much. But at other times he could be just as nice as could be." In February, I wrote, "E— and M— have been fired, and Dr. Russell gave this reason: 'When a person thinks himself bigger than the job, he goes.' I guess it was something like the cheek of the man on your property. I know that M— thought she should have charge of Rita and Mrs. Hart, and was always bossing them. They were very nice people, but Mrs. Russell also said, 'Very jealous of anybody else.'"

Long before the school year began to wind down, my thoughts turned to summer at Muncy Farms. On February 27 I wrote, "Only ten more weeks before I am home. As I told you in my last letter, we were having a Declamatory Contest. By some freak of nature, I won it with my poem 'Soliloquy of the Spanish Cloister.' Have not got the prize yet, but it will probably be a book." A March 7 letter reported, "I got for a prize *The Complete Works of Shakespeare*. It is a beautiful book and will come in handy, because we have to read *Julius Caesar* for English." In April a second Declamatory Contest was held, and on April 11 I reported the results: "I came in second with a very high mention. I was beaten by a longer and a very good poem. Everybody seemed to like mine best, but there were outside judges that judged on everything. Anyway, I am pleased with what I got, because the poems were much better this time." A March 31 letter told Aunt Peggy, "Muncy Farms sounds swell now; it is getting so hot out here. It will be nice to be able to do something again—owing to rationing our activities here are limited. Now we only ride three or four days a week to conserve the horses as they get such lousy food." On April 28, I commented, "Won't it be nice to be at good old Muncy Farms with all the trees. I have forgotten what trees look like. You seem to be hearing from everybody at once, probably after your milk and lambs. It ought to be a swell summer with everybody coming. There will be a lot to do in the garden and it would be a good idea if you got some of the women from the prison to help. They seem to enjoy going out once in a while."

186   Dr. Russell did his best to keep alive my interest in things English. On March 18 he wrote Aunt Peggy, "Last evening I had two young English aviators out to dinner for Brian's special benefit, and they all seemed to have a very happy time together." I wrote about their visit also: "Yesterday Dr. Russell brought out for dinner two R.A.F. pilots from England who were over here instructing at a field near Tucson. I had a very interesting talk with them, but they came from Essex and did not know much about Suffolk."

On March 31 I wrote Aunt Peggy, "By the way, the news lately has not been bad. I wonder how long Hitler can hang on." I must have had in mind recent British successes in North Africa where General Montgomery had forced the Germans and Italians to retreat. The German General Rommel had left North Africa for good on March 9. The newspapers were full of photographs of captured German and Italian prisoners-of-war.

About this time it began to register with me that I had not heard from Father or Mother for quite some time. On April 18 I wrote Aunt Peggy, "I haven't had a letter from Mother and Father for ages. Wonder what is holding them up." And again on April 25, I wrote, "Still haven't received any letters from Mother or Father. Wonder what's keeping them." Aunt Peggy could not give me an answer, as she also had heard nothing.

During the winter of 1942-43, Muncy Farms was a constant source of distress and worry for Aunt Peggy. Very early in 1943, flooding of the Susquehanna River threatened the big house. All the furniture had to be carried up to the second floor. Once the flood waters had subsided, to make things worse, some of the animals died. The first to go was Nell, one of the two big workhorses on the farm.

She and her teammate, Bert, had made a pretty sight pulling the hay wagons in the summer. I wrote Aunt Peggy on January 15, "Poor old Nell. I wonder how Prince [my horse] feels now that they can't talk back and forth. Bert must miss her. I bet Mr. Mattison [the old farmer] is upset about old Nell. He really liked her even though he tried to act as if he didn't."

In February two of the dogs had to be put to sleep. "Poor old Daffy," I wrote on February 9. Daffy was the English setter stray who had adopted the Brocks and was deathly afraid of guns. "It will be awfully lonely without Daffy and Bobby [the show-quality Cocker Spaniel with the bad temper]." Their deaths had been preceded by the deaths of Hakey, the police dog, and Circus, the Irish Terrier who had traveled all over the world with the Brocks. This left only Tumbler, another Irish Terrier, out of the original five dogs who had greeted our arrival in 1940 with so much enthusiasm.

To compound the chaos, near the end of April Aunt Peggy wrote that the old farmer and his son would be retiring. They had been farming Muncy Farms since the 1920s and their loss was a heavy blow. Because of the war it was very difficult to find a replacement farmer. From that time on, Muncy Farms was to have a series of new farmers. But if they were good, they soon left to farm their own land; if they were not competent, they had to be dismissed, much to Aunt Peggy's distress. On April 28 I tried to put a good face on the situation: "Now Mr. Mattison has gone, you will be able to make quite a few small improvements around the farm. I hope the new farmer will be all right."

No sooner had I returned to Muncy Farms for the summer when Dr. Rankin died. Aunt Peggy wrote a friend,

"Perhaps you have heard that my dear old Doctor Rankin died, thank God after only a brief illness at the last, although he has been failing rapidly this past year. For ten days I was hardly home at all as I had to see to all the arrangements at the hospital, send for his niece, make all the funeral arrangements, etc. He was such a darling person, and he and Mrs. Rankin, Henry and I had so many heart-warming lovely times together that I could not bear to see him left alone a minute. Mrs. Rankin was not physically able to go back and forth to the hospital, and he did not want her to see him suffer, and indeed it was frightful to witness, so I stayed there most of the time, and only had her come up when we were fairly sure we could ease him and get him comfortable. Such a dear funny soul he was. I did have to laugh so. The night we took him up in such a hurry, we did not think of much besides getting him to the hospital quickly. About 2 o'clock that morning he came out of the morphia, and with a gleam in his eye asked me if I had remembered his Bible and his bottle of brandy. I shall miss him tremendously, as indeed the whole community will, for he was one of the last of that hardy breed of old-time country doctors who had the sympathy and intelligence and character to heal one's mind and soul along with one's body. I wish I had known others like him, but they are few and far between."

After a long period of silence, Aunt Peggy finally heard from Father on May 26, 1943. "I have been ill since February with nervous breakdown. While ill—unable to walk—relentless litigation was carried on, even at the height of my illness. Everything this time finished for good. No home left. All gone. I tried to protect the mother and children—succeeded the first time, but failed the second. Can you arrange for me to see Susan, Brian, Sheila, Malcolm through Caldwell Johnston? I have plenty of friends near Caldwell. With the children and help of Caldwell and other friends I could soon get back on my feet. Please use your influence by cable to your friends there. It is urgent."

Father wrote Aunt Peggy again on June 10: "Everything is gone, home, etc. I have not slept one night since February 1943. I am ruined, my character defamed, a living death mask for life. I shall not see the children again. It is better to tell them when young. They must spend their lives with their aunts and uncles. Tell Brian it is Daddy's advice, also Susan. Get Caldwell to help you. For the children to think or dream of a home in England would be the greatest calamity. They are safe with you and Caldwell. Picture their misery of life here. It is very difficult to express oneself owing to conventions, but unless you know the truth [that] all my life I have lived for respectability and have 30 years good character as a quiet, respectable man signed by 34 Leading Citizens of Woodbridge and Ipswich—all men of prominent positions—dated Nov. 27, '41, franked by a solicitor, my own solicitor. Sir Malcolm Campbell, who has been my friend for 25 years was one of the "leading citizens" in the first divorce proceedings. I am afraid unless arrangements are made I shall go under. Illness will defeat me because I am defenseless. It is impossible to obtain services of solicitor— all full up with work. My own solicitor is not interested in my case. Picture my position." A postscript was added: "Give my love to the children. I am too ill to write them. I cannot even tell white lies."

Those were Father's last two letters. We did not see them; Aunt Peggy put them away in her files.

On July 9 Aunt Peggy wrote to a friend, "Before I had time to recover [from Dr. Rankin's death], a cable arrived from the children's mother saying their father had died—just the brief cable with no details. I have seldom faced a harder task than that of telling the children. How awful to face one's first tragedy so far away from home. They seem so alone in their grief, poor things, and the news coming as it did just after Doctor's death, when they saw literally dozens and dozens of people so deeply concerned over his illness, somehow has made the contrast of their loneliness more poignant." After Aunt Peggy told us our father had died, I remember that the four of us cried out on the lawn in front of the big house.

It was not until several years after the war ended that I learned that Father had taken his own life on June 20, 1943. Aunt Peggy herself did not learn the details surrounding his death until she received Aunt Cecile's letter dated May 8, 1944. She chose not to share Aunt Cecile's letter with us, and filed it away. I found the letter many years later in Aunt Peg's files. Up until that time, we four children simply assumed our father had died in the war.

Mother learned about Father's death from Mr. Q—, Aunt Cecile's friend. Aunt Cecile had to see to all the details. She wrote Aunt Peggy that, after her brother's death, "I saw heaven knows how many officials—arranged for and attended inquest and cremation. I was alone. I could not think of any friend or any of my few relatives who was free to come. We are all in the forces or in factories over here. We are not free to come and go as we choose at a moment's notice. Mr. Q— told me when I came back from my brother's death that he had hunted for Violet in London till he found her and told her the news. He said she was shaken to the core by my brother's end. She had never dreamed that such a thing could happen."

CHAPTER TWENTY–FIVE

$\mathcal{F}$ather's death made me homesick for England for the first time since my arrival in America in 1940. Whereas in the past I had been uncritical of everybody and everything American, I now tended to be critical of both. Perhaps the fact that I had turned fifteen over the summer had something to do with my becoming a critic. The fun had gone out of the summer vacation as far as I was concerned.

Aunt Peggy probably gave a more balanced view when she wrote a friend on July 9. "I lost my farmer that had been here 30 years, and am now running the place with a 22-year-old boy and an assistant who looks so young that one feels his mouth is hardly dry! Actually, he is 17 and has a seven-months old son! Such a world as this is! In the house I have Mickey, my standby, and two 15-year-old girls. With this ménage and the help of the children, we have 300-plus acres under cultivation, nine milking cows, some chickens, and a bigger garden than I have had when I had two gardeners and five farmers. By dint of some sleepless nights of planning, we manage to stagger along and are gradually getting the house open—after spending the winter with Miss Gibson in Wynnewood—the place is going reasonably smoothly. The children work very hard. Brian drives the farm team and the small tractor as well as running the cultivator and pitching hay, etc. The girls cut the grass, work in the garden, take care of their own rooms, help the laundress, and run the mangle. Malcolm picks up the weeds and grass in his little wagon, and takes entire charge of the chickens, as well as riding on the drill at seeding time. Everybody working this way, we still have time to stop now and again for a little fun. The evenings are spent driving Prince hauling the cart—so crowded with children that you can see nothing but a mountain of children moving down the lane on wheels."

At the end of the summer, I was disappointed to learn that I would not be going back to the Russell Ranch School. I did not know that Dr. Russell had written Aunt Peggy back in April that, "at the moment I am of the opinion that Brian should be in a larger school. He is doing very good work, but perhaps has outgrown our little family." Aunt Peggy took his advice and enrolled me at St. Andrew's School in Middletown, Delaware. St. Andrew's had come to her attention because one of Mr. Brock's cousins had sent his sons there. She had originally planned to send me there in 1941, but I had failed the entrance examination. My failure turned out to be a stroke of good fortune as far as I was concerned because I got to go to the Russell Ranch School instead. This time, however, I passed the entrance exam and was accepted for the fall term of 1943.

St. Andrew's offered a fertile situation for me to criticize, as it was located in the middle of farm country. On October 10, I wrote Aunt Peggy, "Middletown is certainly a one-horse town. There is nothing much to do in it." Two weeks later, I repeated the accusation: "Didn't ride at all this week, but on our day off I went to town instead. It is very dull, but at least there is plenty of ice cream. That's what most of us spend our money on."

However, to be fair, St. Andrew's itself consisted of a cluster of handsome stone buildings surrounded by playing fields. It had been founded by a member of the duPont family, and no expense had been spared to reproduce the look of an English public school. There was even a clock tower on the gymnasium. Even so, to my mind, it lacked the patina of age of my old school in England, Orwell Park, and I was scornful of St. Andrew's "newness."

Knowing that Aunt Peggy was worried I might not like St. Andrew's, I tried to temper my criticisms in my first letters. One letter claimed, "I know quite a few boys now and generally they are all pretty nice. This is a great change, but I don't mind it. There is more to do. The Masters seem pretty good, except for a few that are kind of cross." Another letter, written October 3, said, "I really like it here. It is something like the school in England, but less stiff." The truth, however, was that I missed the warm family atmosphere of the Russell Ranch School, and I felt isolated in rural Delaware, especially since the war permitted few trips away from the school.

My first letter home was my usual mixture of facts and comments. "I have an alcove overlooking the football field. It will be fine in summer, but rather cold in winter. It has been very chilly the last two days. The bed is not too bad. That reminds me, I got all the blankets. You are allowed to hang pictures on the wall of the alcove and you should see some that went up." This last remark referred to pin-ups of scantily dressed women, which were popular with schoolboys as well as soldiers in the war. I did not mention to Aunt Peggy that I talked the boy next to me into throwing our two alcoves together by unscrewing the partitions from the floor.

The new arrangement was such a success that most of the other boys in the dormitory decided to do the same thing. The Master in charge of the dormitory, who was a timid sort, almost had a stroke at the sight of two beds in a single alcove. The Headmaster was called in to put down the rebellion, and a maintenance crew was rushed to the site to put everything back in place. Fortunately, my role in the affair went undiscovered.

Naturally, my first letter mentioned food. "The food is pretty good, but nothing like the wonderful meals we had all summer. Everything tastes kind of boiled." Because of the war the school served uncolored margarine in place of butter. Its white, greasy look was in sad contrast to the home-churned yellow butter we made on the farm. I intensely disliked the milk served, as it smelled and tasted strongly of garlic. The school's dairy herd was pastured in a field full of garlic plants, which the cows ate along with the grass. Also, odd lumps in the milk were rumored among the boys to be saltpeter, added to the milk to dampen down interest in the opposite sex. Daily chapel services were not considered adequate for that task. In any event, whenever a school dance was announced, the older boys would stop drinking the milk.

One thing I did approve of at St. Andrew's was that tea was served every afternoon. In September I told Aunt Peggy, "All you have to do is walk into a Master's room and ask for tea, and then you sit around and talk. I have been to Mr. P—s [the Headmaster's] house for tea." My favorite destination for tea was the apartment of the school's chaplain. He was a bachelor, and his apartment was the most stylish of all. He found living in rural Delaware almost unendurable and would head for the bright lights of New York City at every opportunity. He would return with a terrific hangover but also with tales of the latest Broadway shows and foreign films. I envied his freedom to come and go as he pleased. My same September letter reported, "The next you won't believe, but I am in the choir. I have a red gown and sit next to the altar. How it happened? Well, everybody had to try out and most of them in my group just mumbled, and I just sang lustily."

In October, I wrote more details. "The choir is an easy job as long as you are in it, but today everything went wrong. We did things like not singing when we should or singing the wrong part. To top this all off I sang the wrong hymn, and nobody knew the difference. Also the cross bearer got up to leave halfway through the service, which nearly killed me to stop myself from laughing. So you can see we had a very queer service this morning. And was the Master mad!"

Much to my delight, I discovered that the chaplain was also in charge of the riding squad. In October, I wrote Aunt Peggy, "Today Mr. W— asked me if I wanted to be head of the riding squad. That is to have complete charge of the horses and who rides them. Last year it was held by a Sixth Former, but he left, so you can see it entails responsibility. But it means I get excused from football to look after this job. What do you think I should do? Take the chance of the job, or play football? Both are pretty hard to give up." In the end, I opted to head the riding squad. My charge included the care and feeding of two horses. I wrote home, "One is high-spirited and kind of stupid. By that I mean he does all sorts of silly antics. The other is just a horse, but a nice old horse."

There were about five boys on the riding squad. It was my job to assign times to ride for each boy. The riding trails near St. Andrew's seemed very tame after those I had ridden in Arizona. I wrote Aunt Peggy, "I rode several times, but it is pretty dull riding, as everything is fenced in. This Saturday, however, I found a road that looked interesting and I will try it out the next time I ride."

The news that Aunt Peggy was thinking of buying a horse for Sheila kept me riding as often as I could. I told her, "It is wonderful you made enough [money from a sale] so that maybe we can get another horse. Two would come in very handy, and I bet Malcolm will love to have a dog of his own. We certainly get involved in things. Start off with one horse, now maybe another. One dog, and end up with three by the end of next summer."

In September 1943, there seemed to be no end in sight to the war. Once again, Aunt Peggy found it necessary to request that our temporary permits to stay in the U.S. be extended. Her request was granted by the U.S. Immigration and Naturalization Service, and the four of us were given permission to stay in the U.S. for another year, until September 15, 1944.

The war was coming closer to Americans. My letters home now often included comments about American friends and relatives in uniform. In an October 3 letter I said, "Pity I couldn't see Anne [Aunt Peggy's niece]. Did she have a uniform on? That piece in the newspaper about Fordyce was very interesting." I remembered with fondness fishing and hunting trips with Fordyce at Muncy Farms. Fordyce's sister had written me that her brother was now a paratrooper and had been cited in an Army paper for his bravery. Fordyce and his men had captured the same German town eight times. I commented, "Fordyce will be able to tell some wonderful stories when he gets back. Between Derrick and Fordyce there ought to be enough stories to fill a book." Soon after that, I learned that Fordyce had been wounded and sent back to a U.S. Army hospital. On October 11, I wrote,

"I wonder if he will get a medal. At least now you know for sure where he is, and don't have to worry if he is at the front or not."

On October 23, I noted to Aunt Peggy, "Some of the Masters have been reclassified and think they will have to go into military service." Child refugees continued to turn up at school. One letter to Aunt Peggy about the various boys I had made friends with noted, "I forgot D—. He escaped from China with the Japanese chasing him."

I had not heard from Mother since before my arrival at St. Andrew's. I finally received a letter on November 5. She was still in London, staying at the Park Lane Hotel. She wrote, "Derrick is coming on 7 days' leave on November 10. Part of it he is going to spend here, and then he and Sheila [his current girlfriend] are going to Hampshire to spend two nights with Auntie Eileen. He does not pass out of Officer Training Unit until Christmas, and then hopes to get back to the Glider Regiment again. He seems to miss his flying very much. Anyhow, every Saturday he has been playing rugger and has enjoyed it in spite of getting well knocked about. He has just spent a week in hospital, having been kicked on the knee and it turned septic. However, he is all right now."

Mother was looking for work. "I have some friends who are trying to get me a job with the American Red Cross, as I need a job that is paid. Hope it comes off, as I should like to be able to help the Americans—just a trifle to what Aunt Peggy has been doing for you all. Afraid I have very little to tell you, as I just drive the car about for various Ministries, delivering letters, and hardly ever go out in the evening. Everywhere is so crowded and it is not much fun alone. I expect when Derrick comes we shall go to the theatre. We have been having some air raids, as I expect you have seen in the English papers, but nothing like when you were in London. I firewatch every time there is an alert, and from the roof of the hotel we get a marvelous view of the barrage. Have seen quite a number of American WACs about. They look so nice in their uniforms. The other day for the first time I saw some American Airborne troops. I was not able to get into Westminster Abbey to see the sword that is being sent to Stalingrad. The only short while I had to spare, there was such a crowd of people I had no time to wait. I believe it is very wonderful."

In *The People's War,* Calder described this sword. "In the summer, as the Russian armies began to drive the Germans back, and back, and back, nine out of ten people were willing to give the polls a favorable opinion of Russia. That autumn, the Sword of Stalingrad began a triumphal tour of Britain. The King had commanded that this beautiful weapon of the finest steel should be made as his personal gift to the people of the city [Stalingrad]. In London, where it was exhibited in Westminster Abbey, in Edinburgh, Glasgow, Birmingham and Coventry, people queued for hours to pass before the gorgeous two-edged blade."[1]

Meanwhile, my life at St. Andrew's had its ups and downs whenever I ran afoul of the demerit system. I wrote Aunt Peg, "Last week I got seventeen demerits, and so I and another boy had to shovel coal for three hours, from one end of the cellar to the other. Boy! The sweat really rolled off. Anyway, I only got one demerit this week. I got most of mine last week for being late, but what put me in the red was getting two ringers [six demerits] for pure curiosity. This is how it happened. I was walking down the stairs when three of my friends came down at full speed, and out rushed a

Master. He sent everybody but me back upstairs to the Master at the top of the stairs, who gave each of my friends three ringers. I decided to go upstairs to see what they got and promptly got two ringers myself. I couldn't prove anything, because the Master at the bottom of the stairs, who is very absent-minded, had left and forgotten all about the incident. I think I shoveled coal on very shaky foundations. Anyway, next time I am not going upstairs to see what happened."

At the same time she enrolled me in St. Andrew's, Aunt Peggy enrolled my twin sister Sue at a private girls' school, Garrison Forest, in Baltimore, Maryland. Aunt Peggy and my younger siblings returned to Miss Gibson's house in Wynnewood for the winter. Sheila stayed home as a day student at the Agnes Irwin School in Philadelphia. Much to my astonishment, both my sisters were turning into young ladies. On November 2, I wrote Aunt Peggy, "Just think little Sheila having a long dress. Soon I will have to show my sisters off at school dances." Malcolm had continued at Episcopal Academy in Philadelphia as a day student.

Christmas 1943 was now right around the corner. Mother had closed her November 5 letter with, "Have sent your books off for Christmas. Hope, darling, they will give you a few hours amusement. Hope you will all have a lovely Christmas. You only get a short holiday then, don't you? You are sure to have lots of fun anyhow." What to send Mother for Christmas had been on my mind. I had written Aunt Peggy, "What do you think I could send? What are the others sending? I can't get much around here, so maybe I'd better send you money. What do you think?" A November 11 letter remarked, "I think sending *Life* magazine to Mother is a swell idea, and I will send in a subscription right away. I think she will like it very much. It must be very hard for her to live in England alone. I hope everything will smooth out soon." The choice turned out to have been a good one, because in January 1944, Mother wrote, "Shall simply love to have the paper *Life*. While I was indulging in the flu, some Americans at the hotel sent it up to me."

Aunt Peggy had written to ask where I would like to spend Christmas 1943. I replied, "I would like to go home to Muncy Farms for Christmas. I have also thought of one thing I would like very much for Christmas, and that is a fancy waistcoat—one of those horsy affairs." On December 3, I sent my last letter of the year home from St. Andrew's. "I can't quite believe that in two more weeks I will see you for three weeks. At present we are very busy doing our last homework and preparing for exams. Oh! Oh! The weather has been kind of cold, but it is not too cold to ride. About Christmas—I have fourteen dollars in the bank, so this is the amount of money I would like to spend on presents. You have Sheila's, so could you please get something nice for Sue and Malcolm. Also for Mickey and for Aunt Jo Gorham. Also what do you think Aunt May would like? I guess if I run out of money it would be all right to draw from my school account. Thanks an awful lot for getting the wooden horse for Sheila. They are very nice. How do you think Sue would like a set of watercolors? You can get sixteen different jars and colors for $2.50. Well, that's all the news. Looking forward to seeing you at Christmas. Lots of love, Brian."

Christmas 1943 turned out to be a most enjoyable one, in spite of the fact it was not spent at Muncy Farms. Aunt Peggy had decided that it was not right to use up oil to heat the big house at Muncy while the war was still on, so we remained in Wynnewood.

CHAPTER TWENTY–SIX

*1*944 was to be a difficult year for Mother. On January 25, she wrote Aunt Peggy, "Had two bouts of flu in three weeks, which was rather annoying. Then it became essential that I find a paid job, as some more of my shares [of stock] had decided not to pay until after the war. This, as you may imagine, was rather a blow."

For the first time in her life, Mother was under financial strain. Each month she had been sending Aunt Peggy the small sum allowed by the British government for our support; the monthly check amounted to $144.36 in American money for all four of us. Each month Aunt Peggy put this money into War Bonds for us. Mother's January 25 letter told Aunt Peggy, "I hate to have to write this, but having just received the permit to send out more money, am afraid I shall have to—for the next two quarters—send the amount I have sent in the past. After that, I hope to be able to increase it, as my dividends come in at the end of June. So long as there are no more shares closing down on me, I should be able to manage more, as I am going to endeavor to live on my salary. I do hope you will not think very badly of me, and I really feel rather ashamed after all you are doing for the children. But really I have had a most disastrous twelve

months. Still have the liability of the Eastbourne flat for another year, which is rather a drain, as it is in a closed area and
I cannot let it." Because of the constant threat of invasion,
Eastbourne had been termed a "closed area" by the British
government. It would not be until September 9 that Mother
would be able to write that she had "at last managed to get
rid of the Eastbourne flat, so that is another worry off my
mind."

Mother described her job search to Aunt Peggy. "The
most difficult thing in the world was to find the job. After
wrestling with the American Red Cross for some time, I gave
up the unequal struggle. For the past several weeks, I have
had to carry on with my voluntary driving for the car pools,
otherwise I should have been swept into a factory anywhere
by the Ministry of Labour. In the meantime, an old friend of
my father's tackled 'ENSA,' which is equivalent to the En-
tertainments side of the American Red Cross. Well, after
weeks, have now got a job as manager to several concert parties to tour the hospitals. At the moment I am rather lucky as
most of the dates are round London, so I am able to come
back each night to the comfort of my own room. But shortly
we shall be going off on tour and then will come the dreary
round of billets. However, I am very thankful to get something to do."

Some details about ENSA can be found in *The People's
War*, Angus Calder's book. "By early 1946, ENSA had given
over two and a half million concerts to H. M. Forces and to
Industry, and it employed more than four-fifths of the entertainment industry at one time or another. ENSA paid
poor fees. Though an artist's deferment from national service had come to depend on the offer of six weeks' service
to ENSA, and some major stars—Gracie Fields with her

Lancashire schmaltz, and George Formby with his ukulele—performed under ENSA auspices, ENSA relied heavily on low-grade and near-amateur talent; it was the unsuccessful singers and comedians who relished the security of ENSA contracts, and the entertainment industry was too stretched to provide the manpower necessary for its far-flung commitments. There were, of course, some ENSA discoveries, notably Tony Hancock and Terry Thomas, but in general the complaint from troops and workers alike was not so much that ENSA ... was synonymous with smut, as that the smut was far from funny."[1] Mother must have found working for ENSA quite a novelty, but she did not stay with ENSA very long, and soon returned to her unpaid job as a driver.

While the Eastbourne flat stood empty, Mother made her home at the Park Lane Hotel in London. She wrote Aunt Peggy that the general manager was "a very old and dear friend." Aunt Cecile commented in her May 8, 1944 letter, "I think Violet probably has not yet learned how best to economize. The Park Lane Hotel is terribly expensive. There are some good hotels where she could have gone—not so ultra-fashionable. I imagine this did not even occur to her for quite a time. She has been used to the best."

Aunt Cecile's letter gave examples of how life had changed by 1944 for people of Mother's background. "Ask the children if they remember Bawdsey Manor, Mr. Q—'s home? Their Father and Mother used to visit there. It has about fifty bedrooms and five gardeners were busy keeping the grounds in order. Tell them that now Mr. Q— lives in a flat. He has no maids and every night he cooks the supper. The children may like to know that after living in four boarding houses since I came to the factory, I heard of a flatlet made from one slightly altered room. I jumped at the chance. I am very, very lucky. I used to live in a house with sixteen bedrooms. Let the children know that the cottage I hired after my mother's death—the cottage it took me six months to find, and to which I moved the small, dainty pieces of Chippendale and Sheraton that would go in it, the cottage I paid a woman to look after for me and whose garden I had arranged to be kept tidy, was taken from me last October. The War Agricultural Committee said they wanted it for a farm worker. Against this, there is no appeal. I was ten days touring Norfolk and Suffolk to find storage even, and found it at last by favor of auctioneer friends. The children? You can tell them in your own way that they will never again in England be able to live in a place like Stone House."

Mother also described life in London at the start of 1944. "Things over here seem to be going on much as usual. We are now kept up to pitch by the several raids on London we have had lately. The one last week, when we were visited twice in a few hours, was a marvelous example of defense. I happened to be on firewatch that night, so was on the roof for both raids, and really it was like a super fireworks display except for an awful lot of noise. I must say I was so intrigued watching the barrage I almost forgot the danger until the shrapnel started to rattle down."

These 1944 raids became known as "the Little Blitz". Calder's book, *The People's War*, describes them. "On January 21, 1944, the first of a new series of heavy raids made the 'warble' [of sirens] as menacing as ever. From then on until the end of March, London had thirteen major attacks, far more dispiriting after the long lull than the regular raids had been in November 1940. The Germans used bigger, more destructive bombs, and against their planes the new rocket guns were in action, their crash and swoosh drowning all other sounds of the night. The sheer din was unprecedented. The attacks were short, sharp, and concentrated, and involved a high proportion of incendiaries. In one case, nearly three hundred aircraft took part. The London Fire Guard had their first major test. Operating the new plan, they came out of it very well; they extinguished three-quarters of all the fires created. But once again, there were blazes calling for thirty, fifty, seventy pumps."[2]

London was now full of Americans. Mother reported in her January 25 letter, "I spent New Year's Day with an American Red Cross girl, Jane B—, who comes from Pittsburgh and seems very well known by everyone. She is very charming and tried very hard to pull some strings to get me into the American Red Cross with her. Unfortunately, now she has been sent to Northern Ireland."

That same letter gave us news of Derrick. "Am enclosing a new photo of Derrick [in uniform] … There is such a shortage of photographic materials that I am afraid only one can be sent. Derrick gets his commission in three days time and then comes on ten days leave. He has done very well at his training unit and was Senior Cadet with very high percentage of marks. Am trying very hard to persuade him not to get married yet until he is more settled. After all, he is not 21 until the end of next month."

Mother's January 25 letter does not mention having received Aunt Peggy's letter in which she suggested that they make definite plans for the future of the four of us. Later, Aunt Peggy was to explain to Mother that her "first letter was necessarily vague, and I hesitated to make any concrete suggestions for the future for fear they might be unwelcome to you." Aunt Peggy said we children had begun "to wonder what will happen in the future." She told Mother we were beginning to ask questions about whether "we were to stay on here, whether we were to return, whether Mother will come over, etc. All this is very upsetting to them emotionally. Uncertainty can be devastating to clear thinking. They go through periods when they seem to take the attitude, 'Oh well, what's the use. We may not be here very long.' This is no way for them to accomplish good work and get on with their studies. I have felt, insofar as the children are concerned, it would be best to work out some definite plan, and when this is done, that definite word of the plan be given the children."

It was not until March 20 that a reply to Aunt Peggy's January 20 letter came from Mother. Whatever Mother wrote remains a mystery because, unfortunately, that letter has disappeared. However, in her response to that missing letter of Mother's, Aunt Peggy had written, "Thank you so much for your letter of March 20. We were glad to get news of you, and in particular I was glad to have an answer to my letter of January 20. Your life sounds terribly strenuous these days, and in contrast ours seems so luxurious and easy that it doesn't seem fair. Not that we can do anything much about it, I suppose, but at least some of us here are conscious of our comparative ease. I realize from your letter that YOU are facing uncertainty. Your letter tells me that you cannot maintain a home for the children now at the moment, and that things are even more indefinite now as to the future. This must put an unnecessary worry and burden on you, and I would like to make the following suggestion.

"You speak of the worry you have had should they have been sent home (as others have been). Of course, I should not have even considered this without consulting you and only then if circumstances had changed drastically. Now you have the added worry of being under military rule and the uncertainty of demobilization. I realize that although I may give you my word, this is not as binding or completely protective of the children as it would be if I assumed actual legal guardianship during their minority. This would assure you protection for them during the uncertain days, and would give you sufficient time, perhaps, to find out where you stand financially and what you wish and would be able to do.

"It is somewhat doubtful whether a court would honor the agreement as it now stands. If you will allow me, I shall be glad to make it legal and binding right now. It seems to me this would be a wise view to take. You would be relieved of worry and immediate anxiety; the children would be adequately protected in several ways.

"It is my feeling that once the children were definitely told they were to continue here for their education whether the war ends or not, they will be given a sense of permanence and a definite plan and will lose their attitude of just living from day to day. Instead, they will begin to plan and think in a mature manner of what they want eventually to do and accomplish. They are just standing at the crossroads of childhood and maturity. To be answered every question with 'I don't know' or 'I'll have to ask your Mother' or 'perhaps in a few months or a year we will know' is not conducive to straight thinking and planning for a sound future life. It is sweeping away any attempt they make toward stability—the very thing we want to encourage in them in their teens, instead of adding to their uncertainties.

"Then, too, if I adopt them, I can more adequately protect them. As my legal wards, I should have no trouble in assuring them financial care. As it is now, I am not sure how well I could protect them in case of disaster or death, to me or you. All this must be considered (although far from cheerful) and, of course, we hope is being considered unnecessarily."

Mother had evidently asked Aunt Peggy what career goals we had in mind, because she went on to say, "As to what the children are likely to prepare themselves for, this has not as yet gotten on a very firm basis. Partly because of their age, but also because of the uncertainty as to where they would eventually go and how they would live. You, of course, spoke in your letters of the necessity of their earning their living, and I have tried to make this point clear whenever the question arose naturally. Having been so young when they left England, it is beyond their comprehension to visualize what earning their living there would be like, or even possible. As they have never known surely whether they were to stay here, they have not been able to settle the matter clearly. Sue really has no ideas. Sheila thinks she wants to be a journalist—a photographic reporter if possible—although sometimes after some successful games at school, she feels she might like to be a physical director. Brian toys with the idea of architecture or engineering—says he wants to 'build things'—but does not know if there would be any chance for him as an architect in England, and does not know how he would obtain an engineering training there. Since things were so indefinite, I have not 'pushed' any of the children to a decision, although in about a year they must begin to aim towards something or they will never get through.

"One other thing I believe carried weight in this decision about adoption—the question of service in arms. Of course, the children are liable for service at the same age in

210 either country. If they continue under your guardianship, they would, of course, be liable to the British Army and demobilization under your laws. If adoptees of mine, they would be liable under our laws, and under our service, the government makes more provision for university training before service and, if aptitude and ability are shown, provision is now being made for continuation of that education (under government expense, if necessary) on discharge from the Army."

In the final part of her long letter, Aunt Peggy summed up her proposal. "I may be getting way ahead of necessity in mentioning these things, but it takes so much time to write back and forth, and I am trying to give as clear a picture as possible, so that you can weigh all these and come to a decision that you feel is right and wise.

"As to our personal relations with the children, I do not see that they are altered in the least, simply because the matter of finances becomes legal and binding on me. As I told you, my intention would be to bring the children to England as quickly as visitors are allowed passage.

"I hope you realize that it would give *me* great pleasure, as well as the children, to have you come over for a long visit, so that you might see and really know what sort of life we lead—how and where the children have spent their life apart from you. I suppose it would be more gracious if I simply asked you to come over, and all of us live together. I feel, however, that would hardly be taking a realistic point of view. It might prove quite feasible, but in my experience I have seldom seen two adults make a completely successful attempt at this sort of thing. I would hate to risk our friendly relations or jeopardize our whole relationship with each other or the children. I would like, however, to say that if after a visit you were able and would like to come over, while I could not probably maintain two households, I want you to know that I am quite willing to help with the children's education and support, whether they live directly under my roof or not."

Weeks went by without a reply from Mother to the proposal. When she did write, on June 12, her letter said, "Hope you got my cable alright." [The cable has been lost, so whatever it said is unknown.] "But I thought that if you did not get a letter, you would be wondering if I had received your marvelous letter. Really the children are the luckiest in the world to have someone so kind as you are to take an interest in them ... In a few days time I will write you another letter in answer to your letter about the children as I feel I must get this off so that you will not think I have forgotten all about you. Very many thanks for all your kindness, and promise I will let you have an answer to your letter in a few days."

In the meantime, having heard nothing from Mother, Aunt Peggy began to worry that her April 24 letter had offended Mother. She wrote to Aunt Cecile for advice. Aunt Cecile's reply took the form of an explanation for Mother's silence. "Violet must miss having someone to do all the odd jobs in life for her. Her son Derrick is making his own life. I think the responsibility [for the four of us in America] must frighten Violet rather. Violet hoped to get a big flat in London to which the children could come, she told me. She CANNOT get any flat—anywhere. The furniture still stands at Eastbourne, her only home. She cannot find another. THIS IS SIMPLE FACT. Violet feels homeless. She could not go and live in *that* flat. I, who wanted a home in case the factory got bombed, now have no home. I have no idea when I shall be able to have one, or where. Millions more are in the same

212 case, and we, at least, still have our furniture, even if we cannot use it. But here we are, without a home between us. Recently I tried to book for two nights at a hotel near Fleet
Street where I often stayed. I gave six weeks notice. They
regret they are booked up and cannot take me. You can carry
a suitcase to a dozen hotels in London or anywhere before
you can find a bed. I think Violet's uncertainty is personal as
well as 'national.'

"It is possible that one other thing may be worrying to
Violet. She said to me that, when it was all over, she should
try to repay you for all you had done and spent. She evidently intended to reimburse you for some, at least, of the
money you have expended on the children. Then, it was
possible to plan such a thing. Now she may know she cannot
balance things at all. She is not accustomed to receiving, so
much as giving—can you see what I mean? Violet never explains, at least so slightly.

"I have not enough money to live on without earning.
That does not mean that if it were some little help that I
could not occasionally give money help to one of the children for some special purpose out of what I am trying to put
by, some weeks, for 'after the war.' I want to buy a house, so
that never again can I be made homeless. I will write Violet
next week; show her my willingness to help her insofar as I
can with the children. It was stupid of me to think she would
take it for granted."

Although Mother's June 12 letter did not finally settle
the question of Aunt Peggy's adoption of the four of us, it
did reveal that she was aware of problems stemming from
the return of English children from overseas. "Have had a
letter from Mrs. K—, who has just arrived with her children
from America ... Several of my friends have brought their

children back from America, which under the present state of the war, I personally think is a bit stupid ... The children do not think much of life here after America. Most of the parents just don't know what to do with them now that they are here."

Mother's June 12 letter described D-Day. "As you may imagine, now that the great Invasion Day [D-Day, June 6, 1944] has arrived, we are all very thrilled and very busy. As far as I know, Derrick went over with the first wave of gliders and I am anxiously awaiting news of him, as you may imagine. Luckily, the week before the invasion, Derrick had 48-hour leave, so we spent it together in London. He looked marvelously fit and has decided not to get married for some time, as he felt he must be free to get on with this war job.

"At present things are quiet over here in spite of the battles in France. It is the most wonderful sight in the world watching our planes go out. I happened to see one of the enormous wave of gliders leaving England, and in spite of Derrick being a glider pilot, I must say I got a tremendous thrill to see the sky absolutely black with gliders and their tugs. This was in the afternoon of D-Day, when I was changing over commands."

Derrick was one of 800 glider pilots on D-Day. Pandemonium broke out as all 800 planes were released and headed for the landing zones. In spite of poles placed by the Germans in the landing field, which sliced off the wings of his glider, Derrick managed to land safely with his cargo of 34 fully equipped soldiers. Within 48 hours, he was returned to England to bring another flight across. Fortunately, the second flight was cancelled due to the success of the Allied landings.

Angus Calder also describes D-Day in *The People's War*.

"D-Day was scheduled for June 5th. But stormy weather postponed it for one day. In the small hours of June 6, British and American Airborne Divisions dropped in France. At about 6:30 AM the first American seaborne troops went ashore; the first British troop followed an hour later. By breakfast time the Germans had announced the invasion, and the BBC, independent as ever, was anticipating the official Allied release by quoting the German reports. By the end of the day 156,000 troops had reached France."[3]

Another description comes from Shirley Joseph's *Land Army Hospital.* "That night [June 6] was the first (and last) time that there was complete silence during the six o'clock news. After the nine o'clock news, the BBC broadcast the first of its war reports with an eye-witness account from the French beaches. That day, and thereafter, the newspapers were snapped up in the streets as soon as they went on sale. Soon there were queues outside the news cinemas showing the latest sequences from France; many of those who watched were close to tears, and some wept. The convoys of fresh troops rattled down the streets of the outer suburbs of London, and when they stopped at appointed places, women and girls rushed up with jugs, even pails of tea, thrust packets of cigarettes in 'the boys' hands, joked a while, and cheered as they drew away; a Dunkirk in reverse."[4]

Mother commented in her June 12 letter, "I don't suppose the peace will remain over here. Suppose we shall get some raids when the Germans get desperate." Ironically, on the very day Mother made her prediction, Calder's book describes "the night of June 12/13, when an unusual, spluttering noise was heard over southeastern England. Astonishingly powerful explosions took place in several parts of London and the home counties. As

Churchill had warned, Britain had something worse in kind to suffer than it had endured before. The first V-1s produced no panic, but many rumors. Three days later, a heavy and sustained bombardment began from bases in the Pas de Calais. On the 15th there was a general alert in London just after 11:30 AM; the all-clear did not sound until 9:30 PM. From the next morning onwards, a procession of V-1s came over, by day and by night. On the 16th Morrison announced the beginning of an attack by pilotless planes, and shortly afterwards, the Cabinet ruled they should be called 'flying bombs.'

"For a fortnight, the attack went on at the rate of about a hundred V-1s a day. The fast new British fighters would bring down about thirty of these, the static defenses would halt perhaps ten, but more than half reached the target— greater London—nosing inexorably through all snares. In Croyden, the unlucky borough which lay on their route to the city, one might see nine V-1s in the air at the same time.

"One of the frustrations of the battle against the V-1s was that they caused as much damage if they were shot down over built-up areas as if they had been allowed to proceed on their way. On June 21, the A.A. guns were moved out of London to the North Downs. On July 6, Churchill described to the House of Commons the dimensions of the threat and the action taken against it."[5]

On June 21, 1944 Aunt Cecile wrote to Malcolm to wish him a happy birthday. "At this state, I will say I am at my desk in my office in the parachute factory; staying here for a while as 'Wailing Winnie' has just sounded and I wait to be near my microphone. 'Wailing Winnie' wailed twice last night; the all-clear went only half an hour ago. Do you remember 'Wailing Winnie'? It is as though all the cows in England and all donkeys that are alive in the land raise their voices in one awful howl as though they have toothache!

"These are lively days; no one here is sleeping very much, but we all turn up for work at the proper time. I think you would be interested to see the new robot planes. Perhaps in the night, you think you hear a Ger-rumph-er ... then Winnie wails, and as the din dies away, you hear, coming closer and closer, Ger-rumph-er—rumpher—rumpher— and perhaps, if you look out of the window, you see a wicked, fiendishly beautiful flying torpedo sailing along in the sky, quite low down, pursuing a dead straight course. The way in which the bomb solemnly follows the direct line seems one moment to add to its deadliness; next the thought occurs that perhaps it appears stupid to go so blindly forward. If you stood and watched, I think you would feel as apparently everyone who gazes at the approaching torpedo feels—that it is heading directly for *you*! The red light on it glows with a fiery crimson ... the torpedo glides swiftly on, perhaps out of sight, and then gunfire from all around makes a shattering din so that everything in the house shakes and rattles; then presently a different sort of crashing noise hits your ears: the flying bomb has struck the earth.

"A few experiences like this in the night add to the interest of life. And most of us are keeping ears and eyes open by day as well. How stupid Hitler is! Not once have we stopped work, even for a minute, because of his 'secret invention.' Even when the bombs are about in the daytime, people in this country watch out and go on with what they are doing. Just as if we would waste time because he has sent over robots! Such senseless procedure, which would mean we would play into Germany's hands, is not for us—and not in 1944 above all. How strange it is that Hitler cannot understand us better. We are such a long time before we get *really* angry, before we are *really* roused. Why has he not learned that when at last we are truly annoyed we begin to act and do not leave off till we have done to our complete satisfaction that which we set out to do. When he has grasped that essential, he will be wiser than he is now."

Aunt Cecile told Malcolm about her work as a Welfare Officer in the parachute factory at Woking, Surrey. "I expect you know I am a Welfare Supervisor in Mr. Q—'s factory. In its broad sense that means I am responsible for the domestic organization of the works—for seeing to the general conditions of health, and to help the employees with individual problems which they bring to me—anything from getting their leaking roofs mended for them, helping them to replace lost clothing coupons, telling them where to take their ill dog or cat, getting manufacturers to send batteries for bicycle lamps to a local shop so that our people can obtain them, writing business letters for them, watching that a girl is not straining her eyes at her work, keeping in touch with invalids, go with a girl to hospital. (We had a case we felt sure was an emergency appendix yesterday morning. We were right. I took her to the hospital and they detained her. Then I went and told the girl's mother.) So on and so on, all day. In simple words, it is my job to keep people happy and to make them feel they have a friend ready to help them if they need help."

Aunt Cecile closed her letter, "Do tell me about the nice things you have to eat in the USA. We just love to hear about luscious fruit and rich sauces and chickens and game and fine fish. Nowadays we here go in for plain living and high thinking; no doubt it is good for our bodies and our minds. We shall all get such elevating thoughts that we shall become too virtuous and noble to be bearable, I expect!"

Another letter from Aunt Cecile, dated June 27, was to Aunt Peggy. "I heard from Violet not long since that you have offered to adopt the children till they are twenty-one. She added that the 'government Authorities' were making 'difficulties'—nothing more. She made no personal comments. In my reply I said that you had been so extraordinarily good to them, in truth taking the place of father and mother, that it was in all probability the best thing that could be for the children. You must love them very dearly. The debt to you is something immeasurable, utterly incalculable. I know my Brother realized this. I do, too."

Despite Mother's consent to Aunt Peggy's adopting us, many legal roadblocks had to be overcome. On August 22, the British Consulate in New York informed Aunt Peggy, "The adoption of British children abroad is prohibited by British law." However, the letter went on to say they agreed "to put the whole case up to London for its opinion." On August 30, Aunt Peggy heard from Mother's law firm in London. Their letter stated, "On her [Violet's] instructions we have prepared the enclosed Adoption Agreement and same has been notarially executed by our client. We think the terms of the Agreement will be satisfactory to you, but we should, of course, have preferred to submit a draft to you for your approval, so that you could have consulted your legal advisors on it."

On September 9, Mother wrote Aunt Peggy, "Before you get this letter, you will probably have heard from my lawyer. Do hope the document will meet with your approval. To me it seemed very stiff and formal and if you want to have it altered, please do, because you know I will agree to whatever you say. Am so grateful to you; I could not dispute anything you say. I can hardly realize how the children are now nearly grown up—naturally, it seems very strange to me. It gives me great pleasure to think how happy they are with you. They write wonderful letters of your goodness to them and really have a grand time."

Aunt Peggy's lawyer insisted on certain changes in the documents, and it wasn't until December 14 that he wrote her, "I am enclosing the other letter from Lazarus [Mother's law firm], along with the Deed of Adoption, so that you may have them when you consult with the U.S. State Department. They should certainly convince the authorities that nothing is left to do except go through the formalities. Were I in your position, I should not hesitate to do any wire-pulling I could, and I certainly hope that you do it successfully."

Meanwhile, "The pause in the flying-bomb war is a relief," Aunt Cecile wrote to Sheila on September 9. "We no longer look out of windows to see where the bombs are going, and it is a rest not to have the wail of the siren piercing one's ears by night and by day." However, her comment that "our Home Guard can now have a little rest" turned out to be premature. She wrote, "They have worked from 8 AM till 6 PM or longer, with dreadfully uncomfortable traveling to and from work. We have elderly folk catching a bus at 6:45 AM each weekday; getting back at nearly 9 PM. Then all Sundays on Home Guard duties and various evenings as well, lectures, on-duty spells, parades, practices. The Home Guard is a star turn. They deserve a little rest from it all. They were Britain's bulwarks against the enemy if they landed on our shores … drilling with broomsticks before you left England."

Mother confirmed "the pause" on September 10. "Life

seems very peaceful here at the moment, since the 'doodle bugs' have stopped. We are not under the delusion that we shall not get any more, but in the meantime it is a chance to get some sleep. They certainly were the most peculiar and devastating things. However, everyone stood up to them wonderfully. The news is all so good now London is beginning to fill up again, and everyone seems to have the impression that the war is nearly over, in spite of the government trying to warn against over-optimism. Certainly in London we have lived through some amazing times."

Angus Calder describes this period in *The People's War.* "On the 25th [August 1944] the German commander in Paris surrendered to the Allies. Four days later, Montgomery began an offensive which took the British Second Army from the Seine to Antwerp in five days, and for once justified his reputation for dash. On the way, he overran the V-1 launching sites in the Pas de Calais, bringing the first phase of the V bomb attack to a close. By then 6,725 V-1s had been seen over Britain (while many others seem to have gone astray entirely). Nearly 3,500 had been destroyed by the fighters, the guns or the balloon barrage, and only 2,340 had reached the London target area. Altogether, the bombs had killed 5,475 people, and had severely injured 16,000 more."[6]

The "pause" Aunt Cecile mentioned turned out to be just that. On September 8, 1944, a different menace, V-2 rockets, began falling on England. In a letter dated September 9, she describes a shopping trip to London just after the V-2 attacks started. "Not long since I took a Saturday morning off—it is more than *owing* to me! And rose at 5:40 AM to catch a workman's train to London to buy shoes. I have tried in vain in Woking [where she lived], Guildford, Kingston. By 12:50 PM I had bought two pairs, one Lotus, which many of us regard as England's best. It rained in sheets ... and I saw notices, 'closed during Staff holiday, Quota sold till Tuesday next, open for business Tuesdays, Thursdays, Fridays only.' At the shop where I got my Lotus shoes, I was told 300 were queueing before 9 AM. While I was having a late lunch in a theater-land restaurant, some people dashed into the entrance—masonry, etc. started crashing down outside. There were two bumps a little way off, then quiet again. No one moved or left their tables. Then those who had run in looked out up at the sky, then went off. We others continued our meal. Quite what happened I do not know. Then I went and saw *While the Sun Shines* at the Globe Theater. It was very amusing. I would have liked to see Sybil Thorndike and the Old Vic Players but could not get in."

Calder describes the V-2 attacks. "518 reached London. In all 2,724 people were killed, and over 6,000 badly injured, but this, after what had gone before, was not intolerable. In any case, the rate of arrival was falling by the end of the year. What the V bombs had achieved was not the collapse of British morale, but yet another aggravation of the housing problem. At the peak of the V-1 attacks, more than 20,000 houses a day were being damaged. By the end of September, 25,000 houses in the London region had been totally destroyed or damaged beyond repair, to add to the 84,000 written off after earlier raids. A million more had been less seriously damaged."[7]

"Today the great news has come that blackout is to be eased on the 17th," wrote Aunt Cecile in her September 9 letter. "Oh! The heaven-sent relief! The eternal care that not a match-stalk of light might show from a window, torches [flashlights] dimmed with two thicknesses of tissue paper— to be directed downwards—cycle lamps half blacked out, the insides to be gummed with black paper, the Stygian blackness of the world from 3:30 PM on a winter's afternoon ... we thank God at thought of light, at a touch of carefree mood, at thought of seeing where we go and put our feet."

On November 9 Aunt Cecile wrote Sheila, "We have starlight street lighting in some streets at night now, and dimout instead of blackout for our windows. When the siren sounds—as it often does just when I am having supper or am reading in bed—I have to spring out and instantly black out, so not a matchstick of light shows outdoors. Southern England, which spreads from a line more or less level with London on the map of England from the east to the west coast, still has flying bombs coming down on it. They fall on the loneliest cottages, in fields, in streets, in little towns, villages, anywhere."

On September 10, 1944 we got good news from Mother. "Derrick came back from Normandy safely and had seven days leave with me in London. He is in great form and is now back with his unit." On November 30, she wrote, "Derrick has been on leave again and has now gone fairly far abroad for some long time. He looked very well and seemed quite thrilled at the idea of seeing another country."

Derrick would see Holland by taking part in the debacle at Arnhem, which American General Patton called "the most momentous error of the war." The operation, known as "Market Garden", was the largest and most ambitious deployment of airborne troops in World War II. It was the brainchild of the British General Montgomery and was a bold plan to "open a carpet" for an end run through Holland, around the northern terminus of the Siegfried Line. American General Bradley had deep misgivings about the plan, but Eisenhower approved it because he was anxious to overrun the V-1 and V-2 launching sites and open up the ports of the Low Countries. The operation got underway on September 17, 1944.

On the morning of September 17, Derrick was stunned, along with most of his fellow glider pilots, to learn of the Arnhem assignment. There was a feeling that the mission was virtually doomed to fail because of the limited armor with which the planes were equipped. Derrick's Horsa glider had been altered to carry a detachable tail in order to offload a jeep and six soldiers as quickly as possible. Six bolts had to be loosened to allow the tail to swing free. Although the crews had practiced removing these bolts many times in England before the actual mission, it was very different under German fire. Derrick and his men managed to unload the jeep successfully. They raced the five miles to Arnhem only to arrive at precisely the same time as the German troop reinforcements when, as Derrick put it, "things became very unpleasant."

In his book *Eisenhower's Lieutenants*, Russell Weigley gives an account of the Arnhem operation. "Coming in at one o'clock on a clear Sunday afternoon, all three airborne divisions (one British, two American) enjoyed the most accurate drop they had ever experienced in training or in combat. Nearly all 16,500 paratroopers and 3,500 glidermen assembled quickly on the ground. The British chose to send their gliders in first. Although none of their 358 Horsas or Hamilcars were shot down, thirty-eight failed to arrive at the landing zones, mainly because their tow ropes broke. By extreme bad luck, the missing gliders happened to contain almost all the armored jeeps of the 1st Airborne Division Reconnaissance Squadron. With the jeeps, the Squadron was supposed to compensate for the distance between landing zones and Arnhem by rushing to the railway and highway bridges and seizing them by *coup de*

224   *main*—a distance of nine and a half to thirteen kilometers. The bulk of the 1st Air Landing Brigade and a Regiment of Airborne Artillery fanned out to protect the landing zones, and it was not until the 1st Parachute Brigade dropped following the glider troops and marched a detachment to Arnhem on foot—a matter of four hours—that an effort could be mounted against the bridges.

"One battalion of British paratroopers manages to take control of one end of the Arnhem bridge, while the Germans retain control of the other end, but in doing so find themselves cut off from the rest of the British forces in the area. All the British forces come under attack from an SS Panzer Division, which happens to be in the area to recover from a mauling on the Russian front. The Germans capture a copy of the Allied battle plan and use it for directing their counter attack. Only if the tanks of the British XXX Corps can come quickly to their rescue will certain defeat at the hands of the Germans be prevented. Despite heroic efforts, the British tanks are unable to relieve the beleaguered paratroopers.

"On September 25, the British General Urquhart learned he was to pull back his perimeter to the river for withdrawal during the night. Only fifteen boats were available, and these ferried back and forth through a night fortunately darkened, though made still more miserable by heavy rain. At daybreak, some men began swimming as machine gun fire terminated the ferry service. Some 2,163 men of the 1st Airborne and Glider Pilot Regiment, along with 160 Poles and 75 Dorsets, were taken prisoner. The Germans captured more than 6,000 prisoners in all, north of the Neder Rijn, nearly half of them wounded."[8] Derrick was one of the lucky ones who managed to reach safety that night.

In 1945 Mother sent me a slim volume entitled *Arnhem Lift*. It was written anonymously by a glider pilot like Derrick, who also evaded capture by the Germans. The author gives a remarkable account of how the British troops reacted to being cut off from all help. "The life we had led at Arnhem was nearer to an animal existence than anything we could have conceived, and yet the more savage the fighting got, the more civilized the men seemed to become. By civilized, I don't mean having baths and being clean and shaving and eating with a knife and fork, but the relations between man and man. They became increasingly polite and helpful. There was such gentleness and friendship among them as would have made any of them almost uncomfortable back on the station. Although they were fighting like tigers, and in that fight had to be completely ruthless, there was no tough behavior or coarseness of speech. It was almost uncanny. The familiar Army swear words and idiom were absent from their conversation, probably for the first time since any of them joined the service. They were courteous, kind, and considerate, without any self-consciousness."[9]

About the withdrawal the author wrote, "No pushing or jostling; the complete self-control of the men crouching in the mud, waiting for the boats; the way they passed the lightly wounded to the front; their concern for the Dutch civilians, and the complete absence of grumbling and bitterness. That is what I call civilized behavior."[9]

Mother's September 10th letter not only told us that Derrick had come back from D-Day unharmed, but also that she had landed another paid job. "Have been living for the past month back at the above address [the Park Lane Hotel], as I am now a driver at the American Embassy in London and we really are very busy. Could not keep on with the

226   Ambulance Unit, as I had to have a paid job, and was very lucky to get on at the Embassy. Am with the Office of War Information." Mother got rather fed up with some of the O.W.I. top brass, as they seemed mostly interested in living well in London, and pumping her for names of the "best" shops and restaurants.

Despite her paying job at the American Embassy, Mother said, "Am afraid I am still in a great state of uncertainty as to my life after the war. Of course, my job with the American Embassy will probably continue for some time. Anyhow, I hope long enough for me to organize myself a bit. At present, am still feeling in a sort of haze, but once my finances start readjusting themselves, shall probably get more stabilized. Of course, I miss a home very much, but luckily have a very staunch friend in the general manager here, and he advises me to stay on at the Park Lane Hotel, rather than get depressed alone in a flat. I suspect he is right really. I should very much like to visit America. It sounds a wonderful country, and certainly your boys over here are a grand crowd, but as I have said, life for me at the moment is full of uncertainty."

Mother's last letter in 1944 was written to Sheila on November 30. After her comments about the advice given to her by the general manager of the Park Lane Hotel, we were surprised when she wrote, "Note my new address: St. George's Court, Gloucester Road, London. By the time this letter reaches you, I shall be installed in my new flat. Am going to be busy the next three days moving into the flat. Will write and tell you all about it in my next letter." Mother was no longer homeless.

In the same letter she says, "I haven't sampled *Coca-Cola* yet. They have it in our canteen [at the American Embassy], but I have been so busy getting used to the other kinds of

American dishes and drinks, I haven't gotten round to that yet. (There you are, even I can manage some American expressions.) I do eat doughnuts when I am on night duty. Went to a show called *Merrie England* the other day and took a friend's boy and girl with me. The boy is 14 and the girl 12. They thoroughly enjoyed it. It was all about Queen Elizabeth I. The clothes were lovely and [so was] the singing. Also saw a film show last week—Wallace Beery in *American Gentleman.* Quite good. Will be thinking of you all at Christmas. I shall be working all the time, as we are very busy. Hope you have a simply lovely time. Am sure you will, as you always do."

Aunt Cecile described her 1944 Christmas in a letter to Aunt Peggy. "I could not face the appalling crowds and delays of trying to get to Suffolk for Christmas—about 110 miles, and the last time it took me from 10:45 pm till 6:45 PM. I had my own sandwiches, but no cup, so could get no tea at the stations. We did not know what holiday we were having till it was too late for me to book at a hotel, either by the sea or in London for Christmas. So I stayed here—four days of blessed quietude and rest, four days with the clock not mattering, no din of machines, no girls in tears, no girls and boys scrapping, no woman placing a domestic problem before me, no cleaner suddenly absent on account of her father's illness, no racketing 'Music While You Work,' no leaking cistern with the plumbers working in the next village. Silence, and time to loll, and time to think, and time to dream a little and remember."

For the English, Christmas 1944 was far from a return to carefree, prewar Christmas holidays. Angus Calder explains in *The People's War*, "The Allies in Western Europe now held a long line stretching from the Channel to the

228   Swiss border. On December 16th the Germans opened a surprise offensive against the weakly-held sector in the Ardennes. In three days they advanced 45 miles, driving towards Antwerp. The British public heard only slowly of the real seriousness of the fighting. It took much of the pleasure out of Christmas—the coldest, it was reported, for more than 50 years—though small boys who were enjoying the war and wanted it to last a while longer found it hard to conceal their delight in this new turn of events; and that sporting instinct which had made Rommel a popular hero now prompted some ungrudging admiration for General Rundstedt. The 'Bulge' was not finally squeezed off until January 16th, when it had cost about 80,000 Allied casualties."[10]

Hopes for the end of the war in Europe in 1944 were dashed.

CHAPTER TWENTY–SEVEN

$\mathcal{U}$naware of any adoption plan on Aunt Peggy's part, my main concern in January 1944 seems to have been to wangle for my twin sister Sue an invitation to a dance at St. Andrew's School without becoming entangled myself. This was not easy to do, as every boy with a sister of the right age was trying to do the same thing. On January 30 I wrote Aunt Peggy, "I have written Sue twice and have not got an answer yet. I found out that one doesn't usually take his sister, but gets a friend to take her to the dance. I have several friends that would be glad to, so I asked Sue to send a photo so they know at least what she looks like. So there will be two of us to give Sue a good time. Quite a few in my Fourth Form are taking girls to the dance, but quite a few don't. As far as I can find out, they don't use dance cards, but in certain dances you are allowed to cut in. There will be a lot of boys without girls, so there won't be much rest for the girls."

My ignorance about dance etiquette was because this was the first time boys in my Form were allowed to attend the school dance. Eventually, it turned out that Sue was unable to get away from the Garrison Forest School in Baltimore, so I wrote Aunt Peggy, "The dance was very lively, but I decided to save money and so did not go to it. It was really much the best thing, because although I did not dance, I got all the food I could eat from my friends who did go. As I only go to eat, I thought I had been very smart not to go. During the dance, a boy named G— and I skipped out and went in town to see a movie. We saw a double feature Western and had a good time. Luckily we didn't get caught on the way back, as town is out of bounds at night. My total expense over dance weekend was forty cents, instead of five dollars. The girls were all pretty nice and the school was quite lively. Of course, as I didn't go to the dance, I had to wait on table, but it wasn't too bad." It was predictable that future party-givers in Philadelphia would have to spend an inordinate amount of time trying to pry me loose from the buffet tables to dance with the young ladies.

That January I wrote Aunt Peggy that I also tried out for a part in the school play. "I will be very busy getting ready for the play and that won't give me much time to entertain you. I hope you will come and see the play. I had quite a time getting in, as I had to try out with several other boys. The play is called *The Saturday Evening Ghost* and it is extremely funny. I have a very good part, a major part, and am a P.G. Wodehouse lord named Archie."

Aunt Peggy did come from Wynnewood to see me in the play. I wrote her in February, "It was wonderful of you to come, and I really enjoyed seeing you." Aunt Peggy always made a great effort to attend all of our school performances.

At age 15, my passion was movies. Much of my time at St. Andrew's was spent trying to gain enough credits to take a weekend away from school, which meant a chance to go to the movies in Philadelphia. Credits could be earned by participating in various school activities. Not untypical was a comment in an April letter, "Now about the weekend. I have two-thirds credit signed up already, but need one-third more. Now I have the extra third earned for work in the Library Club and all I have to do is get it signed up if I can." Evidently I was successful because I later wrote Aunt Peggy, "We had a hard time making up our mind from the list of things you made to do. We finally decided we would like to see *Lifeboat*, the most talked-about film of the day. There certainly are some good movies up there. I wish I could see them all." Films were shown on Saturday nights at school, and my letters home often mentioned movies I enjoyed. In one letter I said, "Saw a very good movie, *Citizen Kane*, by Orson Welles—a queer movie, but interesting."

Another interest of mine at the time was writing for the school literary magazine, *The Adrian*. In April I told Aunt Peggy, "I submitted a story for *The Adrian* and am pretty near sure that it will be published. It is quite an honor, if it is. Mr. W— read it, unknown to me, and said he enjoyed it a lot. I won't tell you what it is called or anything, but will send you a copy. I have made it a true story. However it is not exactly the truth." The story was based on a caning I had gotten at my school in England, and it was published.

As can be imagined, marks or grades in academic courses were a constant concern. Most of my letters home made guesses as to how I was doing. Most of these guesses turned out to be overly optimistic. If a grade in one subject went up, a grade in another was sure to go down. Anything to do with math was usually a disaster.

On one horrible occasion I had to write Aunt Peggy, "Now, however, comes the confession. The whole French class was caught cribbing, and sorry to say, I am mixed up in it, too. This is how I got mixed up in it. We had a reading assignment to do, so as I didn't have time to read it, I just put the words I didn't know in English. Of course, the Master had to collect the books that day, and I have told you the rest. Please forgive me, and I won't try it again. But at the time it seemed much easier than handing in a bad lesson. It looks pretty bad, as even the boys who get 90s did it, too. The Master is very mad." On May 14, I reported, "For the French, we all got zero for two weeks." Two weeks later I wrote Aunt Peggy, "I knew you would understand about the French. You should have seen the letter Joe got. Frank, also, was caught smoking that week, and he really got a lively letter from home, too."

In April 1944 Aunt Peggy wrote that she had made a visit to Muncy Farms. I replied, "It must have been nice to get back to Muncy again. Glad to hear that Prince is in good shape, but of course Prince can stay fat while eating anything. Also glad to hear that you got the tennis court weeds burned off. How does it look? Will it be in good shape for this summer?" At school I was on the tennis team. In May, I wrote "I bought a tennis racquet, but could you send a check for $12.50 so I can pay for it. Reason: I only have $10 in the bank, so can't draw. I will have to work it off this summer. Will that be all right? Everything looks very springy here, as I suppose it is there. Isn't it nice to see green again. Can't wait to get back to Muncy and see you all. I hear Sue and I may go to Muncy alone, as you will already be there. I wish I got out earlier, so I could help you open the house. Maybe if you wrote Mr. P— [the Headmaster], you could arrange for me to leave after my last exam." To my disappointment, nothing came of that suggestion.

The most exciting news for me that spring was that Aunt Peggy was looking around for a horse for Sheila. I wrote Aunt

Peggy on May 14, "At the price Mrs. S— wants, I doubt if she will sell her horses. That's an awful lot of money for one pony." Fortuitously, it seemed, Aunt Peggy started to read the early farm ledgers for Muncy Farms. She discovered that a certain family had provided horses for the farm for many years. Checking on this, she found that a member of that family was still alive, and she contracted with him to purchase a horse for Sheila. In June, a grizzled-looking character appeared at Muncy Farms in a beat-up truck, with a chestnut gelding named Pat in the back. When unloaded on the front circle, Pat looked more like a cart horse than a riding horse. Pat was a "cribber" and he had spent his time in the truck sucking in air to the bursting point. Only with difficulty was the saddle cinched around the horse's belly, and then only because the dealer gave him a hearty kick in the ribs. With this kick, Pat let out air like a child's balloon which had been blown up and released. Even minus some gas, the best Sheila could do was to get Pat to amble around the circle in front of the house. While Sheila was trying out the horse, the dealer was busy shrewdly telling Aunt Peggy how much he admired the Brock family, and how he had known Mr. Brock when he was a ten-year-old boy. The upshot was that Mrs. S—'s price would have been a bargain. I was amazed to find horseflesh worth such a handsome sum.

The summer of 1944 seems to have been the year that scatology tickled my funny bone. Perhaps the fact that I turned 16 that summer had something to do with it. Every time I think of Sheila and that horse, I have to laugh. One day we were cleaning out the stables together. I had trained Prince to move on command from the area I wanted to muck out. Sheila tried out the command on Pat, but he just ignored her. Finally in desperation, she poked him in the ribs with the pitchfork handle. There was the usual whistling noise from Pat, and he reluctantly moved over. Then Sheila made the mistake of walking behind him. Pat backed up and pinned her to the wall like a butterfly in a display case. As I watched in fascination, Pat raised his tail right in her face, and the sound of released gas reverberated around the stable. Sheila turned bright red, then an interesting shade of yellow, and finally a sickly green color. Pulling myself together, I grabbed Pat's halter and yanked him off Sheila, who staggered to the stable door. With that I laughed so hard that tears came to my eyes. It took Sheila quite a while to recover, and she never did recover her lukewarm affection for Pat. She wasn't too pleased with me, either.

The summer passed all too quickly. All four of us worked to put Muncy Farms in order, although the big house was beginning to look shabby from lack of fresh paint, and the plaster walls inside were beginning to crack from the absence of heat during the winter months. We all played a lot of tennis, and Sheila got her picture in the local newspaper for winning a tennis tournament. On September 7 Aunt Cecile wrote Sheila, "I was interested to learn from Mrs. Brock that you all undertake various duties in your holidays so that you are really helping with things. That has been the way of life here for a long time. Even the very youngest—any child old enough to go out into the road or street—has done a job of work directly linked up with the war effort. It had to be so; if we had not all put our backs into it, the cycle of events would not have evolved to the present state of things."

Mother wrote Aunt Peggy on September 10 that she was "so glad Brian is turning out so useful to you." But there must have been times that summer when Aunt Peggy had second thoughts about my usefulness. One of them I recall

vividly. Aunt Peggy had been attending to the rental proper-
ties on the farm herself. Several of them were a constant head-
ache. They had been cheaply built during Victorian times,
when ten families farmed Muncy Farms. The fact that these
wooden cottages had belonged to her husband made Aunt
Peggy look upon them as rose-covered gems. I saw them as
buildings with peeling paint and with plumbing about to
give up the ghost. In many cases, the tenants did not help
the buildings by letting bathtubs overflow, leaving kitchen
pots on the stove to explode, running the furnace full blast
with all the windows open. The best thing that could be said
for these houses was that the rent was extremely low, and
because of the war, there was a big demand for them. Another plus was that Aunt Peggy could never say "no" to rent-
ers with children or dogs; the sorrier-looking the children
and the dogs, the more her heart went out to them. One day
Aunt Peggy asked me to go with her to look at a plumbing
problem. When we arrived at the house, the tenant shooed
away a raft of unappealing kids, and then took us to the upstairs landing. There he showed us a wide crack in the ceiling, which he said had been caused by a leaking toilet above.
Aunt Peggy told him she wanted to see the leak for herself,
and for him to go upstairs and flush the toilet. Before doing
so, he suggested that we step back off the landing, which I
did. Aunt Peggy ignored this advice and continued to stand
under the crack, looking up. With that, there was a sound of
rushing water and the entire contents of the bowl landed on
Aunt Peggy's head. I laughed so hard I fell backwards down
the flight of stairs. Fortunately, the water was clean, but I was
no more popular with Aunt Peggy than I had been with
Sheila.

That summer Aunt Peggy decided that Sheila should go

to boarding school in the fall. She chose the Foxhollow School in Lenox, Massachusetts. She was attracted to the school because its Headmistress was English, and the school was run along the lines of an English girls' school, with school uniforms, etc. Aunt Peggy was amused at Sheila's first report home from Foxhollow: "Sheila is apt to become excited and rather rough in a mob, but alone she is reasonable and courteous. Her intelligence will, I hope, surmount her coltish inclinations."

Once again, I returned to St. Andrew's. I told Aunt Peggy on September 28, "It does feel different to be an 'old boy' and a Fourth Former. However, it feels different in a different way than you think. You see, there were so many Fourth Formers that they had to turn the Second Form dorm into a Fourth dorm. Every time I enter, I feel like a Second Former. So did everybody else, but the feeling is beginning to wear off. We really have quite a good time, because we are allowed to do much more. The radio is coming in very useful. We now know what is happening in the world. I listen to the news every day, and so does everybody else in the dorm. The radio booms jazz all day long. Also, as I am doing right now, we usually listen to at least ten of those dramas—*Lonely Wife* or *Bill's Other Wife*, etc. Frank [my roommate] knows every one of them from 9:15 in the morning until they quit. He is especially fond of *Just Plain Bill*, the barber of Heartville, which nearly drives you crazy with his monotonous voice. There are quite a few nice boys here this year and—not like last year—everybody is on chummy terms with everybody else. So far it has been a very pleasant term. If the new Sixth Form can weather their new gained power, it will continue to be so. I am permanently on Chapel, which cuts out any chance of my having to do a kitchen job—thank God! This year, instead of Miss N— [the school nurse], there is a Miss M—. She owns an amazing parrot. He can whistle and sing the '*Marseillaise*' and '*Claire de Lune.*' He can also talk a blue streak. He belonged to a French sailor, and every once in a while he will utter some French swear words, which evokes a sharp 'Pete, stop it!' from Miss M—."

My twin sister, Sue, returned to Garrison Forest that September. On November 6 the Headmistress wrote Aunt Peggy, "Although we know that sometime Susan will want to go back to the 'Old Country,' we *hope* she will be able to finish her schoolwork here, and love and enjoy her senior year in the Senior House. She is such a good child—one of the people we shall need to interpret us to our English brothers and sisters in the days that are coming. She looks well, and you would be glad if you could see her tonight helping her class with the square dance party."

Malcolm returned as a day student to Episcopal Academy in Philadelphia, where Aunt Peggy was again spending the winter months. His school reports showed him doing "B" work in all his major subjects. His attitude was listed as "satisfactory", unlike my own, which was described by the headmaster of St. Andrew's in this way: "Brian persists in his easy going attitude toward life. In fact he is rather pleased with himself in the pose of a dilettante." Fortunately for me, Aunt Peggy tended to ignore any negative comments about the four of us, convinced that most behavior changes for the better over time.

None of us knew about Aunt Peggy's correspondence with our mother about her adoption plan. Sheila was the first to know, when Mother wrote her in September 1944 and suggested she ask Aunt Peggy about "the new arrangements." Mother explained to Aunt Peggy, "When I wrote to Sheila the other day, I told her to ask you about the new arrangements, as I felt you could explain them so much better than I could by letter. Hope you don't mind. Always think the spoken word is easier."

I didn't learn about the plan until Thanksgiving, when Aunt Peggy wrote to tell me that Mother had agreed to let her adopt the four of us. On December 2, I replied, "Received your wonderful Thanksgiving letter. I have read it over many times, and I cannot express the glad feeling I felt on receiving it. In some way, I hope we have already shown you how much we love and admire you, but if there is any doubt in your mind, I can only say that next to our Mother, we love you most in the world. I might add that I worry about you and praise you as much as any boy would praise his own mother. I am, indeed, proud to be seen with you. You do not have to worry about future plans, for whatever they are, they will include our Aunt Peggy. It wouldn't seem like home without you, and anyway we could never forget a person whom we love as much as you. I will try to fulfill your trust in me with my best efforts. And again, I cannot express how much I appreciate your faith in me. I pray that someday it will be in my power to pay back a little of what I owe you. I hope this letter can at least express my love and gratitude to you, for if it can, its task is accomplished."

Aunt Cecile was involved in the plan, too. She wrote Aunt Peggy on December 16, 1944, "I want you to know that I have carefully read all you tell me about your worries concerning the business of adopting the children. I have today been relaying your account of these matters to Violet. I really think the silence is not all due to fault on her part. She has written me for Christmas and tells me she has heard from you, but that she has 'not had much from the children lately.'

I *hope* Violet deals with matters at once. I have asked her to do so."

Aunt Peggy was feeling the strain of the war in much the same way as Mother. In one of her 1944 letters to Mother, she wrote, "I noticed what you said in your letter about feeling you had aged. Life seems so hard these last few years. Everyone has had to adjust and re-adjust their lives in so many ways, great and small. Sometimes I feel (and I have known comparatively nothing to what millions have undergone) that I am just a shell, making the motions but not really living. I have not really suffered the changes that you and countless others have, and may not know truly as you do, yet I have faced enough so that I wish to understand and be as helpful as is possible, according to my ability."

Aunt Cecile's Christmas greetings to Aunt Peggy concluded with, "I should think all your strenuous efforts on behalf of the children must have tired you. May you have some rest, as well as happiness, this Christmastide."

CHAPTER TWENTY–EIGHT

*A*s 1945 got underway, Aunt Peggy was ready to do battle with the bureaucratic red tape on both sides of the Atlantic which was preventing her from carrying out her plan to adopt the four of us. With the war winding down, she felt a sense of urgency, since in December she had been notified by the U.S. Committee for the Care of European Children in New York that she should "fill out embarkation papers for the children, with the view that all arrangements would be in order so that immediately on cessation of European hostilities, the children's passage would be engaged without delay for their immediate return to England." Aunt Peggy's attention was called to the fact that our visas would not be valid after August 8, 1945.

We had spent Christmas 1944 in Pittsburgh. The four of us thought we were there so that Aunt Peggy could see her family, and we could go to dances over the holiday. However, the real purpose of the visit was so that Aunt Peggy could obtain from her prominent Pittsburgh friends letters of introduction to top U.S. State Department officials and the British Embassy in Washington D. C. She had decided to follow her lawyer's advice. Also, because of the importance of the steel industry to the American economy, Pittsburghers had close ties with government officials in Washington. With the help of the letters of introduction, Aunt Peggy was able to discuss our case with the Secretary of State, Edward Stettinius. He gave Aunt Peggy a letter of introduction to the First Secretary of the British Embassy in Washington D. C., and promised that "the State Department will be glad to give you any further advice or help you may need."

Aunt Peggy evidently told Mother about her visit to Mr. Stettinius, because in July, Mother wrote "there seem to be rumors going round that Mr. Stettinius may come to England. If he does, I hope I may come in contact with him some time." The rumors turned out to be true; Mother wrote on August 11, "I see from the newspapers that Mr. Stettinius is coming to London." There is no record of Mother's having ever met with him, however.

The results of such efforts were rather discouraging. The British Ambassador, Lord Halifax, wrote to one of Aunt Peggy's Pittsburgh contacts, "I fully sympathize with Mrs. Brock's desire to adopt the children and wish that I could be of some assistance to her. Unfortunately, the English law, as it now stands, definitely prevents the adoption by persons resident abroad of British children who are still minors. This is not even a case in which the Foreign Office could be of any help, as it would be necessary to change the law, and only an act of Parliament can do that. The legal question must therefore, I fear, be left over for the time being."

Lord Halifax was more encouraging about our being allowed to stay in the U.S. to complete our education. "I do not think Mrs. Brock need be unduly worried, however. I feel certain that it should be possible to renew the children's visas when they expire in August this year, and I have asked a member of my staff to look into the question. It is certainly not our intention to force any British children who received care and hospitality in this country during the dark days to be obliged to return to England if they have no home to go to there, and I will let you know as soon as possible what steps, if any, Mrs. Brock may have to take to ensure keeping the children with her at least until such time as they have a home of their own." In the end, the British Foreign Office did renew our visas.

Determined to deal with the obstructions, Aunt Peggy next contacted Father's old friend, Caldwell Johnston, who was still at the American Consulate in Montreal, Canada. He advised her that British officials might be willing to accept a *fait accompli*. "My experience and study of similar cases has been that British officials are too proud to admit their willingness for British subjects to forswear their allegiance and become Americans, even when they are economically unable to provide for their well being." He suggested that the *fait accompli* might be brought about by having the four of us re-enter the U.S. from Canada on permanent U.S. Immigration visas. These visas would entitle us to become American citizens when we became of age. The matter of our adoption would be of less concern to British officials under those circumstances. Aunt Peggy accepted his advice and immediately sought permission from the U.S. Committee for the Care of European Children in New York to allow the four of us to re-enter the U.S. from Canada on permanent Immigration visas. The Committee told Aunt Peggy they would have to study the matter.

In the meantime, the U.S. Committee had asked their

English social worker to interview Mother about her decision to allow the four of us to be adopted by Aunt Peggy.
Evidently the social worker did not approve of Mother's
decision and tried to talk her out of it. This annoyed
Mother no end, as she thought it was none of the social
worker's business. On February 11, 1945, Mother wrote
Aunt Peggy about their meeting. "She [the social worker]
was inclined to be difficult at first, and thought the children should be brought back to England first, and then
sent back on the quota. I told her I had already inquired
into the quota business, and it appeared to be full up for the
next two years after the war. She then suggested they might
go to Canada and come in on that quota, but I could not see
the sense in that. Her other suggestion was they should return
here and then go back on a student's permit. She admitted to
me there were quite a few parents leaving their children in
America. Eventually she asked for a copy of the Agreement
that I had sent you, which I believe my lawyer has already sent
to her. At the end of much talk, she said she would transmit
my views to New York, and try to fix things as we wish. So I
trust now things will come to a satisfactory conclusion."

Throughout this period of time, Mother never seems to
have had any second thoughts about giving the four of us up
for adoption. As early as January 22, 1945, she wrote Aunt
Peggy, "By the next time I write, and also when I get your
next letter, I do hope we shall have settled the children problem, as I feel very strongly about the desirability of them remaining with you. As an example, two friends of mine have
had their children sent back from the States and are now
bitterly regretting it, as the children are missing the life in
the States and are finding the English schooling so utterly
different that they are not settling down at all, and are most

discontented and making their parents' life a misery. They have been away so long that now they have no friends here and miss their American friends."

In an article written for the July 29, 1985 issue of *The New Yorker* magazine, Anthony Bailey, who had left England on the same ship we did, described what it was like to return to an English school after being in America. "For several days, I was the object of curiosity, disdain and—from one or two lads—downright hostility. My American accent prompted feelings that the person speaking was over-privileged—a junior, civilian version of the American soldiers who dispensed cigarettes and chewing gum, and, no doubt helped by their higher pay, all too successfully romanced English girls. 'Yank' was the obvious nickname for me, and 'Yank' stuck, long after my nasal, Ohio manner of talking had faded into a mere undertone modifying basic British speech. ...'Yank,' was yelled as a challenge by a fellow-member of 2b, a freckled pug-faced lad named Ginger, whose gray uniform showed more than usual wear and tear because of playground fights, in which he was generally the victor. Ginger's version of the war to date gave no credit at all to the Americans. In Dayton, Ohio, I had been compelled on several occasions to stand up for England, but now I found myself forced into the role of spokesman for the United States: for Generals MacArthur and Mark Clark, for PT boats and Mustang fighter planes, for Sherman tanks."[1]

Pittsburgh had been very festive that Christmas of 1944. I wrote Aunt Jo Gorham, "We had a wonderful time and went to all the dances. It was very nice for a change, but I think on the whole I'd rather spend vacations at Muncy. At last we have seen all of Aunt Peggy's family; they were at different parties. I am taking piano lessons, believe it or not. I can now play with great gusto the notes C, E and G, and what's more remarkable, backwards, too. Right now the school is in the midst of a St. Andrew's plague. When civilization steps back a bit, we get the plague, which gives you terrible pains and you feel like vomiting. Every time the boys do not wash before meals, this happens, but this year it is worse than last. Everybody has it. Wait till I tell Aunt Peggy that after all her talk about my neck being dirty, I am about the only person who hasn't had it and I feel all right. Touch wood!"

Christmas 1944 had been enjoyable for Mother too. In January she wrote Sheila, "The Christmas food parcel arrived quite safely. Thanks very much for it. Was quite lucky Christmas. Had a lovely, lined sheepskin waistcoat and a bottle of gin from Derrick, and an American friend of mine who was in France sent me some scent and powder, etc. My old maid, who I had at the flat in Eastbourne, sent me a Christmas pudding and mince pies and sausage rolls, so I did very well. Another American friend gave me a large comb and a tail comb. It probably sounds funny to you, but these are some of the things we have not been able to get for a long while. Hairpins and haircurl grips are practically unseen. She also gave me a pair of stockings, as she had a dozen pair sent her from America. It will seem funny when one can buy these things again."

As usual at the start of a new year at school, my mind was on food, my studies, and—for the first time—on girls. I was now 16 ½ years old. In a January 14 letter I told Aunt Peggy, "I certainly missed Mr. W— [the school chaplain, who had fled rural Delaware], as did his other advisees, when the first advisee meetings were held at the beginning of the school year."

I also reported to Aunt Peggy that I had to see Mr. P—— the headmaster, about my academic work. "He did not sound too displeased with my report and congratulated me on passing English, much to my surprise. He also said something to the effect that if I passed French, I would have a good (excellent) group. I only got three [demerit] marks this week, so I hope you will like better this term's [conduct] record. I like to please you, but I also like a good time. Often they don't balance quite right."

As for girls, I wrote Aunt Jo Gorham, "The school dance and play are coming up soon, but I'm rather annoyed about the whole matter, for after getting a girl and making all arrangements, the School announced that Fourth Formers couldn't bring girls, because there wasn't enough room to put them up. Everybody was caught with a girl on his hands. I feel like a fish that has just been landed."

As usual, Mother wrote us about Derrick's news. In her January 14 letter, she said that he was now a full Lieutenant and hoped to get his Captaincy soon. On January 22 she told us, "Derrick is now in Italy and seems to be having quite a good time in his off moments. He has been there since November and has been lucky enough to be posted to a squadron which was the original one in which he started his glider career." In February, "Derrick has had several visits to Rome and funnily enough met several of his school pals out there who are in different regiments." In April, "Had a letter from Derrick yesterday. He said it was getting very hot in Italy and the towns very smelly."

Mother had begun 1945 living in a London flat of her own. So we were surprised to learn that after only a few weeks in the flat, she reported, "Am now back living at the Park Lane Hotel, as I found I could not run a flat and work at the Embassy as well. Am now a permanent night driver at O.W.I. and work longer hours. So as I think the job is more important, when I have finished getting the flat straight, I shall let it furnished. We have been tremendously busy, as now that things have got moving again in Europe, your countrymen over here are certainly doing an American hustle and seem to work all hours of the night. The weather has been atrocious for weeks. In fact, every kind of weather, and most people have had a form of 'flu,' which leaves one with no energy at all. I have been battling with it for days, as I could not get time off. Really, at last think I have got the upper hand of it, although I still have to exert a lot of will power to struggle to my job. The V-2s are still about just to remind us that the war is not over yet." Eventually Mother rented her flat to a Spanish couple.

Aunt Cecile gave a different explanation for Mother's giving up the London flat so soon. Being surrounded by my father's possessions and furniture was too much to bear. On February 13, she wrote Aunt Peggy, "I wrote to Violet regarding your difficulties with the adoption of the children at once, as I promised to do. With seeing to the removal of the furniture from Eastbourne to London, getting into the flat, then deciding she could not live in it, returning to the hotel etc., she had not written me. On top of the rest, her ears had troubled her ever since she was caught by the blast of a rocket that fell in Oxford Street. Actually, I am not surprised that Violet did not stay in the flat. I consider that Violet is made of stern stuff. I am sure she felt convinced she *could* live with the *tares et penates* that just breathed of former associations ... but the week I spent at Eastbourne, going through my brother's things, was a trial that called for all my powers of endurance. I felt taut as a piece of stretched elastic, and now that Violet tells me she became so dejected she could no longer endure it, I feel no surprise. I have said if the home were mine, I would sell the lot. I still cannot bear to look at my brother's silver cigar box, etc., the things I want the children to have. As for sitting at his desk, reclining in his chair—No." That silver cigar box stands on my own dresser today.

Mother wrote Aunt Peggy about her finances. "As to my financial state, things have improved slightly this last year, but I never know from year to year whether my shares will fluctuate or not. As I told you, I have been paying up debts left by Mr. Barlow. I suppose living at the Park Lane Hotel may sound extravagant to you, but actually the management has been very good to me. I pay Service terms, as now the O.W.I. is more or less under the American Army as far as our branch is concerned. From this month I have an increase in pay and will instruct my bank to add one month's pay in three months to the draft that is sent to you. It will not be a lot, but it will give the children a small sum more. Living in London at the moment is very high, and as all American staffs get a salary and then high living expenses as well, it is almost impossible for any English staff, who only get a salary, to find accommodations at a reasonable price. Also with the V-1s, the housing problem is very acute. Although our men who do the emergency repairs are helped enormously by the American Army, it is still difficult to get houses habitable quickly. Another factor which makes the housing question difficult is the return of most of the people who were evacuated at the beginning of the war."

Mother's comments about the housing situation in London are borne out by Angus Calder in *The People's War*. "The War Cabinet [in 1945] agreed to give the highest priority to repair. The Armed Forces released men to help.

Forty-five thousand builders were drafted in from the provinces, many of whom, because of the very shortage of accommodations which they were to correct, had to sleep in Wembly Station or in improvised camps. Altogether, 130,000 men were employed in repair work on London in January 1945. By the end of March, nearly 800,000 houses had been repaired after a fashion, but many bombed-out families were living in huts erected with the help of American troops and former Italian prisoners of war."[2]

Mother closed her January 22 letter, "My American friends over here are always saying I should go to the States. I must say, I seem to get on with them well and am now the complete American as regards food." This was quite a change from an earlier letter she had written Sheila: "Have now got quite used to American food, as I have quite a lot of meals in the Canteen at the American Embassy, but the one thing I had a lot of trouble with was peanut butter. Wasn't sure whether I liked it or not. Don't like *Coca Cola*. There is always an uproar when I say so to any Americans."

Despite my isolation in rural Delaware at St. Andrew's, I continued to follow the progress of the war in Europe with keen interest. Mother's letters helped, and so did lectures and war movies shown at school. On February 12 I wrote, "Last Saturday we had a very good movie called *This Is My Country*. It was about the German occupation of The Netherlands and was very well done." In an April 25 letter, written the day the Russians and Americans linked up on the Elbe River in Germany, I told Aunt Peggy, "Mike D— lectured here again and made his usual sweeping statements, but it was rather interesting. He lectured on Russia again, and showed us some very good war pictures. We saw Russia, the re-capture of Paris, and movies of the D-Day invasion. Very interesting, but couldn't see anybody we know in any of them, although there were quite a few close-ups of men, especially the parachutists." I always searched documentary films for a glimpse of Derrick or Fordyce.

Aunt Peggy still received from me in my letters home a miscellany of information. I mentioned food a lot. "I am at Mr. H——'s table now, thank God, for it is right next to the food." I apologized a lot. "I feel thoroughly ashamed that I haven't thanked you for your wonderful Easter present. It certainly tasted wonderful. I felt very well fed for a couple of weeks. Frank's mother came down for his birthday this week, which was celebrated by a big cake and tea. I ate most of the cake, needless to say." I apologized for fouling things up. "You remember that you told me to get my ration book from your room. I disappeared into your room, only to return to ask you some question. After that I forgot that I hadn't yet got my ration book. I *don't* have Sheila's or anybody else's." I made requests. "I have one request, which I offer up in the humblest manner. I forgot, I admit it without strings, my tennis racquet. Will you please, without too much hate in your heart, send it to me." I asked for money. "My bank account is low again due to causes out of my control. I enclose a statement of what I have spent so far, which I believe is a modest sum. Can you refill?" "By the way, you didn't mention you received my accounts. Did I mail them to somebody else?" "I think the present plan for an allowance is very generous of you." I shared school gossip. "Today a startling event happened, for somebody stole the chapel wine and a silver stopper given by an alumnus." "Yesterday one of the Masters had a serious heart attack and is now in the hospital. He has something like the Trombone." [This must have been my attempt at spelling "thrombosis".] "Mr. P— took the Easter service and for once was interesting. I enjoyed the service very much. Sat with Frank and Joe, which gave it sort of a family air." "The holiday for the H— baby was outstandingly dull. No, wait—Sunday afternoon we went swimming off the dock. Tom and Frank were playing around and tripped over a glass fishbowl on the dock. It smashed the bowl to pieces, nearly cutting Tom's foot off. Frank and I carried him to the infirmary, and later went to town with him to the doctor. His tendon was halfway cut. The doctor said if we hadn't carried him—Tom didn't want us to—he would be out the use of his foot. Anyway, he is now on crutches and on the road to recovery." Finally, a parting shot in one letter was, "I cannot say exactly what I did with the key to the gas tank, but I am sure I gave it to you."

Mother wrote on April 16, "Just at the moment the weather is lovely, and as I have a few hours off duty, am able to sit in the park. Things are very peaceful here now, since it is nearly two weeks and no V-1s or V-2s about. Hope we have heard the last of them. Things in London are really getting cleaned up now. The parks are looking lovely with the flowering trees, and a lot of the bomb damage has been removed and tidied up." According to *The People's War*, "On March 27, the last V-2 fell in Kent; the last V-1 was launched two days later. The sirens after five years and seven months had lost their occupation."[3]

The war in Europe was coming to an operatic close. Calder writes, "On April 28, the first of the dictators came to an ignominious end. Italian Partisans strung the bodies of Mussolini and his mistress head downwards from meat hooks in a petrol station in Milan. Next day the German

252 armies in Italy surrendered. The Russians had encircled Berlin. On the 30th Adolf Hitler and his mistress committed suicide in the ruins of the city. The first reports which reached Britain from German radio said that he had died bravely defending his post. With quaint formality, Admiral Doenitz was designated his successor. On the day that his hero, Hitler, perished, William Joyce, a British subject known as 'Lord Haw Haw,' made his last broadcast from Germany. Roaring drunk at the microphone, he said 'You may not hear from me again for a few months,' shouted '*Es lebe Deutschland,*' then dropped his voice: '*Heil Hitler.* And farewell.'"[4]

Calder comments, "Had these impossible creatures ever lived? Had Low (a British cartoonist) imagined them, like Colonel Blimp? The ruins of Hamburg, from which Joyce spoke, proved otherwise. The stage was grandly littered with corpses, but there was no Fortinbras to round off the drama with dignity. Against a banal background of wrecked streets and hungry children, the next act, which was to end with the Berlin Wall, was opening quietly.

"On May 4th, the German forces in northwestern Europe surrendered at Montgomery's headquarters on Lunenburg Heath. His old adversary Rommel, implicated in the July plot against Hitler, had long since died at his own hand; it was a little known admiral whom Doenitz sent to complete the formalities. On May 7th, the German Supreme Command surrendered at Rheims. Unbelievably, the war in Europe was over."[5] The war with Japan would continue for four more months, ending with formal surrender on September 2, 1945.

"When V-E Day was announced," I wrote Aunt Peggy on May 17 from St. Andrew's, "I spent the entire day listening to the radio, and heard Truman (what a flat speech he made) and Churchill (I thought his speech beautifully delivered), and The King (very good in content, but how his voice has aged) plus numerous other officials. In fact, I must have listened to everybody, for I spent most of the night listening to re-broadcasts. However, like you, I felt that the gaiety was vulgar and uncalled for. I can understand why England might celebrate, but I think people might have celebrated in some different fashion than getting drunk, as it appeared the general population did." I was glad when both Mother and Aunt Cecile refuted the idea of any general drunkenness at the V-E celebrations. I did not like the idea of Britons dancing on my Father's grave, because I considered him a casualty of war. I remember feeling sad that V-E Day would not mean a reunion with my Father. However, I looked forward to seeing Mother again at long last.

Aunt Cecile was the first of our relatives to write about V-E Day. "Of late, naturally, the near approach of V-E Day, then the actual occurrence, threw all normal working procedure out of gear. Hour by hour, by special permission of the management, I was at the radiogram, and on the day preceding V-E Day, to broadcast the news. We left the factory that night still uncertain, and honor-bound to come in the next day if nothing definite was broadcast in the evening. Then at 8 PM we heard that for which we have waited so long. By government decree, all factories were to have two days' holiday. That has been followed by the Whitsun break, and in addition to other reasons this has just meant lots of extra work for me. The Welfare Supervisor must keep the domestic side always geared.

"I went to London on V-E Day in the guard's van, sitting on a soldier's kit bag. In the afternoon and evening we went

254   to the West End. Traffic was forbidden in the main streets, and all the world just filled the streets and walked happily and quietly along. They just walked and walked, quite slowly. Here and there a little group just formed up, did a round dance, then moved on again—still quietly, decorously almost. At 9 PM we went to Trafalgar Square to join the immense throng assembled to hear the King's speech. After that, a sailor climbed a very high standard in the middle of a street by Trafalgar Square. With foothold for one toe-tip only, he did an acrobatic dance. Was later joined by a brother A.B. and the two of them, on either side of the standard, gave a comical show to the strains of merry songs sung by the crowds below. It was one of the funniest things I have ever seen. No single case of drunkenness. When my friend and I tried to get some wine—anything—nothing but ginger beer [non-alcoholic] was available."

Mother wrote about V-E Day on May 28. Unlike Aunt Cecile, she had to work during the two-day celebration. She told Aunt Peggy, "The two V-E nights were quite hectic. We had an awful job to get about as most of the main streets were roped off, and all the taxis were taken off the roads. None of the American organizations shut down like the English ones, so you can imagine that, as we were the only means of transport, we just never stopped. In fact, the second day, I started at 6 PM and finished at 7 AM. If the few of us who were on duty had not known our London well, we should never have coped with it, as we had to use all the back streets and covered over a hundred miles each. The crowd in general behaved very well, and except for bonfires in most of the streets and crowds dancing all night, it was not too bad.

"Things over here seem very strange. Even now one expects to hear the very familiar noise of a buzz bomb or rocket.

However I expect that feeling will soon wear off. In the meantime, evidently the food question is going to get more difficult. However, having survived six years of food rationing, I don't suppose another year will do us any harm."

In *The People's War*, Calder describes this time period. "There was a world shortage of food, reflected in famine in India, hunger and even cannibalism in Europe. There was less meat on sale in Britain in 1945 than there had been in 1944, less in the second half of the year than there had been in the first, and the improved supply of fish which followed the release of trawlers and fishermen from naval service could not compensate psychologically. With coarse irony, Dame Austerity whittled the bacon ration from four ounces to three, and the lard ration from two ounces to one in the victorious month of May 1945. Then, as the shortage of labor in the mills was causing a new crisis in textile production, she turned to and cut the clothing ration in September to only 36 coupons per year."[6]

Aunt Cecile reported on May 22, "Shopping becomes increasingly difficult. I have had my old *Daily Mail* friend enquiring for me in London for a lot of things I shall shortly need. Only six cabin trunks to be found; one store only with black leather shoes, size 6. No soft leather slippers, size 6, *anywhere*. A few silk dressing gowns, and no navy blue sweaters. As for finding brassieres in my size, well, she says the sooner I go up and start my shopping, the better. A shop that has six dressing gowns today may have none tomorrow."

"Derrick is still in Italy," Mother informed us on May 28. "He has just had a marvelous tour of North Italy, where the 8th Army made its last stand. He said he did 14,000 miles in a jeep and has hardly been able to sit down since. Anyhow, now he seems to have seen the greater part of Italy and has just come back from Venice. He does not know yet whether he will get back to England, but says he is in the wrong age group for any such piece of luck, and may be sent straight to the Far East. He is also having a great time keeping his flying up by flying American planes." In July, she told us, "Derrick has just arrived home last week and has a month's leave before going to the Pacific. He looks very well."

Both Mother and Aunt Cecile made plans for the future now that Victory Day in Europe was part of history. On May 28 Mother wrote, "At the moment I shall continue with O.W.I., as I am not the sort of person to sit about a hotel doing nothing. The O.W.I. is gradually closing down, but I think there will still be some departments here for some time to come. Anyhow, at the moment we are busier than ever."

In July Mother wrote, "The O.W.I. has been cut down considerably, but I am still being kept on. In fact, only 14 out of 78 drivers are left. As a matter of fact, we are busier than we were all through the war, but I think the reason for that is that so many of the personnel are returning home. At the moment, I am just working and returning home to bed. However, I really thrive on work. At the moment we have some lovely new Packards (autos), so am really enjoying myself."

Aunt Cecile, on the other hand, decided to change jobs. "Since soon after D-Day, I began my efforts to obtain a position overseas. I have filled in countless forms; between other duties, have been before a Selection Board; got well away with things; then was ordered by Dame Oliver Boyle, president of the British Red Cross, to begin all over again by filling in their forms. This had to be done. I had an entire day of medical examinations and tests in London. I had to give my life's history and references. Mr. Q— [the owner of the parachute factory and a personal friend] was regretful that I want to leave, but agrees that at this stage of the war, work in the liberated countries is more important. He would not have released me for another factory, but was reluctantly willing to let me go for *this* work. The National Service Officer after a little while took this point of view also. I gather the Factory Inspector thought differently ... but, well, my release from the factory took effect a few days ago. But I am still doing my duties at the factory till I am sent for to go to London—there to have a fortnight's intensive course, inoculations and vaccination, collect my kit, etc., for a Welfare job perhaps in Italy, perhaps northwest Europe. I shall have commissioned rank, British Red Cross, wear a uniform all the time, and be attached to a Medical Unit under military organization and law. I may sometimes (not very often) sleep in a hotel; will live mostly under canvas, and sometimes sleep in my sleeping bag on 'a heap of rubble.' I have had an interesting, useful, and happy job here. It has been worthwhile, but after 4 2/3 years in a factory, I just want a change—change from confinement, the same routine, the narrow life we have had to live. I want to travel, to see fresh scenes, and Europe in these days."

A July 10 letter from Mother to Aunt Peggy said, "Cecile Bunn has gone to Italy as a Welfare Officer with the British Red Cross."

As soon as V-E Day was announced, Mother began looking into the possibility of a visit to America. "I am told that at the moment the chances of getting to America are very slim for some time to come. Probably easier from your side than mine, as every bit of available shipping from this side is being used to convey troops back to America and the Far East. However, as things progress, all this may alter. Well, I do hope, Mrs. Brock, that the time is not far distant when at last we shall meet, and I shall at last personally be able to thank you for all your kindness. Since you wrote, I have had your telegram, stating that you now have permanent visas. My lawyer is sending you the birth certificates, but for some reason was having trouble in finding Sheila's. When they had passports to go to America, we certainly had to have copies of the certificates then, so cannot understand it. However, I hope you will receive them quickly."

Aunt Peggy finally heard from the U.S. Committee for European Children on May 18. "We have no objection to your making temporary arrangements for the Barlow children through readmission from Canada, as long as it does not involve a permanent plan for the children's stay in the United States or a change of sponsorship at this time." The Committee had failed to understand the whole point of our re-entry into the U.S. on permanent visas. Fed up with the U.S. Committee, Aunt Peggy decided to ignore their prohibitions. On July 5, we flew with her from Burlington, Vermont, to Montreal, Canada. On July 6, we were given non-quota Immigration visas and were re-admitted to the U.S. through St. Albans, Vermont, on July 9, 1945. An August 11 letter from Mother said, "What a lovely time the children have had in Montreal. They seem very thrilled at having their first papers." The question of our adoption remained unresolved.

Mother was doing her best to obtain passage on a ship to America. It turned out to be a frustrating endeavor. A July 10 letter told us, "Well, I have been making some inquiries as to the possibility of getting to America by Christmas, but as far as I can make out, it is quite impossible. Also, had a talk with an American regular naval captain, a friend of mine, who is well up in this kind of travel, and he told me the same thing. Apparently surface traveling is impossible, and air travel very much priority. In fact, the authorities depressed me by saying it might be a year and a half. However, after a few months, I am hoping things may progress quicker than they anticipate. I cannot imagine anything more lovely than a real country family Christmas, but it is evidently not to be. Having been alone every Christmas since the children left, you can imagine how I should enjoy it."

Mother described what England was like that summer of 1945. "At the moment, we are having dull, hot weather that seems to sap the last bit of energy left. Am hoping about August to get a week's leave to go to my sister. She has a lovely house on the Hampshire coast with her own sands, and if only the weather will be kind, I could relax in the sea and the garden.

"Things in London are beginning to get back to normal. Most of the bombed sites have been cleared up, and the blast walls removed, and some painting is being done. On July 15 the street lighting goes on, then we shall be able to see our way about. The only serious situation is the food, which has deteriorated since the war, but even that is not too bad. The clothing situation is improving, and I had a great thrill in buying a new dress in spite of it costing over double the price of pre-war days. I believe the petrol will come off ration shortly, and then people with cars will get a break. Unfortunately, I sold mine, and at the price they are now should not dream of buying one. London is very full. Everyone from the country seems to be spending their holidays here, and by the terrific queues at the railroad stations, all Londoners are heading for the country and seaside. Driving a car in London is a nightmare. Half the people have forgotten how to drive and the traffic jams are dreadful. Since the basic ration of 5 gallons a month, life as far as we in the car service are concerned has become intolerable."

By July 1945, the war with Japan was in its final phase, although that was generally not recognized to be the case by either the American or British public. In Britain, the general public did know that Churchill had predicted the war against Japan would take 18 months to complete after the victory over Germany. On July 13, the Japanese Foreign Office formally notified the Russian government that "the Emperor is desirous of peace." The message reached Stalin just as he was setting off for the Potsdam Conference in Germany. He sent a chilly reply saying that the proposal was not definite enough for him to take action or agree to receiving a diplomatic mission. A fortnight later, the Japanese government sent a second message to Stalin, trying to make still clearer the purpose of the mission, but received a similar negative reply.

On August 6, the first atomic bomb was dropped on Hiroshima, destroying most of the city and killing some 80,000 people, a quarter of its inhabitants. Three days later, the second atomic bomb was dropped on Nagasaki. On August 8, Russia declared war on Japan and moved immediately into Manchuria. On August 14, Hirohito himself made the determination to surrender, and Japan's surrender was announced over the radio. However it was not until September 2, 1945 that Japan signed the "Instruments of Surrender" on board the U.S. battleship *Missouri* in Tokyo Bay. The Second World War ended six years and one day after it had been started by Hitler's attack on Poland, and four months after Germany's surrender.

The dropping of the second atomic bomb convinced Brit-

ons that Japan's surrender was a foregone conclusion. Mother
wrote on August 11 (four days before the surrender announcement on Japanese radio), "The celebrations in London last night at the news of the Japanese surrender did not
compare with V-E night. All the American boys have got a
tremendous thrill from the news and were climbing lamp
posts and dancing round bonfires in Picadilly."

Malcolm remembers we were enjoying a picnic at Muncy
Farms, down at the log cabin on the Susquehanna River,
when the fire siren and all the factory whistles in Muncy—
five miles from the farm—sounded to signal the end of the
war with Japan.

Mother's letter about V-J Day also told us, "The Army
are still holding Derrick's squadron back, so I hope now he
will not have to go to the Pacific. He is very anxious to get
released soon, as he wants to go into a perfumery business in
which I hold some shares." However, like other servicemen,
Derrick would have to wait his turn to be released from the
army under a carefully worked-out demobilization plan.

Angus Calder describes the plan. "There was to be no
chaos of priorities as there had been after the First World
War. The plan created two classes for demobilization. Class
B would cover builders and others urgently required for
reconstruction work, who would have priority in release,
but would be subject to recall if they left the vital work to
which they were directed. The remainder, the vast majority of servicemen, would be formed in an orderly queue,
with their position established according to an ingenious
scale which combined simplicity with self-evident justice.
Both age and length of service would be taken into account.
Two months' service would be taken to equal a year of age,
so that a man of 22 with four years' service would be re-

leased with the same priority as a man of 40 with one years' service, while a man of 24 with four years' service would 'equal' a man of 30 with three. Each 'demobbed' man in Class A would get eight weeks' paid leave on his release. A week after V-E Day, Bevin cut the suspense short by announcing that releases would begin on June 18th, forecasting that three-quarters of a million men would be out of uniform by the end of the year. In the latter months of 1945, some 30,000 men a week were turning to the Resettlement Advice Service, which answered questions on anything from domestic problems to those of men wishing to set up shops. And, as Bevin had prophesied, with startling confidence, there was no mass unemployment of returned warriors."[7] Derrick's turn for release would not come until June 1946.

Mother kept on with her efforts to obtain passage on a ship to America. Her V-J Day letter told us, "Have not been very successful at the moment finding out about a passage, but next week a friend of mine has given me an introduction to the head of Cook's Travel Agency, so am hoping I may get some information and help. From the newspapers I see that civilian travel begins on September 1, but that all passages are booked until January. However, I am still hoping and will let you know as soon as I hear something. I cannot tell you how anxious I am to come and see you all. Although I am working harder than ever, there are times when I feel very much alone and certainly miss having a home. One gets very fed up with a hotel however nice it is. In any case, I never did like London except for an odd week or so. Have always been very fond of the country."

"All the O.W.I. organizations are either going home or to the Continent," Mother wrote on August 11. "The O.W.I. have made tremendous cuts in their personnel, and I am one of the eight left, so as they seem to need me, shall go on working until I can start my visit to you. Must go on night duty, so will close."

On October 20, Mother wrote, "At the moment, I am feeling a bit desperate as my job is now finished, and I just don't know what to do with myself all day. Hotel life bores me to tears, and while there is any hope of getting to the States, I do not want to look for another job." Evidently Mother was re-hired by the O.W.I. because on December 2 she told us, "This week the remainder of O.W.I. personnel go back to the States on the *Queen Mary*, and I am then transferred to the British Division of the American Embassy."

The four of us returned to school in September 1945. Malcolm stayed on with Aunt Peggy at Muncy Farms and was enrolled in the 5th grade of the Muncy public school district. Now that the war was over, it was no longer necessary for Aunt Peggy to close the big house for the winter months to save oil. Susan returned to Garrison Forest School in Baltimore; Sheila went back to Foxhollow School; I returned to St. Andrew's School as a Fifth Former. On September 29, I wrote Aunt Peggy, "I arrived safe and sound, if that is of any interest, without too much trouble. Frank and I have the first room on the Sixth Form corridor. Although not beautiful, it is one of the nicest rooms and we are very pleased with it. We got hold of two small rugs, and these, with the pictures, make the room quite nice. However, if you run across a nice armchair, we would love to have it." A later letter reported, "One rug was stolen from us, but we stole someone else's, which in turn was taken from us, and so on without end. Therefore I won't need any rugs from home, because they might get borrowed, and we trust we can come out on top."

Frank's and my main accomplishment that fall was to introduce the Fifth Form to cocktail parties. On October 9, I wrote Aunt Peggy, "Last Saturday we went into town and bought lime cola, root beer, ginger ale, Canada Dry water, and mixed them all together to make a vile tasting but powerful potion, which afforded us much amusement and entertainment." At age 17, I had the good sense not to tell her that the "power" came from vanilla extract, which we added, thinking it contained alcohol. Secret cocktail parties soon became the rage of the Fifth Form.

That same letter mentioned that Frank had started teaching English to the French chef. I left out the information that the teaching took place after lights out, when we would sneak down to the kitchen and work our way to his apartment above the kitchen. I told Aunt Peggy, "I had a try [teaching the chef English], but his French is off in the deep blue sea. However, Frank manages to bluff by, although I know he hasn't the slightest idea sometimes of what the old boy is saying. I went to bed well pleased when he said I pronounced some words very well, and that he thought Mr. F—'s pronunciation pretty bad." Mr. F— was the school's French teacher, and he spoke French with a southern accent.

The English lessons continued, and might have gone on forever, as we were making much headway teaching the chef English. However, one night the chef made a big mistake. Frank had a bad cold, so the chef offered him a cognac with lemon juice, diluted with hot water. I claimed to have a cold, too, so he gave me a cognac. Soon we gave up any pretense of teaching the chef English, and spent our time cadging cognac. Eventually the chef caught on and threw us out of his apartment for good.

To replace the lost liquor supply, Frank and I decided to brew beer. Off to town we went to purchase the necessary supplies, including a bottle stopper. Our first attempt at making beer was a failure, so we decided it didn't work unless you made beer in big batches. Back to town we went for more supplies, being careful to buy each item in a different store, as we had seen done in various crime movies. We ended up making three cases of beer, which we stored in the attic of the gym tower. A week later, I happened to be standing next to the headmaster, watching a basketball game, when a cannonade went off above our heads. The headmaster tried to locate where the explosions were coming from, but fortunately the noise stopped after three loud volleys. Sadly, not a single bottle of beer survived to be enjoyed. We decided not to risk brewing another batch.

"It certainly is wonderful to think we may see Mother before Christmas," I wrote Aunt Peggy on October 26. But such was not to be the case. Mother had written Malcolm on September 6, "Had hoped I should be able to get out and see you, but at present there are so many American soldiers going home, it looks as if I shall not be able to see you all until after Christmas." By October 20, Mother's news was even gloomier. "Well, the travel situation at the moment is not much better. In fact, as regards civilian travel, it seems worse. Even the O.W.I. people who were going home have been curtailed, but I have not given up hope yet. For the past fortnight, I have been waiting for the return of my passport, and now the Travel Section of O.W.I. are going to see if they can hurry it up. When I have that, am then going to tackle the American Embassy for a visa. There is now no longer any need for an exit permit, so that simplifies things. The father of a friend of mine is head of a large travel agency, and is going to give me all the help he can. Over these matters I am very lost, as I have never traveled except once to the Continent."

Mother told Aunt Peggy, "Your idea of a permanent basis [moving to America to live] interests me very much. Really I have nothing to keep me in England, as Derrick is old enough to look after himself. Somehow, in this letter, I do not feel I am being very helpful towards your suggestion of cooperation. All I can say is, that the sooner I get to the States, the more pleased I shall be, and am just hoping that things will straighten out. The lease of my flat is up in February, so I shall not have anything to worry about. At the moment, cannot make up my mind whether to store the furniture or get rid of it altogether."

Mother's last letter for 1945 was dated December 2. "Lately I have got to know the Second Secretary of the American Embassy, and he has given me lots of advice on getting to the States. The Embassy has suggested that I wait until about April, when travel facilities will be very much easier. I believe the school holidays begin in May or June, so I thought perhaps that might be a good idea, as then I could come for 3 months or so. Then make some plans. As regards finance, I shall be able to give you a better idea later, as now that cosmetics, etc., are starting to be released, my income should increase. At the moment the government takes nearly ¾ in tax. Even my poor little salary from the American government, out of every £200 I get, the government taxes me £108 on it. Living costs in Britain at the moment are very high. Well, I hope you all have a lovely Christmas. Shall be going down to my sister in Hampshire if we are given any holiday. Last year the Americans made us work."

However, Mother was to be ill with flu before the end of the year. At the beginning of 1946, she wrote, "In bed with a good attack of flu, but am recovering and shall probably be back at work at the end of the week. It is a most annoying disease, as one's temperature seems to dash up very high and then drop suddenly, so that one is left feeling too limp for words." Mother, like so many others in England, was emotionally and physically drained by six years of war.

CHAPTER TWENTY–NINE

"On 10 January 1946 the Tory M.P. and diarist 'Chips' Channon attended a society wedding in London and remarked to another guest, Lady 'Emerald' Cunard, 'How quickly normal life has been resumed. After all, I said, pointing to the crowded room, this is what we have been fighting for.' 'What?' said Emerald, 'are they all Poles?'"[1] This anecdote is found in *Modern Times* by Paul Johnson.

"Normal life" did not resume for Mother for several more long years. Christmas of 1945 was spent with her sister, who could still afford to live on a pre-war scale, unlike Mother. "My sister has a large house in Hampshire and all through the war she has had plenty of servants. Have now come back from spending Christmas there. Unfortunately, the weather was awful. We had terrific gales, and as her house is on the cliff overlooking the sea, we quite expected to be blown up by loose mines. However, we were lucky this time. A short while ago, a mine blew up under her cliff and took out all the windows."

For the first time, no Christmas presents arrived for us from Mother. She explained, "Owing to a concession last month allowing parcels to be sent to America, I scoured the shops for days and eventually sent Susan a bead necklace with earrings, and Sheila a gold bar brooch with an aquamarine on it, and Brian a year's subscription to the Book Society. Over Malcolm, I was completely defeated, as there was absolutely nothing I could buy for him. The toys over here are just rubbish, and there are no such things as fountain pens, etc." Mother asked Aunt Peggy, "I wonder if you would be very kind and get him some little thing, just so he should not think he had been left out. The weather here now is very cold, but no snow as yet. At the moment, there does not seem to be any improvement in things over here. In fact, in a lot of ways we are worse off than we were during the war. During Christmas there was literally nothing in the shops to buy. It's the first time I have seen big stores such as Harrod's with bare shelves." The presents Mother got for us never arrived.

Aunt Peggy sent Mother a nightdress, two petticoats, and some panties. Mother wrote back, "The things from you were almost right, but could have been a size larger. I think with all this starchy food we have been having, I have put on a bit of weight. It is now about 136 lbs. You might be interested to know the price of underclothes here, that is when any worth buying can be found. In one of the stores the other day I looked at a flowered nightie, and it was £27.5.0. Of course cheaper ones are about £6.8, but do not last. Before I went away, I had to use some of my precious coupons for a pair of cami-knickers, and having searched London I eventually tracked quite a nice pair down at Fortnum and Mason in rayon satin, and not quite as skimpy as usual. Had to pay £8.15.0 for them. While I was in Bournemouth last week, I looked at quite a plain dinner frock. Just a long straight black skirt and a short black and gold coat, no trimming on it, and the price was £57.10.0, so you see, until something is done about the clothing situation, most people just don't buy anything.

"The biggest racket here is the secondhand car market. The prices are just enormous. My sister had a large Daimler, which was too extravagant on petrol ration to use, so in 1940 she bought a 13 HP car for £300 new. Having run it ever since 1940, she has been offered over £800 for it. Second-hand American cars are beyond most people's money. I was offered a 1937 Terraplane the other day for £900. New cars are being made now in small quantities, but with 100% purchase tax, the cheapest 9 HP car will cost over £500, so really to have any of the things one has been used to, one has to be a millionaire."

The four of us had chipped in together to send Mother a food parcel for Christmas. Her January 3 letter told us that the food parcel had not arrived by Christmas Day. "At present the food parcel has not arrived, and so many of my friends who have had parcels sent have also not received theirs." A February 2 letter told us, "Haven't received the food parcel. A friend of mine has had five parcels sent her since November and has only received one." The parcel finally arrived on April 11.

Mother's letter about her Christmas also told us about Derrick. "Derrick spent Christmas with me at my sister's. He is now a Captain and off to Palestine at the end of the month. Right into the fighting arena again." On February 5, she told us, "Derrick leaves for Palestine on Friday. He seems quite thrilled at the idea of getting abroad again." On March 5 she wrote, "Derrick has arrived in the Middle East, and although at the moment he seems to be living in a tent in the middle of the desert, he says it is quite comfortable. In about three weeks time he is getting a new job, and will be permanently in Cairo." An April 11 letter told us, "Heard from Derrick today. He seems to be having a grand time in Cairo. He has paid a visit to the Pyramids and done all the usual tourist visits." Derrick was to meet his first wife in Cairo, where she worked at the Military Headquarters and outranked him. They were married in Egypt.

At the time, Mother had good reason to be worried about Derrick in Palestine and Egypt. Palestine was about to explode; the British were caught between the warring Arabs and Jews. The seeds of this conflict had been sown by the British White Paper of 1939, which had placed the future of Palestine on ice for the duration of the war. It was agreed at the time that land transfers from Arabs to Jews would be halted, and total immigration for the next five years would be held to 75,000.

In his book *The Middle East—A History*, Sydney Fisher writes, "As the war in Europe drew to a close, the drive to obtain fulfillment of the Biltmore Program (to establish a Jewish Commonwealth in Palestine and permit unlimited immigration) was intensified by pressures from all sides. Jews from Germany, Poland, and Eastern Europe fled from their homes behind the Iron Curtain and found temporary refuge in German and Italian displaced-persons camps.

"World Jewry in the West, in memory of the Jews massacred by the Nazis, felt a 'Divine Impatience' over procrastination in finding homes for these displaced persons. Illegal entries into Palestine multiplied, and thousands filtered through the lines held by the Jewish Brigade in Italy. Others came by ships of every description. Crises arose when British authorities would not permit them to land, turned them back, or interned them in Cyprus or Mauritius. The *S.S. Patria*, crowded with visa-less refugees, was sunk off Haifa, and passengers were allowed to land and remain. On the other hand, passengers on an old cattle boat, *S.S. Struma*, were denied visas, and all lives but one were lost when she sank in the Black Sea. Incidents such as these heightened the irritation at the delay in opening the gates of Palestine to the homeless Jews."[2]

Ben-Gurion, head of the Jewish Agency in Palestine, covertly authorized a resistance movement against British authority. Resistance took the form of terrorist deeds: munitions thefts, explosions, sabotage, bank robberies, killing of English soldiers, and destruction of bridges. The British retaliated by arresting Jewish Agency leaders, rounding up members of various Resistance groups, and seizing great caches of arms. On July 22, 1946, Jewish terrorism culminated in the blowing up of the King David Hotel, the British military headquarters, killing 91 people and wounding 45 others. Fortunately, Derrick had been posted to Egypt before the conflict with the Jewish Agency had reached its terrorist stage.

Derrick's tour of duty in Cairo coincided with serious tensions existing between the British and the Egyptian government. Having declared war against Germany, the Egyptian government at the end of the war sought to renegotiate the Anglo-Egyptian Treaty of 1936, which allowed British troops to occupy Egypt to protect the Suez Canal. The Attlee government in Britain was unable to reach any agreement about British troops in Egypt, when the Egyptian government insisted that any agreement must recognize Egypt's sovereignty over Sudan, which the British government was unwilling to do. The end result was that the British government did agree to pull British troops out of Cairo and Alexandria, but kept them in positions to protect the Suez Canal. It was during these times of negotiation that Derrick served in Egypt.

After getting over our disappointment that Mother would not be sharing Christmas 1945 with us, we were still delighted to be able to enjoy a Christmas at Muncy Farms. To see the house decorated for the holiday and to see snow on the ground for skiing and sledding was for us a re-run of that first magical Christmas in 1940. When it came time to return to our boarding schools, Sue, Sheila, and I envied Malcolm that he could remain at home. Aunt Peggy must have found that Christmas as joyous as we did. By then she knew that the last problems over the adoption of the four of us had been resolved. On February 5, Mother wrote, "Was delighted to hear that you have at last sorted out the status of the children. If you could see the chaos everything is over here [referring to strikes], you would understand my pleasure at the news."

It came as a surprise when Mother told us in her January 3, 1946 letter that she had finished her job with the American Embassy "as I really felt I could not cope with it any longer. Shall anyhow stay here until I have disposed of the furniture out of the Eastbourne flat, and then I may go down and join my sister for a while, as I much prefer the country to London. At the moment, I cannot find any storage rooms anywhere for the furniture. Have been trying to find a small house or flat in Hampshire to put it in, and then let it furnished, but they also seem non-existent, so that at the moment I can see myself sitting on the pavement in February, surrounded with furniture." Eventually Mother did find a small house in a rural area to store the furniture in, but before she could rent the house, all of the furniture was stolen. It was never recovered.

Now that she was no longer working, Mother concentrated on getting to America. "I shall certainly try to time my arrival to see you all about the first week in June. It may be difficult to time it exactly, as apparently the shipping situation will not be too good then, but I have a friend who knows the shipping line well, and he thinks he will be able to get me a passage all right. You need not worry about it being a hot period then, because I love the heat, especially after having been virtually frozen for the last five years. Really, I am looking forward to my trip. It is going to be quite an adventure."

The adventure turned out to be trying to obtain the necessary papers to make the trip to the U.S. On February 5, Mother wrote, "This morning, I went to see the Second Secretary of the American Embassy. He does not think I shall have any trouble to get out, provided I go on a Visitor's visa and not on an Immigrant's. The Visitor's visa is valid for 12 months and can be used for going backwards and forwards several times. He seems to think, if after I have been to visit you, should I think I would like to live in the States, I could come back to England and apply for an Immigrant's visa. He has given me an introduction to the Head of the Visa Department, but tells me not to apply for a visa yet, as it is too soon if I am not coming until May or June. My very good friend, who is the general manager of this hotel, has applied for me to two shipping lines for a passage around the end of May."

Mother needed a letter from Aunt Peggy saying that she would be staying with her and would not "become a financial embarrassment to the U.S.A." Mother wrote, "I have tackled my bank, and as soon as I have a visa and passage, they are going to ask the government for permission to send money out for me. If this should fail, the general manager knows many American businessmen

Standing, left to right: Sue, Aunt Peg, Violet Layman Jamieson, Brian on his 18th birthday, July 1946; Sheila is kneeling in front.

personally, who have business on both sides of the Atlantic, so probably I can have an arrangement with them. At the moment, am getting such a thrill at coming out. Now that I have no job, I feel absolutely lost, as I really dislike hotel life. Lately, have been trying to find another flat—at the sea if possible—but unbelievable as it sounds, all the estate agents tell me the same tale. There just isn't such a thing at any price, and not likely to be any for some years, so that is that. If you could only see the chaos everything is in over here. Really, things seem to be getting worse. People here are more fed up than they were during the war. Food hasn't improved. In fact, it is getting more difficult, and having been on this diet so long, everyone is beginning to lose their energy and adopt a don't-care attitude. Certainly, when I get on the boat to the States, it's going to save my life. Cannot tell you how I am looking forward to seeing you all. The farm sounds Heaven."

"I really have got a little nearer the States," Mother wrote Aunt Peggy on February 9. "I enclose a slip that was given me by the Visa Office of the American Embassy. The Second Secretary of the Embassy was most helpful. Now I can do no more until you comply with the slip, if you don't mind. There must be *two* affidavits. As soon as these are returned to me, I can get a passage on the United States Line through a friend. The Cunard was not very helpful, and would not name any time within 8 weeks of June, if then, so I got in touch with Mr. M— of Pan American, who has a lot to do with the United States Line, and he promised me a passage either the end of May or first week in June, but, of course, I must have my visa first."

Mother described conditions in England. "Suppose you have read that our rations are cut again. Really, everyone here is getting a bit fed up with life. We are worse off now than we were during the war, what with food, and nowhere to live. I tried to get a flat or small house anywhere in London or south of England. Was told I was asking the impossible." Mother had great difficulty finding Sheila a birthday present. A March 20 letter said, "You will probably think it sounds crazy, but I am still trying to find something to send Sheila for her birthday [which was February 15th]. Being limited to five pounds rather curbs my efforts, as everything here is just soaring in price." Not until April 11 did Mother report, "Last week I sent Sheila a white pigskin handbag for her birthday."

Near the end of March 1946 Mother began to despair about her chances of getting to the States to see us. "Very many thanks for the papers for the Embassy, which I took along, and thought my troubles were ended. In fact, I was quite wrong, and they were only just beginning. After nearly a month, am right back where I started. As far as I can see, there is so much 'red tape' and it all works in a vicious circle. After your papers were handed in, I found I could not get a visa until I have a permit from the Bank of England to leave this country with £100 in my possession. No one can leave England for anywhere without this, so as it is a regulation, you would think the permit would automatically be sent. Not a bit of it. I had to apply, which I have done, and my Bank suggested that I should at the same time apply for an extra £100, but not for more, as they were sure it would not be possible. Well, after filling up many more forms, the application has gone in, but no result at the moment. The Visa Office told me that the visa is definitely waiting for me as soon as I have the money permit. Everyone I meet here scares me to death by saying if I get the £200 allotment, everything in the States is so expensive that it would be very little use to me. I hope this isn't so, as it would be quite useless my applying for more than that, and I may only get away with £100."

Mother's tale of woe seemed endless. "On this money application, I had to state a definite date for sailing, which, of course, is quite stupid, as shipping companies will not give a definite date. So as you will see by all this, everything just keeps going around in a circle. Anyhow, I hope to be able to write and tell you something definite soon. While I was at the Embassy, I asked how long I was allowed to stay in the States, and they told me this was decided by the American authorities when I arrived there, so again I shall have no idea until I am actually in the States."

On April 11, Aunt Peggy heard from Mother again. "This is just a few lines to tell you how I am progressing. Really, am having a terrific struggle. After spending several days at the Visa Office with no result, I was beginning to get so despondent, thought I should have to throw the whole idea up. However, yesterday I made one more determined effort and was lucky enough to sit next to a businessman who really knew the ropes, and he was good enough to get me in with him, with the result that after we had sat for *five* hours, at last I came away with a visa. So now the battle starts all over again with shipping lines. Shipping is more chaotic than ever, and I might even have to come on a cargo boat. The new order has come out that I can only travel on an English line. Then I pay my fare here and am allowed to land with £75. Before, out of the £100 allowance, the fare was deducted. I tried to get more from the Bank of England, but they would not pass it and if I had insisted would quite definitely have stopped my passage. Also, not until I land in the States will they tell me how long I may stay. I stated,

'I hoped two to three months,' so, much as I hate asking it, if I run short of money, perhaps you would lend me some. I, for the time being, can only put it in your name here. Really, am getting rather thrilled at the idea of coming. Have suggested to Cunard any time after May 20, but I might have to sail on 48 hours' notice, if there was a vacancy any time before then. Am told, if you once refuse, it might be months before another chance, so I hope you will not have a shock, if you suddenly get a cable from me. Have enclosed one of my visa photos, just in case you had to find me on a crowded dock. It isn't too bad a photo, so I am told by my friends.

"Everyone at the moment seems very excited at the Budget. Actually, the Labour government is pandering to the working class again. My income, being unearned, does not get any help, and may eventually cost me still more in taxes. There will certainly not be any more large estates in England, as the really wealthy people are going to be taxed to the hilt. The government has openly said so."

Earlier than she had planned, Mother at long last cabled Aunt Peggy that she was about to sail to America. The cable was followed by a letter dated May 5, 1946. "Am sailing next Thursday on *S.S. Washington* for New York. Believe it takes about six days. Have been very lucky, as a Mr. C—, a geologist staying at the hotel, is returning to the States on the same ship. He has been kind enough to say he will look after me on the voyage. As you suggested in your last letter, if I do not see you on the dock, shall meet you in the Customs' shed under 'L'." [After her divorce from Father, Mother had resumed her maiden name of Layman.] "At the moment, I have the most awful cold. Worst I have had for years, but perhaps the sea voyage will get rid of it. Am really getting very excited now. Had a passage last Friday on a Swedish boat, but could not take it, as the Bank was closed, so could not get any traveler's checks. As it happens, shall do much better with the U.S. Shipping Lines." Evidently the British government had by this time dropped its demand that travel be done only on English ships.

Aunt Peggy immediately contacted all our schools to have us meet her in New York the day before Mother's ship was to arrive. In my case, the summons arrived when I was not in very good standing with the headmaster. The previous week, I had written Aunt Peggy, "Now I had better mention the rather sore spot, which I hope you will not think too bad. Last week I somehow got 28 demerit marks. This is extremely annoying and will probably put me on bounds. Up to now, I was doing fine and hoped to get on the White List. These marks were gotten in the first week this way: 2 Ringers (6 marks) for our dorm raiding the Third Form, 2 Ringers for overdrawing my bank account, 4 marks on account of my friend and me feeling too good one night, which resulted in the removal of my sheets, which I was rather noisy about reclaiming, 7 marks for being late, 4 of which I consider unjust, and 1 Ringer for Frank and I talking before the end of study hall. Now to this week, in which I reaped a mighty harvest. The 30 marks, by the way, include 9 carry-overs from last week, unless somebody else has given me more marks, for I am not able to go and see. Well, I got three Ringers from Miss M—, which I consider unjust, for she kicked me out of the choir for no reason; she suddenly turned around and told me to leave, which I did without arguing at the time. The next day I went up and politely asked her why I got them, and she said two words: 'Get out'. The other Ringer Frank and I got for arriving at 22 minutes after, instead of 20, and even then she had no right to give it. Got 1 Ringer last night for walking into the dining room late, and again 5 from Mr. C—, as did the rest of the table. There, I think, is all about the marks, and I'll try to get none next week. Again, hope you won't mind this number too much— a very unfortunate 2 weeks." The number of marks does not appear to add up correctly, but then, math was never my strong point. The end result was that the headmaster only reluctantly granted me a three-day weekend to go see Mother.

As was my custom, this "bad" news about the demerits was sandwiched between "good" news in the hope that Aunt Peggy might skip over it. The system never worked, but I never lost faith in it. The "good" news was, "At last, I'm among the stars for in some unknown manner I got a Third Group and no flunks. There are only five people who have higher Groups in school, but there are about 13 who have Thirds. Anyway, it's right up there and I still can't believe it. Now maybe I'll have time to write Sheila and Sue, who have been begging for letters. Today I'll just stay here and write them each a long letter. Also I hope to write old Malcolm if I get time."

All three of us reached New York on schedule to join Malcolm and Aunt Peggy. Mother's ship docked on May 15, 1946. We took a taxi to where the ocean liners were berthed. Mother's ship was already tied up at the dock when we arrived, and passengers lined the rails of the *S. S. Washington* three or four deep. As people on board recognized friends on the dock, there was frantic arm-waving. There was growing excitement as the sailors jockeyed the gangplank into position. I searched the faces of the passengers lining the railings for a glimpse of Mother, but none of the faces looked even remotely familiar. As the passengers began to disembark, there was still no one who looked like Mother.

Then I noticed a woman coming towards us, but it wasn't until she had all but reached us that I realized it was Mother. She looked quite different from the way I remembered her in 1940. She wore her hair in a style which was popular during the war years in England because it did not require curling. Her lithe, pre-war figure had thickened from the starchy wartime diet. She wore bright red lipstick; in England I did not remember her ever wearing it. She wore a rayon dress, but it did not have the elegant cut I remembered her wearing in England.

However, Mother still moved through the crowd with the complete self-assurance which English women from her background seemed to be born with. She was obviously somebody of importance. She greeted us with complete composure, no tears. To the observer, it would seem that we had been apart for just a short time. I gave her a polite peck on the cheek. I thought I detected some feeling on her part, as she looked at each one of us, that she thought us very American-looking. This might have upset her except for the fact that she had made many American friends in London during the war, and rather admired them.

The plan was that we would take the train from New York to Philadelphia, where we would spend the weekend at Aunt May's. I remember one rather silly incident on that train ride to Philadelphia. As we were making our way to the dining car for lunch, I was walking behind Mother and noticed that her slip was showing. Whenever this happened to Aunt Peggy, we were supposed to tell her "it's snowing down south." I said this to Mother. She replied in her English accent, "How extraordinary!" which nonplussed me to the point where I did not pursue the matter.

As the weekend progressed, we began to feel more comfortable with Mother, and she in turn began to kid us about our American ways. I think she was a bit taken aback by our easy manner with Aunt Peggy. We expressed our own opinions freely; we teased her; we joked with her; we protested if we didn't want to do what she asked, although we usually did it willingly in the end.

After a pleasant weekend of good food and talk, the three oldest of us returned to our boarding schools. Mother, Aunt Peggy and Malcolm journeyed on to Muncy Farms. Mother spent the summer with us at the farm. It was like one long country weekend, so familiar to the English. We did our best to keep Mother amused with picnics, swimming, tennis, and rides in the buggy behind my horse Prince. Mother loved walking the farm, and quickly made friends by her gracious manner.

After an initial politeness toward each other, Mother and Aunt Peggy became friends. They found they shared a common basic outlook, but I think they were both careful to choose their words. Aunt Peggy's best friend, Aunt Josie Molten, who had met us when we first arrived at Muncy Farms, remembers hearing Aunt Peggy correct Malcolm in front of Mother and then apologize to her. Josie reported that Mother replied, "As long as the children are under your roof, they are to do what you wish." As time passed, I think Mother came to recognize that she was not the center of our world. She had to share us with Aunt Peggy, although it had never been Aunt Peggy's intention to bring about such a situation.

Near the end of the summer, we all returned to New York to see Mother off to England by ship. Her departure was not the wrench I expected it to be. In fact, after Mother had kissed us good-bye and was walking towards the gangplank, my attention was attracted toward a smartly-dressed couple from the Midwest who were there to meet their son. The son had spent the summer in Italy. I heard the mother gasp, "Oh my God!" as the teenaged son approached with long hair curling over his collar, a bright bottle-green Italian suit, and the most extraordinarily colored shoes, a bright yellow-brown. When I turned my attention back in Mother's direction, she had vanished from sight.

Mother left with the promise to return the following summer. A letter written after her return to England said, "Got home to find a nice large Income Tax claim waiting for me. The government took all the money I earned at the Embassy, plus some. So, really, I paid to work there. It may curb any ideas I have of coming over next year, but we shall see."

On October 13, Mother wrote Aunt Peggy, "First of all, let me thank you for your very great kindness in giving me such a lovely time in America. I really did enjoy it and everyone says I look so well. After I left you at the barrier, we stood in a queue for 1½ hours before our passports were seen. Was very glad I was there early, as the cabin accommodation was not so good, on B-Deck, an inside cabin with no ventilation and 12 berths, so was able to get a bunk near the door. My traveling companions were quite nice and included a very good-looking black girl going over to be married to a boy at the London University. My deck steward looked after me well, so was able to keep very much to myself. The first two days were lovely, very hot and calm, after that a Northeast gale. Practically everyone was seasick until we reached Ireland on the following Thursday. Thank goodness I was not. I stayed firmly on deck and only went down to meals and sleep.

"We landed the Irish lot at 2 AM Friday morning. As we

were sailing for Southampton, a crane workers' strike was reported, so we put into Plymouth at 1 PM. We eventually got off at 9 PM, and were then kept until 2 AM Saturday waiting for the Customs, who were so fed up with the whole thing that they did not open anyone's luggage. Arrived Paddington at 8 AM and to my joy found the general manager of the Park Lane Hotel had come to meet me, and brought a car and porter, so was able to really relax."

Mother's visit to America in 1946 seems to have convinced her that it was not possible for us to be divided in our loyalties. She recognized that our adoption by Aunt Peggy in truth only confirmed what had transpired since our arrival in October 1940. "Home" for the four of us had come to mean Aunt Peggy and Muncy Farms. Aunt Peggy never intended this outcome, but too much time had elapsed after our departure from England to bring about a different result. Even though Aunt Peggy and Mother would share us for the rest of their lives, because of World War II, in Mother's heart she really had only one child—Derrick.

Margaret Burgwin Brock, "Aunt Peg."

Aunt Cecile's first visit to the United States.

Violet Layman (Barlow) Jamieson in Connecticut.

Aunt May Gibson.

Sheila Bohun Barlow O'Brien, the author's younger sister.

Malcolm Bohun Barlow, the author's younger brother.

Derrick Crombie-Steedman at The Morny Perfume Company.

Susan Bohun Barlow, the author's twin sister.

Derrick, Brian, and Malcolm in Dartmouth in 1990.

Malcolm Bohun Barlow in front of the Stone House, on a return trip to England after the war.

ENDNOTES
&
BIBILIOGRAPHY

ENDNOTES

Chapter 2
1. Angus Calder, *The People's War*, 55.

Chapter 4
1. The date of these *N.Y. Times* quotations is unknown.
2. Calder, 40.
3. Arthur Marwick, *The Home Front*, 27.

Chapter 5
1. The date of these *N.Y. Times* quotations is unknown.
2. Anthony Bailey, *America, Lost and Found*, 23.

Chapter 6
1. Calder, 144–145.
2. Ibid., 140–141.
3. Ibid., 153–154.
4. Ibid., 170.
5. Ibid., 181.
6. Ibid., 184.
7. Ibid.
8. Ibid., 178.
9. Ibid., 214.
10. Bernice Grohskoph, *The Treasure of Sutton Hoo*.

292   Chapter 8
        1. Bailey, 20-21.
        2. Ibid., 3.
        3. Ibid., 23.
        4. Ibid., 24–25.
        5. Ibid.

        Chapter 9
        1. Bailey, 25. The Edwin Gould Foundation for Children was located at 1761 Stillwell Avenue in the Bronx. It was founded by Edwin Gould, one of the sons of the railroad magnate Jay Gould, to be a home for "orphaned and underprivileged children."

        Chapter 11
        1. Carl Van Doren, *Secret History of the American Revolution.* Page numbers are unknown.
        2. Further information about this booklet published by the Williamsport Junior League is not available.

        Chapter 12
        1. The Lend-Lease Bill was intended to supply war materiel and supplies to Britain. Such aid was to be repaid after the war ended.

        Chapter 13
        1. The source of this quoted letter about the politeness of English children is unknown.
        2. The source of this quoted letter from an English father to his son's host family is unknown.

        Chapter 16
        1. Marwick.

Chapter 18
1. A stone is equivalent to 14 pounds.
2. Marwick.

Chapter 25
1. Calder. A more detailed description of the sword presentation can be found in Simon Sebag Montefiore, *Stalin: The Court of the Red Tsar*, 468. The actual presentation of the Sword of Stalingrad to Stalin is described in *Stalin, The Court of the Red Tsar:* "A guard of honour formed up of British infantry with bayonets and NKVD troops in blue uniforms, red tables and slung tommy guns. An orchestra played their national anthems, in the Soviet case, the old one. The music stopped. There was silence. Then the officer of the British guard approached the large black box on the table and opened it. A gleaming sword lay on a bed of 'claret-coloured velvet.' He handed it to Churchill, who, laying the sword across his hands, turned to Stalin: 'I've been commanded by His Majesty King George VI to present to you ... this sword of honour ... The blade of the sword bears the inscription: To the steel-hearted citizens of Stalingrad, a gift from George VI as a token of the homage of the British People.' "Churchill stepped forward and presented the sword to Stalin who held it reverently in his hands for a long moment and then, with tears in his eyes, raised it to his lips and kissed it. Stalin was moved. ... He walked round to Roosevelt to show him the sword. The American [president] read out the inscription: 'Truly they had hearts of steel.'"

Chapter 26
1. Calder, 371–2.
2. Ibid., 555.
3. Ibid., 558.
4. Shirley Joseph, *Land Army Hospital* is an untraceable source.
5. Calder, 559.
6. Ibid., 561–2.
7. Ibid., 562–3.
8. Russell Weigley, page numbers unknown.
9. Anonymous, *Arnhem Lift: Diary of a Glider Pilot*, 94–5.
10. Calder, 564.

Chapter 28
1. Bailey, "A Wartime Childhood, England, First and Last," *The New Yorker*, July 29, 1985, 51.
2. Calder, 563.
3. Ibid., 565.
4. Ibid., 566.
5. Ibid.
6. Ibid., 571.
7. Ibid., 570–571.

Chapter 29
1. Paul Johnson, *Modern Times*, page number unknown.
2. Sydney Fisher, *The Middle East, A History*, pages unknown.

BIBLIOGRAPHY

Anonymous. *Arnhem Lift, Diary of a Glider Pilot.* London: Pilot   295
Press, 1945.

Author unknown. *An Airman's Letter to His Mother.* New York:
E.P. Dutton & Co., Inc., 1940.

Bailey, Anthony. *America, Lost & Found.* New York: Random
House, 1980. Portions of this book were reprinted in *The
New Yorker,* July 29, 1985.

Beevor, Anthony. *The Mystery of Olga Chekhova.* New York:
Penguin Books, 2004.

Beevor, Anthony. *Stalingrad.* New York: Viking, 1998.

Brecher, Elinor J. *Schindler's Legacy, True Stories of the List
Survivors.* New York: The Penguin Group, 1994.

Bryant, Arthur. *The Turn of the Tide, A History of the War Years.*
Garden City, New York: Doubleday & Company, 1957.

Calder, Angus. *The People's War, Britain 1939–45.* London:
Jonathan Cape, 1969.

Clayton, Tim and Phil Craig. *Finest Hour, The Battle of Britain.*
New York: Simon & Schuster, 1999.

Fifty-Fifth Commemoration of the Battle of Arnhem, 1999.
Commemorative Book, Dedicated to the Arnhem Veterans.
Translated by Henk Diunhoven. Printed by Tamminga
Siegers, Duiven, 1999.

Figes, Eva. *Little Eden, A Child at War.* New York: Persea Books,
1978.

296   Fisher, Sidney. *The Middle East—A History*. New York: Alfred A. Knopf, 1968.

Gilbert, Martin. *The Boys, The Untold Story of 732 Young Concentration Camp Survivors*. New York: Henry Holt and Company, 1996.

Gill, Anton. *An Honourable Defeat, a History of German Resistance to Hitler, 1933–1945*. New York: Henry Holt and Company, 1994.

Goodwin, Doris Kearns. *No Ordinary Time. Franklin and Eleanor Roosevelt: The Home Front in World War II*. New York: Simon & Schuster, 1994.

Grohskopf, Bernice. *The Treasure of Sutton Hoo; Ship-Burial for an Anglo-Saxon King*. New York: Athenaeum, 1970.

Hackett, John Winthrop. *I Was A Stranger*. Boston: Houghton Mifflin Company, 1978.

Hastings, Max. *Armageddon: The Battle for Germany, 1944–1945*. New York: Knopf Publishing Group, 2004.

Hough, Richard and Denis Richards. *The Battle of Britain, The Greatest Air Battle of World War II*. New York: W.W. Norton & Company, 1989.

Inglis, Ruth. *The Children's War, Evacuation 1939–1945*. London: Collins, 1989.

Jackson, Carlton. *Who Will Take Our Children?* London: Methuen, 1985.

Johnson, Eric. *Nazi Terror, The Gestapo, Jews, and Ordinary Germans*. New York: The Perseus Books Group, 1999.

Johnson, Paul. *Modern Times*. New York: Harper & Row, 1983.

Joseph, Shirley. *Land Army Hospital*. (publisher and date unknown).

Keegan, John. *The Second World War*. New York: Viking Penguin, 1990.

Loftus, Harry. *East Anglia*. London: Charles Letts & Co. Ltd., 1976.

Lukacs, John. *Five Days In London, May 1940*. New Haven: Yale University Press, 1999.

Marwick, Arthur. *The Home Front: The British and the Second World War.* London: Thames and Hudson, 1976.

Milbourn, Louise. *A Very Different War.* Cambridge, England: Isis Publishing Ltd., 2003.

Montefiore, Simon Sebag. *Stalin, The Court of the Red Tsar.* New York: Knopf, 2004.

Pahor, Boris. *Pilgrim Among the Shadows*, translated from the Slovene by Michael Biggins. New York: Harcourt Brace & Company, 1995.

Rosenbaum, Ron. *Explaining Hitler, The Search for the Origins of His Evil.* New York: Harper Collins, 1999.

Van Doren, Carl. *Secret History of the American Revolution.* New York: The Viking Press, 1941.

Weigley, Russell. *Eisenhower's Lieutenants: The Campaign of France and Germany 1944–1945.* Bloomington, Indiana: Indiana University Press, 1981.

Williamsport Junior League. *Homes and Heritage of the West Branch Valley.* Williamsport, Pennsylvania: Grit Publishing Co., 1968.

Yurchak, Katherine. *Where Wigwams Stood. A History of Muncy, Pennsylvania, as Seen Through the Pages of Now and Then.* Bloomsburg, Pennsylvania: Spectrum Publishers, 1994.

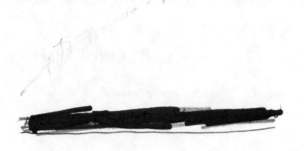

Printed in the United States
111770LV00004B/1-48/A